*No More Masks!*
*An Anthology of Poems by Women*

ELLEN BASS received her B.A. from Goucher College, where she studied with Florence Howe, and an M.A. in creative writing from Boston University. She has had poems published in *Preface, Prickly Pear, Softball, Women: A Journal of Liberation,* and *Earth's Daughters.* She edited the feminist issue of *New Magazine,* entitled, "If you want something done, do it yourself." She lives in Cambridge and works at Project Place, leading groups which use writing and acting out poetry as the medium for exploring feelings. She also leads poetry workshops at the Cambridge and Boston Centers for Adult Education.

FLORENCE HOWE teaches women's studies and literature at the new Old Westbury campus of the State University of New York. There, she also coordinates the work of The Feminist Press and its several educational projects, including The Clearinghouse on Women's Studies and the *Women's Studies Newsletter.* She has published essays and monographs on teaching, literature, politics, women's studies, sexism, and sexual stereotyping in the public schools. She is coauthor (with Paul Lauter) of *The Conspiracy of the Young.* In 1964, she taught in Mississippi Freedom Schools and worked in Mississippi in 1965. Since 1967, she has been active in *Resist* and other anti-war movements. From 1969–71, she was the first chairman of the MLAs Commission on Women. Currently, she is president of The Modern Language Association. In progress are a monograph on Virginia Woolf and a book on the education of women.

# No More Masks!

*An Anthology of Poems by Women*

*Edited by Florence Howe & Ellen Bass*

*Introduction by Florence Howe*

*Anchor Press/Doubleday Anchor Books*

*Garden City, New York, 1973*

The Anchor Books edition is the first publication of NO MORE MASKS!
AN ANTHOLOGY OF POEMS BY WOMEN

Anchor Books edition: 1973
ISBN: 0-385-02553-x
Library of Congress Catalog Card Number 72–89675
Copyright © 1973 by Florence Howe & Ellen Bass
All Rights Reserved
Printed in the United States of America

Grateful acknowledgment is made to the following for permission to reprint
material copyrighted or controlled by them:

"The Garden by Moonlight," "Interlude," "Autumn," and "The Sisters" by
 Amy Lowell are reprinted from *The Complete Poetical Works of Amy
 Lowell,* copyright 1955 by Houghton Mifflin Company, by permission of
 the publisher, Houghton Mifflin Company.
"A Petticoat," "A Waist," and "A Time to Eat" by Gertrude Stein, from
 "Tender Buttons," are from *Selected Writings of Gertrude Stein,* edited
 by Carl Van Vechten. Copyright 1946 by Random House, Inc. Reprinted
 by permission of the publisher. "XVIII," "XXII," and "XXIX" from "Be-
 fore the Flowers of Friendship Faded Friendship Faded," by Gertrude
 Stein, are reprinted here by permission of the Estate of Gertrude Stein
 and Daniel C. Joseph, Administrator of the Gertrude Stein Estate.
"The Puritan's Ballad," copyright 1928 by Alfred A. Knopf, Inc., and re-
 newed 1956 by Edwina C. Rubenstein, and "Little Eclogue," copyright
 1932 by Alfred A. Knopf, Inc., and renewed 1960 by Edwina C. Ruben-
 stein, by Elinor Wylie are reprinted from *Collected Poems of Elinor Wylie*
 by permission of Alfred A. Knopf, Inc.
"Helen" and "XXIX," "XXX," "XXXI," "XXXII" from "Tribute to the
 Angels" by H.D. are reprinted from *Selected Poems* by H.D., Grove
 Press, copyright © 1957 by Norman Holmes Pearson. Reprinted by per-
 mission of Norman Holmes Pearson.
"Marriage" by Marianne Moore is reprinted with permission of The Macmillan
 Co. from *Collected Poems* by Marianne Moore. Copyright © 1935 by
 Marianne Moore, renewed 1963 by Marianne Moore and T. S. Eliot.
 "O To Be A Dragon" by Marianne Moore is from *The Complete Poems*

to our sisters
in jail
underground
at war
whose lives are their poems

# Contents

# Foreword

When we first thought about an anthology, we had in mind poems *about* women, not simply *by* them. It was the summer of 1970, we were at the beach, and with the women's movement very much on my mind, Ellen and I began to talk about poetry. "What would happen, do you suppose," I mused, "if we began to put together, side by side, what male poets have said of women with what women have written of themselves?"

"Why not also include women poets on men?"

We began to play what became a daily game. Reach into your memory for a poem about a woman, any poem: Donne's "Goe and catch a falling star/Get with child a mandrake root"; Shakespeare's "My mistress' eyes are nothing like the sun"; Wordsworth's Lucy poems. Try for a series of archetypal images: Herrick's "Corinna," Keats' "La Belle Dame," Eliot's "Portrait of a Lady," Yeats' "Leda." Again and again, the poets were male, the women, objects of worship, derision, wonder, or fear, if not victims. We knew hundreds of poems by men about women. But apart from Browning's sonnets to Robert, we could not think of a man immortalized by a woman poet.

"Why not?"

They weren't usually anthologized.

"Why not?"

That summer we were also reading back issues of women's movement magazines and newspapers. The poems caught us: was their introspection or anger new? Or had women poets always written about themselves and about other women? We did not know, nor had we any real idea of the *number* of poets, American women, who had produced good or excellent poetry in this century.

We set about collecting poems in two groups: male poets on women; women poets on men and women. Both collections grew large enough for two separate volumes, and in the end we decided to drop the men, chiefly because their poems were either well known or easily accessible in many anthologies. But few volumes have included more than a token woman—Emily Dickinson or Christina Rossetti—and fewer still, if any, their poems about women. In the end we narrowed our focus still further, to twentieth-century American poets,* since they were numerous and excellent enough to claim a volume of their own.

Beyond the variety and excellence of poems by women, beyond their omission from most anthologies as well as the literary curriculum, there was another reason for this volume to come into being. A nagging doubt: are women victims of prejudiced editors or are women poets out of the mainstream of modern poetry? What is the mainstream? And what do women write about?

Men, we know, write about women at least part of the time. They also write about themselves as artists, their (female) muse, their lust for fame. They write sometimes about their fathers, and occasionally their mothers; occasionally, too, their children. But on the whole, and in spite of their interest in the public world of affairs, men stand at the center of their poems. They create and re-create themselves, their feelings, in thought or in action.

What do women write when they are artists as well as subjects of poems? What can they tell us about ourselves? We are just beginning to look for the answers to these questions.

The most important reason for this volume to exist, finally, is an ideological one: a belief in the uniqueness of women. We are not men, nor do we want to be. We are interested in our differences, in the range and possibilities of our development. We want to know ourselves and our history. We want to examine our relationships with men, with our children and our parents; we want to discover our relationships with women.

Most of all, we want to shout NO MORE MASKS! This is what we feel and what we hear most women poets saying today. No more masks, especially not the oldest of these, the mask of maleness.

Is this a political or a literary document? It is neither one nor the other, and yet it is always both. We made conscious literary choices as we read poems: this poem and not that; this poet and not that. We include poems by women who are not primarily poets but fiction writers (Boyle, Paley) because we thought their poems had something

---

* There is one Canadian poet in the collection—Margaret Atwood. We found her early, when we thought we might be able to include British, Australian, and other English-speaking women poets in the volume. We have left her in, as a sign of the riches that might fill still another anthology.

to add to the collection. Yet is it a literary or a political fact that of those included in the volume, and born before 1920, only half were publishing poets all their life? That of those poets, few married and fewer still bore children? Is it a political or a literary fact that as the century moved on, the number of women poets increased? Finally, we know from past experience that poetry often springs from revolutionary spirit. Much, if not most, of the poetry in this volume follows the revival/renewal of the women's movement in the mid-sixties.

We took two years to collect and sift poems, asking ourselves always whether the poems reflected each poet's strength as a writer as well as her concerns as a woman. We wanted a volume of representative and excellent poems, various enough to reflect a multiplicity of themes, feelings, forms, ideas. We invited some 90 poets to participate, only three of whom declined on the grounds that they did not wish to appear in a "segregated" volume. Happily, none of those three was a black woman, and we are very pleased, therefore, to be publishing a volume of contemporary poetry that is, for once, truly non-segregated, in which black poets are not tokens.

Many people have helped make this book possible. Leone Stein of the University of Massachusetts Press first believed in the idea of the book—in 1970—when no one else in the publishing world was listening. Many poets have been most generous about fees because they believed in the book. We are especially grateful to Muriel Rukeyser, who made it possible for us to use seven of her poems and gave us as well a new unpublished one. To her we owe also the title of this volume.

FLORENCE HOWE

## The Poem as Mask

Orpheus

When I wrote of the women in their dances and wildness, it was a
    mask,
on their mountain, god-hunting, singing, in orgy,
it was a mask; when I wrote of the god,
fragmented, exiled from himself, his life, the love gone down with
    song,
it was myself, split open, unable to speak, in exile from myself.

There is no mountain, there is no god, there is memory
of my torn life, myself split open in sleep, the rescued child
beside me among the doctors, and a word
of rescue from the great eyes.

No more masks! No more mythologies!

Now, for the first time, the god lifts his hand,
the fragments join in me with their own music.

Muriel Rukeyser, 1971

# Introduction

This is not the last word on women poets. Indeed, in some respects it is more like the first word, since so little has been written about them as a group. Many of these poets are out of print; others are not yet into print; still others are not yet available in libraries. If your life has been like mine, you will come to this volume with years of male poems in your heart and head. You will be amazed by what you find here. Perhaps you will also share the sense of discovery and revelation we felt as we collected the poems for this volume. If you are not a reader of poetry, you will be surprised in yet a different way: to find the concerns of your life, your feelings and beliefs, vividly on some of these pages.

The poem distinctively by a woman is not always a private one. Some poets speak mainly in public voices—Marianne Moore, for one. Other poets, like Kay Boyle, characteristically choose public subjects: the alleged rape in the Scottsboro case or "For James Baldwin." While Shirley Kaufman frames "Watts" with her own body, it is nevertheless a poem about the racist fears of a well-to-do middle-class elite world. And while most of the poems in this volume are "private" ones, we have included as well, for diversity and in order to suggest the range of women's poems, a representative body of public poems whose themes quite naturally reflect our world: war, poverty, racism, drugs, pure air, poverty. But among young poets, for whom the life of a woman is a public matter, such distinctions between public and private fall away. For young feminists the poem that celebrates their sexuality is as political as the one that defines them as women in a hitherto male world.

The collection is a rich source of poems on themes usually ignored in literature courses or by literary critics, but now receiving careful attention at least in women's studies courses: the relationship of mothers and daughters (as distinct from fathers and sons); female sexuality, including breast-feeding and homosexuality; female identity; abortion; childbirth; female creativity. The theme of the divided woman runs through the volume as does the search for wholeness. Another theme is less distinct, if as interesting: who is the creative woman's muse? how does woman function as an artist?

But first, who are the poets in the volume?

We call them all moderns, but in point of fact one of the oldest of them, Amy Lowell, was born ninety-nine years ago and has been dead for nearly half a century. The youngest are in their early twenties. The poets are organized chronologically to note the shifts in sensibility—in tone, theme, and style—through the century, and to provide a sense of history and tradition for poets writing today. The subtitles suggest the flavor of that changing sensibility. They catch especially the poet's view of her self early and late in the century: from Amy Lowell's pensive perception of her kind as "a queer lot/We women who write poetry" to Jean Tepperman's delight in being a "Witch" among witches—"We are screaming,/we are flying/laughing, and won't stop." The central subtitle, Adrienne Rich's "The Will to Change,"[1] obviously stretches beyond the period assigned to it. As subtitle, it could easily serve for the volume as a whole.

All but eight of the poets are living, and from almost all those living we include poems written within the past decade. Of the 220 poems in the volume, nearly half (95) were published in the 1960s, less than two-fifths (77) in the first three years of this decade, and more than one-fifth (48) before 1959.[2] It is on that healthy one-fifth that we lay the weight of tradition. These poems assure us that long before the 1960s, women poets were thinking and writing about themselves. At the same time, the volume is strongly contemporary. Whether they are in their twenties or sixties, the 79 living poets in this volume represent the variety of women's voices to be heard today.

There is no representative woman poet, and it is as difficult (and unrewarding) to generalize about women poets as about men. I shall first describe the changing sensibility of poets and poems through the several parts of this volume before turning to unifying themes.

---

[1] This was originally Charles Olson's phrase.

[2] The date following each poem is usually the date of first publication in a volume by the poet, although in a number of instances, we were able to track the poem to its first magazine appearance. Especially for younger poets, the date that appears is the date of publication in a magazine. We include two dates within brackets when the date of composition preceded the date of publication sufficiently to warrant its inclusion.

4

That women should be poets at all was the question in the early decades of the century. And so many of them. Before the twentieth century, at least in English-speaking countries, there had been a couple of tokens—a Rossetti, a Barrett Browning, a Dickinson. And there was Sappho to whom all could look:

> . . . a burning birch-tree
> All tall and glittering fire . . .
> —Amy Lowell, "The Sisters"

But quite suddenly, in the second and third decades of the century, here were a handful of contemporary women poets, not exactly part of a group, but with some knowledge of each other. Some of these women (H.D., Amy Lowell, Elinor Wylie, and Gertrude Stein) were also known by a small group of male poets. H.D., as Richard Aldington's wife, could keep her place as a woman in relation to those men, and was tolerable therefore as a female poet. Amy Lowell, on the other hand, did not keep her place—whatever that might have been for her. She was as independent and as troublesome in her way as Pound was in his, but of course as a woman she was not likely to get away with unique behavior without a few derogatory labels.

It is not surprising, therefore, that Lowell felt unique, and not unique in relation to men merely, but rather in relation to women. This is the most significant difference between the poets who open and those who close this volume. For a woman to feel "chosen" or "special" enough to take on a male role has, in the past, meant that she was separated from other women, and that she had to make some kind of adjustment in order to survive in a male world. She might have to deny her sexuality and her human need for family and live out her days as a spinster. Or she might allow her sexuality to bloom in non-heterosexual ways. And she might also, like Elizabeth Barrett, who chose the first route, feel that she had to write as though she were a man. Until she met and loved Robert, that is; and then she established for women one of the most devastating traditions we have had to live with; the lovesick woman, prostrate before her heroic, accomplished love. (Toward the end of her life, Barrett Browning did write a poem from an unconventional woman's point of view and was notorious for it. *Aurora Leigh* is, of course, the one important piece of her work not generally known today.)

The handful of American poets with which this volume begins are especially to be treasured because, unlike their sisters of the more distant past, they tried at least occasionally to write about the condition of being a poet among men. And it was not easy, either to write about it or to live it out. Their lives are known to us only faintly, for we have not yet turned to them. (And by "we" I mean the new breed of conscious feminist scholars—historians and literary critics—who must review and write our history and restore our literature.)

The early selections in this volume attempt to begin some of that enormous task. We chose to reflect the note that was new and the one that, looking back now, was most auspicious for women of this century. The wry or bitter note. The wistfully reflective poem. The poem that queries what it is to be a woman, rather than the one that performs the role unthinkingly. But the tone was relatively comfortable, compared especially with poems written later in the century, even relaxed:

> Taking us by and large, we're a queer lot
> We women who write poetry. And when you think
> How few of us there've been, it's queerer still.
> I wonder what it is that makes us do it,
> Singles us out to scribble down, man-wise,
> The fragments of ourselves.
>
> —Amy Lowell

We were *queer* not only in relation to men who were poets but to women who were not. We could be comfortable in neither world. Especially if we were Amy Lowell, we could join neither: we could live only in isolation from both, calling upon those sisters of the past—Sappho, Barrett Browning, and especially Dickinson—for comfort (what sociologists call "role models"). And we could, even if we were Lowell in the last year of her life, look also for comfort to the future.

But not all of the women in the first section lived as Lowell did. Several were expatriates, choosing less conventional sites than Boston or New York—then the literary meccas of the U.S.—for their lives. But among both those who left and those who stayed, there were what we might today call "tokens"—those women especially selected by males (or accepted by them) as women/artists. Thus, Gertrude Stein in Paris, and much more quietly, Marianne Moore in New York.

I do not mean to disparage the work of Stein or Moore. They were both significant innovators who left behind a bulk of literature that will be lovingly elaborated upon for some time to come. But I think it is important to mention—however painful or embarrassing this may seem . . . that neither is known for poems written about their lives as women. Moore, in fact, wrote no "personal" poems, let alone "confessional" ones. Their poetry might be described as sexually and otherwise "objective." And such a label would not detract from its value. I would make the point, however, that Yeats could write from his maleness when he chose, as could those allegedly "objective" artists, Eliot and Joyce. It is significant to note that women writers esteemed by men are not, on the whole, allowed similar privileges. Or, to put it another way, those women artists esteemed by men are not ones to declaim themselves women. Neither in puzzlement or pain (like Lowell) nor in bitterness (like Louise Bogan).

Nor indeed in defiance, like Muriel Rukeyser. She is our first and most persistent rebel. If she is the favorite older poet of many students today, it is because she is also yea-saying. She does not suffer nor will she be silent. From the first, she could write lines to and about women that shock us still:

> destroy the leaden heart,
> we've a new race to start.
> > —"More of a Corpse Than a Woman"

In a rare openly autobiographical work, "Poem Out of Childhood," she tells us two pieces of information about herself: "Not Sappho, Sacco," she says, as she names the source of her "rebellion." And when she turns to her "adolescence," she remembers her father shaving:

> "Oh, and you," he said, scraping his jaw. "What will you be?"
> "Maybe—something—like—Joan—of—Arc . . ."

It is, of course, her early political commitments that make her so contemporary a feminist today. (Kay Boyle strikes a similar chord for us.) But it is also something else. The opening lines of "Poem Out of Childhood" set the tone of her work and her life:

Breathe in experience, breathe out poetry—
Not Angles, angels—and the magnificent past
shot deep illuminations into high-school.

She is a mystic, and for her this life recalls illuminations of the past not unlike Wordsworth's "Intimations of Immortality," though of course he was no Jungian. Like Wordsworth, too, it is her own daily life, the commonplaceness of it, from which her poems are made. The cry of the child and the experience of breast-feeding set off the mystical experience in "Night Feeding." And in her later poems, we find similar transformations.

Few of Rukeyser's contemporaries have been as prolific as she. Of them, only Gwendolyn Brooks and May Swenson have had relatively long publishing lives as poets. The "silences"[3] of several others are painful to enumerate. The one-volume poet: Margaret Walker, who, in 1942 at age twenty-seven, was published in the Yale Younger Poets series, and who only very recently published a second volume. The late-starter: Ruth Stone's first volume was published in her mid-forties, the second more than a decade later. And Naomi Replansky, who, along with Rukeyser, was the only still living poet of note to have appeared in an anthology of "1,311 Living Writers" (1936)[4]—she was only eighteen at the time—published no volume until 1952 and none since that time.[5]

PART TWO

The heart of the book: the will to change. Thirty-eight poets, twice as many as in part one, and twice as many poems as in either of the other sections of the volume. These poets were all born after 1920, more than two-thirds of them after 1930 and the crash. They were born after World War I, and as they reached adolescence or maturity, World War II began. Doris Lessing calls their generation the "children of violence," their chief heritage war (Anne Halley calls her 1965 volume *Between Two Wars*). They are also the first generation of women

[3] See Tillie Olsen's essay, "Silences," *Harper's,* October 1965.
[4] The volume was called *Contemporary American Women Poets,* edited by Tooni Gordi, and issued under the auspices of *The Spinners: A Bi-Monthly of Women's Verse* by Henry Harrison, Poetry Publisher, 430 Sixth Avenue, New York, in 1936.
[5] One is in preparation now.

to follow the victory of suffrage and the death of the women's move-
ment. In their more recent lifetimes and with the assistance or assent of
some of them, a new women's movement has begun.

Neither young nor established—the youngest is nearly thirty-five,
the oldest fifty-two—they are the poets of our time. But do we know
them?

Probably not, or not yet. Only a few of these poets have appeared
with even moderate frequency in contemporary male anthologies. Of
those, Sylvia Plath is most famous—not for her life or her poems, but
for her death. Suicides attract us. We feel terror and awe for the crea-
tures of talent or accomplishment who take their lives. Why do they
throw it all away? More than most poets in the volume, to be a
woman was Plath's chief subject. More than most poets in the volume,
Plath found being a woman unbearable.

Plath's life has still hardly been touched. Mostly she has been
the victim of a male mystique that of course cannot account either for
the extreme feelings in her poems or the violence of her life. Men see
her, and she appears in male anthologies, as woman *in extremis*—the
only good woman poet is a crazy woman. Cassandra.

She is not Cassandra, but one of our cassandras, one most filled
with the kind of self-loathing that kills. Placed here, for the first time
in the company not of male contemporaries but of women, Plath may
seem more and less unique. She is our only suicide, though other
poets also write of the self-hatred most women have experienced and
the pressures of life she found murderous.

I am not demeaning the youthful brilliance of her work. There
are few poets of any age capable of her intensities. Our selection also
deliberately reflects the tenderness of which Plath was also capable.
And I would not dispose lightly of her death, as necessary to her art.
I am suggesting only that the Plaths who could and did survive de-
spair also claim our attention.

As a group these poets are different from those of previous genera-
tions. In 1939, Louise Bogan could write of women poets:

> It is difficult to say what a woman poet should con-
> cern herself with as she grows older, because women
> poets who have produced an impressively bulky body
> of work are few.[6]

[6] *Selected Criticism* (New York: The Noonday Press, 1955), p. 155.

Nearly thirty-five years later, we would not make the same statement. Half of these poets have published considerably more than four volumes of poems, in addition to prose or drama. And relatively few have been late-starters. Many of these women, moreover, are also wives and mothers as well as teachers and professional readers of their poems. While the group includes Cynthia Macdonald, who published her first volume at age forty, and Jane Cooper, who did not publish poems in the fifties for fear that their subject matter—women—would meet disapproval, such women are rarer than they would have been several generations earlier. In short, the "silences" of women poets seem fewer or briefer than before.

Perhaps the survival of these poets in numbers is related to two important facts about their poems: they address women directly; they write openly of the differences between male and female lives and points of view. And not only in an occasional poem and not only incidentally. As a group, they have been freer than older poets to write as women, and to speak to women.

"Hypocrite women," Denise Levertov opens a poem of the early sixties, "how seldom we speak/of our own doubts."

> And if at Mill Valley perched in the trees
> the sweet rain drifting through western air
> a white sweating bull of a poet told us
>
> our cunts are ugly—why didn't we
> admit we have thought so too? (And
> what shame? They are not for the eye!)

Blunt, colloquial, Levertov goes on to criticize women for other forms of hypocrisy. Three years later, in the early days of the new movement, Carolyn Kizer is more impolite still, and again chiefly to women.

Kizer, like Amy Lowell forty years earlier, begins with Sappho to "consider the fate of women." *"Have we begun to arrive in time?"* she asks with some urgency, and a pun. First, with regard to "The Independent Woman," she questions the reality of that alleged independence:

> Our masks, always in peril of smearing or cracking,
> In need of continuous check in the mirror or silverware,
> Keep us in thrall to ourselves, concerned with our surfaces.

10

Kizer asks of this "maimed" independent woman,

> Meanwhile, have you used your mind today?
> What pomegranate raised you from the dead,
> Springing, full-grown, from your own head, Athena?

But she saves her sharpest points for "women of letters," those in her own "racket." And she does not spare either "the sad sonneteers, toast-and-teasdales we loved at thirteen" or those who "try to be ugly by aping the ways of the men." Of the last, she says, they "succeed."

> . . . Swearing, sucking cigars and scorching the bedspread,
> Slopping straight shots, eyes blotted, vanity-blown
> In the expectation of glory: *she writes like a man!*

What does Kizer want? Nothing less than the freedom to write without affectation. After all, she says, women

> . . . are the custodians of the world's best-kept secret:
> Merely the private lives of one-half of humanity.

Her utopia:

> If we submerge our self-pity in disciplined industry;
> If we stand up and be hated, and swear not to sleep with
>     editors;
> If we regard ourselves formally, respecting our true
>     limitations
> Without making an unseemly show of trying to unfreeze
>     our assets;
> Keeping our heads and our pride while remaining unmarried;
> And if wedded, kill guilt in its tracks when we stack up
>     the dishes
> And defect to the typewriter. And if mothers, believe in
>     the luck of our children,
> Whom we forbid to devour us, whom we shall not devour,
> And the luck of our husbands and lovers, who keep free
>     women.

Like Lowell's "The Sisters," this is a relatively loose, discursive poem, quite unlike much that each poet wrote on other subjects. If both are intimate in tone, and addressed to women, Kizer's is deliberately anti-poetic, breezy, written in a loose jargon and long, loping anapests. The chief difference between them, however, is ideological. Gone is the assumption that poetry is male work and that the woman who writes it, therefore, must be part of "a queer lot." Lowell asked in 1925,

> . . . Why are we
> Already mother-creatures, double-bearing,
> With matrices in body and in brain?

And she answers that we (poets) are so few because the task is so impossible:

> The strength of forty thousand Atlases
> Is needed for our every-day concerns.

Given the dual complexities, only a rare woman would be a poet and rarer still the one who would be both poet and mother. But for Kizer, the question (why should a woman be a poet?) does not exist. Women are and have been poets—that's a fact she takes for granted—and they may, if they wish, be mothers as well. The question for Kizer is how can the woman poet be herself, rather than a creature sexually definable as feminine or masculine.

By and large, the poets in this section of the volume begin to answer that question. They write about their daily lives, not only about the gardens they walk in but the work they do in the gardens and kitchens they inhabit:

> I move among my pots and pans
> That have no life except my own,
> Nor warmth save from my flesh and bone,
> That serve my tastes and not a man's.
> —"Trimming the Sails," Vassar Miller

> If I could, I'd write
> how glad I live and cultivate:
> to put tomatoes in and squash,
> green salad on a yellow cloth,
> how especially the white and blue
> plates please me then. Also, I do
> ironing mornings, make my list,

go squeeze fruit, open corn husks, watch
the butcher while he cuts our meat
and tote up prices in my head.
Evenings, I shake the cloth and fold
clean sheets away, count socks, and read
desultorily, and then to bed.
            —"Housewife's Letter: To Mary," Anne Halley

They also write about their children, and especially their daughters.
We have all known the intensity of mother/daughter relationships,
either firsthand or from a short distance. In some of these poems, the
hatred and the pain startle:

> Her face laps up my own
> despair, the sour, brown eyes,
> the heavy hair she won't
> tie back. She's cruel,
> as if my private meanness
> found a way to punish us.
> We gnaw at each other's
> skulls. Give me what's mine.
> I'd haul her back, choking
> myself in her, herself
> in me. . . .
>             —"Mothers, Daughters," Shirley Kaufman

Most women poets have written of relations with men. In the
first section of this volume, such poems are unhappy ones, even bitter,
*grief* poetry for the most part. In the second section, poets are more
angry than bitter, and occasionally devastatingly comic, even scato-
logical:

> When I was seventeen, a man in the Dakar Station
> Men's Room (I couldn't read the signs) said to me:
> You're a real ball cutter. I thought about that
> For months and finally decided
> He was right. Once I knew that was my thing,
> Or whatever we would have said in those days,
> I began to perfect my methods. Until then
> I had never thought of trophies. Preservation

Was at first a problem: pickling worked
But was a lot of trouble. Freezing
Proved to be the answer. . . .
> —"Objets d'Art," Cynthia Macdonald

Or if there is no quarrel with males, the poem may redefine a relationship:

Don't lock me in wedlock, I want
marriage, an
encounter—
> —"About Marriage," Denise Levertov

or explicate a sexual encounter:

The water closing
over us and the
going down is all.
Gills are given.

. . .

Now we are new round
mouths and no spines
letting the water cover.
It happens over
and over, me in
your body and you
in mine.
> —"Together," Maxine Kumin

In contrast to poems that express anger toward men (see Diane Di Prima, Rochelle Owens, Marge Piercy), a new and smaller group of poems expresses the longing for close relationships with women or the regrets of missed opportunities. Denise Levertov's poems to her sister Olga, which could not be included in this volume, are part of this group, as are Piercy's "Night letter," Helen Chasin's "Photograph at the Cloisters," and Kathleen Spivack's "The Meeting."

Finally, women poets have also written about mythological women —not often and not with worship in mind. Indeed, there are few heroines in these poems: Leda, Helen, Hera, and Penelope are transformed into anti-heroines and domesticated. (Mainly, black poets

14

celebrate heroic women and these are, like themselves, real, not mythological. And in poems by white poets, two of the handful of heroines are Harriet Tubman and Mississippi's Fannie Lou Hamer.)

The woman in mythology has as often as not been a sexual vessel of special interest to male poets. Thus, William Butler Yeats immortalizes Leda in a heavily-anthologized sonnet, "Leda and the Swan." It is a poem that most of us trained as readers of poetry cut our teeth on; we can recite it by heart. And perhaps, therefore, it is difficult to review it dispassionately, for its *sense*. But let us try, especially since Yeats concludes the glimpse of sexual encounter between a god, Zeus, in the guise of a swan, and a mortal woman, Leda, with a significant question: would the mortal/woman, "mastered" by the power of the god/male, "put on his knowledge with his power?"

It is a common enough male view to see the act of impregnation in terms of male "power" that allows the female to conceive and bear a child. Such a view is as nonsensical as its reversal, which women have been sensible enough not to promulgate: that woman's power turns the male sperm into a child. Sexual powers are mutually exclusive as well as cooperative. To put the matter another way, a woman's sexuality is controlled by her body's power, just as a man's is, though neither can conceive a child without the other.

The second part of Yeats' rhetorical question is as provoking as the first, since it assumes a connection between male sexual power and male knowledge, one that experience hardly verifies. But more than that, it suggests, as do most of the old fairy tales, that male sexuality awakens a woman's entire self, indeed allows her to be a mature, knowledgeable woman. Whether Yeats' question is rhetorical or whether he means us to answer, why yes, of course, Leda "put on his knowledge with his power," it's all the same. The male act controls; the female responds. In terms of past history that has largely been the case.

Indeed Mona Van Duyn has written two poems in response to Yeats, and the difference between them is as interesting as the responses themselves. In "Leda," which uses the last lines of Yeats' poem as epigraph, Van Duyn's answer is simply "no," and what's more, she casts doubt on Zeus' own knowledge if not his power.

Not even for a moment. He knew, for one thing, what he was.
When he saw the swan in her eyes he could let her drop.

15

In the first look of love men find their great disguise,
And collecting these rare pictures of himself was his life.

The rest of the poem treats Leda's life afterwards, the experience
with the swan having simply put her "to sleep." Along the way, Van
Duyn dismisses the myth-making habits of men. Leda was not "mys-
terious and immortal," but rather pragmatic:

> She tried for a while to understand what it was
> that had happened, and then decided to let it drop.
> She married a smaller man with a beaky nose,
> and melted away in the storm of everyday life.

The second poem, "Leda Reconsidered," is longer and, I think,
more interesting if not as pungent, because it comes at the subject
from another point of view entirely. It is not a question here of put-
ting male poets in their place for turning women into "glassy" ab-
stractions. It is rather an attempt to try the sexual encounter itself,
but from the point of view of Leda, watching the awkward swan step
"out of water," a Leda imaginative enough also to put herself into the
swan's head. She tries, in fact, to understand his god/maleness sympa-
thetically:

> the pain of his transformations,
> which, beautiful or comic,
> came to the world
> with the risk of the whole self.

If there is a tiny bit of condescension in her view of the swan/god/
male, she does not glorify herself at his expense:

> To love with the whole imagination—
> she had never tried.
> Was there a form for that?
> Deep, in her inmost, grubby
> female center
> (how could he know that,
> in his airiness?)
> lay the joy of being used,
> and its heavy peace, perhaps,
> would keep her down.

And then, still before the encounter, she wonders about the aftermath:

> And now, how much would she try
> to see, to take,
> of what was not hers, of what
> was not going to be offered?

She thinks of "that old story/of matching him change for change,"

> pursuing, and at the solstice
> devouring him.
> A man's story.
> No, she was not that hungry
> for experience. She had her loves.

The poem concludes with the sexual encounter itself, one in which her mood controls his manner—it is not the savage "brute force" of Yeats' version:

> She waited for him so quietly that
> he came on her quietly,
> almost with tenderness,
> not treading her.
> Her hand moved into the dense plumes
> on his breast to touch
> the utter stranger.

For our purposes what is interesting is the second "no." No, she does not want his knowledge, or the stories of his knowledge, for they don't suit her. While Van Duyn's Leda is not interested in sexual warfare, Van Duyn herself offers a clear response to standard male points of view on the subject: no, she says, that is not what is meant at all, not at all. But if not the change for Leda prescribed by "A man's story," what then?

There are no clear answers. But for Cassandra, I would choose Adrienne Rich whose poem "Snapshots of a Daughter-in-Law," published in the early sixties but written before then, still seems prophetic. Rich too is critical of women:

> Our blight has been our sinecure:
> mere talent was enough for us—
> glitter in fragments and rough drafts.

and of men:

> . . . we hear
> our mediocrities over-praised,
> indolence read as abnegation,
> slattern thought styled intuition,
> every lapse forgiven, our crime
> only to cast too bold a shadow
> or smash the mould straight off.

But through the coffee-pots, the tap-streams that "scald her arm," the "wooly steam" of the kettle, she too has Leda on her mind:

> A thinking woman sleeps with monsters.
> The beak that grips her, she becomes. . . .

And later,

> . . . Pinned down
> by love, for you the only natural action,
> are you edged more keen
> to prise the secrets of the vault? has Nature shown
> her household books to you, daughter-in-law,
> that her sons never saw?

Her vision may not satisfy us altogether these days because of its image of the beautiful "boy/or helicopter," but a decade ago she caught the spirit of the decade still to come:

>                   Well,
> she's long about her coming, who must be
> more merciless to herself than history.
> Her mind full to the wind, I see her plunge
> breasted and glancing through the currents,
> taking the light upon her
> at least as beautiful as any boy
> or helicopter,
>                 poised, still coming,
> her fine blades making the air wince
> but her cargo
> no promise then:
> delivered
> palpable
> ours

In the late thirties, shortly before her death, Virginia Woolf wrote an essay about the two angels in the house that needed to be slain before a woman could be a writer. And she acknowledged her inability to conquer the second of those angels—the guardian of sexual propriety. Though male writers in Britain and the U.S. have been battling over questions of censorship since the early twenties, not until the early sixties have women written freely about sexuality. The poets in Part Three, born after Virginia Woolf's death, began writing in a literary world already inhabited by *The Second Sex, The Group* and *The Golden Notebook* as well as Denise Levertov's *O Taste and See.*

We know less about the poets in this section than about others, for after all, they are just beginning to live out their lives. Many of them are still students, several are young teachers, a number are young mothers without husbands, and a few are lesbians. Almost all express an affinity with the women's movement. For many of them, the movement is their life, their source of energy and power, their driving force. They—and in this generalization one should include also some of the poets born in the late thirties—they are the political poets of the movement. Though their poems are concerned often with their private or sexual lives and though they are read avidly by other women in the movement, their poems are public manifestations of new ideas and life-styles.

Sexuality in the poems of younger poets is very distinctive. Partly it is the presence of lesbian themes and images:

> the lovers
> lay at one
> another's breasts
> and their hair
>      joined
> like swiftly running
>           rivers
>      the dark murmur
>      and splashed gems
> of deepest waters
>           —"One, The Other, And," Wendy Wieber

Partly it is the direct rendering of sexual acts by women, whether heterosexual or homosexual:

> Last night I licked
> your love, you love,
> like a cat. And
> I watched you rise like
> bread baking, like
> a helium balloon, rise
> with the skill of a soufflé,
> your love, waving like
> passengers on a boat coming in.
> —"In Celebration," Ellen Bass

But even more important it is the expression by women of great pleasure in their own sexuality:

> . . . a snow-
> ball
>
> white on white as one
> as your skin
>
> and mine the night we dared
>
> frost and the moon,
> two
>
> shivering question marks,
> periods
>
> buried,
> luminous (your
>
> thighs your chest your face and) the face
>
> of the snow
>
> we tossed at each other like
> clouds,

like waves exploding,
                    bearing us

into our own motion again,
                    to sleeping

bag blankets,
          warm sheets,

to our mouths.
                    —"Personal Poem," Ingrid Wendt

And the pleasure takes the form of activity, including, perhaps surprisingly, the activity of or the longing for pregnancy. Among most younger poets, women are sexual beings, not objects. And while sometimes the mood comes through as defiance—see Alta's poems—chiefly the emotion is joy.

If one major theme of younger poets is sexuality, a second and probably more inclusive theme is "the second sex" itself. A poem like Robin Morgan's "The Invisible Woman" attempts a generalization on the subject by using the figures of the madwoman and the doctor, paradigms in the history of women; and by adding paradoxical notions of invisibility. On the one hand, the doctor cannot see the woman as she truly is: whether she is sick or well, he cannot know her. On the other hand, she has the power to make herself visible to him: she "pulls on her body/like a rumpled glove":

Better to suffer this prominence
than for the poor young doctor to learn
he himself is insane.
Only the strong can know that.
                    —"The Invisible Woman," Robin Morgan

The poem expresses the ideology of the movement: that sickness and health, far from being absolute states, are socially defined at the expense of women, even in order to control their behavior; and that women now know this and that such knowledge is power.

To flatten a poem into statement does it no service, and yet most of the new poems rest on ideas either not widely known or not accepted. In a classroom, such poems provoke debate, since they invert traditional standards or ideals. It may come as a surprise that to call a woman a "witch" compliments her, and not only because of the existence of a movement group called W.I.T.C.H., but because of the ideological position: what was thought (by male standards) to be bad may indeed be good. That is, what's wrong with being a witch anyway? Let's try it and see:

> I have been invisible,
> weird and supernatural.
> I want my black dress.
> I want my hair
> curling wild around me.
> I want my broomstick
> from the closet where I hid it.
> Tonight I meet my sisters
> in the graveyard.
> Around midnight
> if you stop at a red light
> in the wet city traffic,
> watch for us against the moon.
> We are screaming,
> we are flying,
> laughing, and won't stop.
> —"Witch," Jean Tepperman

Like Tepperman's, many of these are "freedom poems." Typically, they trace the source of a woman's oppression back to her childhood and family or they describe its manifestation in relation to a man. And they declare themselves free of it:

> today i found my temper.
> i said,
> you step on my head
> for 27 years you step on my head
> and though i have been trained
> to excuse you for your inevitable
> clumsiness
> today i think
> i prefer my head to your clumsiness
> —"For Witches," Susan Sutheim

Miriam Palmer uses still another method when she describes the ethnology of raccoons:

> raccoons are selectively polygamous
> they are fond of eggs, nestlings, corn and melons
> their preferred den site
> is a large, hollow branch of a tree

When she turns to herself, to her "raccoon hands," her sharp "body smell," her head "thick and furred," she also breaks free:

> I have been sleeping through a long cold
> in the hollow branch of my mother
> it is time now to splash through
> the thawed ice

> —"Raccoon Poem," Miriam Palmer

The tone of such poems is not always as light, even-tempered or non-threatening to others as Tepperman's, Sutheim's or Palmer's. One of Susan Griffin's poems, "I Like to Think of Harriet Tubman," ends on a note of warning to the men in power who make laws affecting adversely the lives of mothers and children:

> I want them to feel fear now
> as I have felt suffering in the womb, and
> I want them
> to know
> that there is always a time
> there is always a time to make right
> what is wrong,
> there is always a time
> for retribution
> and that time
> is beginning.

> —"I Like to Think of Harriet Tubman," Susan Griffin

If Griffin's poem is more directly self-righteous than some of the others, it is not without cause—or without a more delicate touch on occasion:

> The legal answer
> to the problem of feeding children
> is ten free lunches every month,

being equal, in the child's real life,
to eating lunch every other day.
Monday but not Tuesday.
I like to think of the President
eating lunch Monday, but not
Tuesday.

But of course delicacy is not a virtue among these young poets. Strength, energy, vitality, daring, and joy interest them. Their voices, like some of their models, are "rough" or unpolished. And strong. If they are labeled ideological, they will wear that label as a banner. If they are challenged as poets, they will gladly be woman/poets.

## A NOTE ON BLACK POETS

The most famous young poet in this volume is a black woman, Nikki Giovanni, and much of what I have said above about young poets might be said of her. Her poems are also freedom poems, but with a difference. She celebrates being a sexual woman and being a black sexual woman. She loves men; she would make love to them, however "counterrevolutionary" that may seem to black men. She writes with deliberate roughness rather than with polish, and she can be both comic and urgent, almost at one time:

its knock-need mini skirted
wig wearing died blond mamma's scar
born dead my scorn your whore
rough heeled broken nailed powdered
face me
whose whole life is tied
up to unhappiness
cause it's the only
for real thing
i
know

—"Woman Poem," Nikki Giovanni

For Giovanni and most black women, the struggle for liberation is a racial struggle first, a sexual one second. Indeed, several poems focus on white women, either in laughter or with fury. June Jordan's

24

"What Would I Do White?" imagines aspects of the appearance of white women:

> What would I do white?
> What would I do clearly full
> of not exactly beans nor
> pearls my nose a manicure
> my eyes a picture of your wall?

Her pictured white woman "would disturb" (the streets), "would forget" (her furs), "would acquire" (over her wine), but finally "would do nothing." For Carol Freeman, writing of a lynching, white women provide no comic relief:

> all the limp white women with lymphatic greasy eyelids came
> to watch silent silent in the dusty burning noon
> shifting noiselessly from heavy foot to heavy
> foot licking beast lips showing beast teeth in
> anticipation of the feast

While these white women seem solid, even substantial in their bestiality ("shifting noiselessly from heavy foot to heavy/foot"), like Jordan's version of white women, they are without energy, "limp," and in that respect certainly sharply distinct from the images of black women in the poetry of black women poets.

For one thing, the lives of black women hardly allow inactivity. Carolyn Rodgers describes her youth in Chicago:

> where pee wee cut Lonnell fuh fuckin wid
> his sistuh and blood baptized the street
> at least twice ev'ry week and judy got
> kicked out grammar school fuh bein pregnant
> and died trying to ungrow the seed
> > we was all up in there and
> > just livin was guerilla warfare, yeah.

"Let uh revolution come," Rodgers concludes,

> couldn't be no action like what
> > I dun already seen
> > > —"U Name This One," Carolyn M. Rodgers

Survival itself is evidence of strength.

In a number of poems, the strength of black women is a function of mothering, the key theme the endurance of women despite the suffering of unwanted abortions or difficult pregnancies (see "The Mother" and "Jessie Mitchell's Mother" by Gwendolyn Brooks); despite the ineffectuality, hostility or demands of men (see Carol Gregory, Mari Evans). In Audre Lorde's "The Woman Thing," the two themes—motherhood and hostility to men—are combined. Hunters, "beating the winter's face," "for their children's hunger," return "Emptyhanded . . ./ Snow-maddened, sustained by their rages." Why have they failed? Rather ambiguously, we are told

> They do not watch the sun
> They cannot wear its heat for a sign
> Of triumph or freedom

though we do not associate the sun, until the end of the poem, with the mothers. On the men's return, they eat and then "seek/ Young girls for their amusement." As the poem concludes, the woman's hostility to the hunters crystallizes:

> All this day I have craved
> Food for my child's hunger.
> Emptyhanded the hunters come shouting
> Injustices drip from their mouths
> Like stale snow melted in sunlight.
>
> And this womanthing my mother taught me
> Bakes off its covering of snow
> Like a rising blackening sun.

Race seems not so important as gender, at the end, and gender passed from mother to mother. The "Food for my child's hunger" seems the motivating force, and from that point of view, the hunters are hardly sympathetic figures. And the "blackening sun" rises as the "womanthing's" threat to men.

Besides mothers and grandmothers, there are proportionately more strong women among these poems than in the rest of the volume. Occasionally these heroines are legendary, like Margaret Walker's "Mollie Means," perhaps our first heroic witch. Or "Kissie Lee," "The toughest gal God ever made/ And she drew a dirty, wicked blade." We hear of Kissie's training in self-defense, of her victories, and finally, her noble demise:

> She could shoot glass doors offa the hinges,
> She could take herself on the wildest binges.
> And she died with her boots on switching blades
> On Talledega Mountain in the likker raids.
>> —Margaret Walker

Finally, and perhaps surprisingly, black women celebrate old women, poor and beaten-down women, and without sentimentality, for there is the truth of those lives and the plain language with which it is invoked:

> I say
> when I watch you
> you wet brown bag of a woman
> who used to be the best looking gal in Georgia
> used to be called the Georgia Rose
> I stand up
> through your destruction
> I stand up
>> —"Miss Rosie," Lucille Clifton

The black tradition is distinctive, and only in the recent poems of young white women have we begun to feel something of its effect.

## SOME UNIFYING THEMES AND CONCLUDING QUESTIONS

I have reserved for these concluding pages several interrelated themes not confined to a single part of this volume: the divided self or split woman; the longing for wholeness; the source of creativity for the woman poet. These themes are not unique to women, needless to say, but we come at them from a particular social perspective. Their presence in women's poems opens questions we may not yet be able to answer.

Nine poems in this volume (and others we could not include) attempt a definition of woman by splitting her into two (occasionally three) "sisters" or women. Usually, the poem consists of static characterizations: two women sewing, a third watching "a red crust" on the ocean; a woman "smelling of/ apples or grass" and a second, a "turbulent moon-ridden girl"; a woman "climbing a glass hill/ of clothes and dishes," her double a "bitch." While there are few complexities, and while their images are usually predictable, these poems proved haunting. Partly it was the persistence of the theme; but also it was the presence of narrative in a few of these poems that point toward a search for wholeness.

Elinor Wylie's "Little Eclogue" is an early example (1932) of the division worked out in a narrative poem. Twin sisters named Solitude and Loneliness live, "like birds," in the woods. Much of the poem describes their differences as they serve "their appointed tasks,"

> One like a moth, the other like a mouse.

"Poor," "tame," and "dull" Loneliness, "freckle-faced, and full of sighs," really does not like the life they lead together, though she cannot say why. "Lovely" Solitude, "wild and holy," "fair as cressets in the skies,"

> Preferred the forest, and her private mind.

"One day," the "wild and holy" twin "escaped into the dawn," leaving her sister even more lonely than before. Wandering presumably in search of Solitude, Loneliness

> . . . found a sleeping demigod or man;
> And gazed entranced upon the creature's face,
> Which was adorable and commonplace.

Despite the irony of the last line, we are now prepared for the story's conclusion. Quite so. Even the freckles that had marred her beauty "melted with her heart/ To sun and dew" at the sight of the young man's opening eyes. Though the fairy tale is somewhat reversed— the man rather than the woman is found asleep, and his beauty impresses her—the effect is the same: it is his presence/power that turns Loneliness into a beauty. Wylie ends her poem somewhat quizzically, even sardonically:

> Let you believe, let me unsurely guess
> This wonder wrought upon poor Loneliness;
> But what was done, to what intrinsic end,
> And whether by a brother or a friend,
> And whether by a lover or a foe,
> Let me inquire, and gods obscurely know.

Wylie's point is that allegedly happy endings are not necessarily what they may seem. Who knows how Loneliness will feel about the beautiful young man several years hence? But more interesting is the utter disappearance of the "wild and holy" twin—the sister who might have been poet. Apparently these two, at least in Wylie's day, cannot co-exist, and certainly not in the same individual.

Nearly forty years later, in a narrative poem called "An Embroidery (I)," Denise Levertov draws a pair reminiscent of Loneliness and Solitude. Again, two sisters keep house in the woods, though this time they are not totally solitary. They prepare dinner for a "bear" that one of them will marry. After dinner, the bear falls asleep before the fire and the two sisters go to bed. Rose Red "dreams she is combing the fur of her cubs/ with a golden comb," while "Rose White is lying awake." In the poem, her characteristic post is at the window, looking into the dark forest, or catching its scent from the fur of the visiting bear. The poem concludes, however, not with Rose White's escape to the forest, but with a prediction:

> Rose White shall marry the bear's brother.
> Shall he too
> when the time is ripe,
> step from the bear's hide?
> Is that other, her bridegroom,
> here in the room?

The questions are left unanswered, though the tone is not entirely ambiguous. At least, young students have assumed that Rose White *will* marry the bear's "double," someone as much like her as Rose Red is like the bear. Is that not, after all, what happens in the fairy tale? Read differently, the two sisters are one woman with two desires—for the bear and for the scent (poetry) of the forest. Still, the outcome holds. She shall have them both.

In two very recent poems written by young poets, there is neither young man nor bear, nor a fairy tale ending, but new ingredients, the most important of which is the ascendency of the "wild and holy" woman, Wylie's lost twin, the potential poet. In Ranice Crosby's "thoughts for you," the woman returns from the mountains for a visit, hoping to convince her timid sister to go along on the next trip. In Jean Tepperman's "Going Through Changes," the "wild and holy" sister lives in a department store elevator:

My hair is long and wild
full of little twigs and cockleburrs.
I visit the floors only for water.
I make my own food
from the berries and frightened rabbits—
I pray forgive me brother as I eat—
that grow wild in the elevator.

The two women in this poem, moreover, converse together about their lives, arguing both propriety and purpose. In the end, the "wild and holy" sister notes, other women begin to take up similar habitats in the elevators of "a big department store America."

Yesterday pausing at childrens
I saw another lady
take off all her clothes
and go to live in #7.
We are waiting to fill
all thirteen.

At the end of Crosby's poem, the timid woman, still "trying to climb out of . . . [her] holes," says to her sister, "you are a mountain." In both cases, these poems about split women have become freedom poems. The passive women of the domestic fairy tale have shifted— if so slight a sample may be said to illustrate a shift—into the convention-breaking, mountain-climbing women of the younger poets, who must look to each other, or to themselves, for support, courage, inspiration, creativity.

"Women have no wilderness in them," Louise Bogan wrote nearly fifty years ago. And perhaps it has taken all that time for women to look past domesticity both into their own selves and toward the mountains outside. "Narcissists by necessity," as Carolyn Kizer has more recently called us, we may still feel uncomfortable with that charge. And yet, where else but to women may we look for a sense of possibility and hope? And if we respond, not to the men who have suffocated us—with cords or kindness—it is not out of hostility. There is nothing in tradition, mythology, or in the social history of women, to support the idea that women might conceive of men as their sources of inspiration or creativity. It is not simply that the "muse" is female, for that tradition is not a particularly live one any more.

It is rather that the myth tells us something of the social reality of women's and men's lives together.

The myth tells us that men are poets, but that in order for them to function, they need the support and encouragement of women, either as secretaries, assistants, wives, or mistresses, or in some combination thereof. Men not only make use of women in their daily lives, they idealize them in their poems. They need to name their source of inspiration woman or muse. The naming is not a sharing of power, but an extension of power: it codifies a patriarchal relationship. Women may be mysterious sources of energy, but as muses they are designed to feed their power to poets.

But what if that poet be woman?

Few poems confirm a specific source of creativity of women. Sylvia Plath's "The Disquieting Muses" fancies an offended relative's curse as responsible for the arrival of

> . . . those three ladies
> Nodding by night around my bed,
> Mouthless, eyeless, with stitched bald head.

Not a pretty portrait, and as Plath grows older, the three (more like Fates than muses) function demonically to prevent her from dancing and even from hearing music. Though she says nothing directly of poetry, in the final stanza the dreadful trio petrify:

> Day now, night now, at head, side, feet,
> They stand their vigil in gowns of stone,
> Faces blank as the day I was born,
> Their shadows long in the setting sun
> That never brightens or goes down.

Written forty years before, Louise Bogan's "Medusa" strikes a similar, joyless note. As though in a dream, the poet arrives at "the house, in a cave of trees/Facing a sheer sky." The key to the opening is motion—"Sun and reflection wheeled by." But then there is the vision—Medusa—the legendary figure whose serpent-hair turns men to stone:

> When the bare eyes were before me
> And the hissing hair,

Held up at a window, seen through a door.
The stiff bald eyes, the serpents on the forehead
Formed in the air.

The poet sees Medusa and survives, but the scene becomes the poem: "The water will always fall, and will not fall." And the poet herself is caught forever in the act of vision:

And I shall stand here like a shadow
Under the great balanced day,
My eyes on the yellow dust, that was lifting in the wind,
And does not drift away.

These poems raise several questions. Is the deadly Medusa the woman poet's muse? Why is the experience in each case joyless, if not altogether destructive for the poet? Does the poet's source of creative energy need to be an opposing, unkindly, if not terrifying force? Is this force reminiscent of Solitude, Rose White, and other "wild and holy" sisters?

Yes, I can say, at least to the final question, and perhaps that yes will shed light on the others as well. Amy Lowell concludes in "The Sisters" that "We are one family," and I see a family relationship possible. Young poets today have transformed the Medusa or the stone heads of Plath into "witches" that aren't frightening any more, at least not to them or to us. They are not frightened by their own impulses, to poetry, to the mountains and forests, to sexuality, perhaps because these impulses no longer place them in hidden, painful, and self-destructive conflicts with a male world. Instead, the "wild and holy" witches of the seventies are part of a social movement that validates their existence, even their art.

In the male tradition, the poet also may appear demented, peculiar if not prophetic. As madman, the male poet has had a place in society; given the Isaiahs, Miltons, and Shelleys of the world, he is secure enough even to name woman, the muse, the source of his creative powers. But the woman poet begins in a different position. Hers has not been an acceptable, traditional relationship with the world. If she is no longer "queer," as she was in Lowell's day, she still needs to be labeled not poet but woman poet.

It was not easy or "natural" for Bogan or Plath to be poets—at least they had little personal or social support for the work they did.

A trio of stony muses, a legendary female creature terrifyingly hostile to man—these are not improbable sources of women's creative power, if we remember that their poetry reflects the social reality of their lives.

These days women are glad to be women: a small but remarkable fact. Marge Piercy caught the spirit of these times in 1963 when she concluded "Noon of the sunbather" with the memorable image of the woman burned to cinders by the male sun, yet still fighting back:

But the ashes dance. Each ashfleck leaps at the sun.

Women poets today, young or old, are bound together in ways Lowell, Bogan or Plath could not have imagined. And we provide an audience that women poets have not yet had. A new poetry is in the making. No more masks! No more mythologies! *And the fragments will join in us with their own music.*

October 1972
College at Old Westbury

. . . *we're a queer lot*
*We women who write poetry*—AMY LOWELL

# The Garden by Moonlight

A black cat among roses,
Phlox, lilac-misted under a first-quarter moon,
The sweet smells of heliotrope and night-scented stock.
The garden is very still,
It is dazed with moonlight,
Contented with perfume,
Dreaming the opium dreams of its folded poppies.
Firefly lights open and vanish
High as the tip buds of the golden glow
Low as the sweet alyssum flowers at my feet.
Moon-shimmer on leaves and trellises,
Moon-spikes shafting through the snowball bush.
Only the little faces of the ladies' delight are alert and staring,
Only the cat, padding between the roses,
Shakes a branch and breaks the chequered pattern
As water is broken by the falling of a leaf.
Then you come,
And you are quiet like the garden,
And white like the alyssum flowers,
And beautiful as the silent sparks of the fireflies.
Ah, Beloved, do you see those orange lilies?
They knew my mother,
But who belonging to me will they know
When I am gone.

[1919]

# Interlude

When I have baked white cakes
And grated green almonds to spread upon them;
When I have picked the green crowns from the strawberries
And piled them, cone-pointed, in a blue and yellow platter;
When I have smoothed the seam of the linen I have been working;
What then?
To-morrow it will be the same:
Cakes and strawberries,
And needles in and out of cloth.
If the sun is beautiful on bricks and pewter,
How much more beautiful is the moon,
Slanting down the gauffered branches of a plum-tree;
The moon
Wavering across a bed of tulips;
The moon,
Still,
Upon your face.
You shine, Beloved,
You and the moon.
But which is the reflection?
The clock is striking eleven.
I think, when we have shut and barred the door,
The night will be dark
Outside.

[1919]

# Autumn

They brought me a quilled, yellow dahlia,
Opulent, flaunting.
Round gold
Flung out of a pale green stalk.
Round, ripe gold
Of maturity,
Meticulously frilled and flaming,
A fire-ball of proclamation:
Fecundity decked in staring yellow
For all the world to see.
They brought a quilled, yellow dahlia,
To me who am barren.
Shall I send it to you,
You who have taken with you
All I once possessed?

[1919]

# The Sisters

Taking us by and large, we're a queer lot
We women who write poetry. And when you think
How few of us there've been, it's queerer still.
I wonder what it is that makes us do it,
Singles us out to scribble down, man-wise,
The fragments of ourselves. Why are we
Already mother-creatures, double-bearing,
With matrices in body and in brain?
I rather think that there is just the reason
We are so sparse a kind of human being;
The strength of forty thousand Atlases
Is needed for our every-day concerns.
There's Sapho, now I wonder what was Sapho.
I know a single slender thing about her:
That, loving, she was like a burning birch-tree
All tall and glittering fire, and that she wrote
Like the same fire caught up to Heaven and held there,
A frozen blaze before it broke and fell.
Ah, me! I wish I could have talked to Sapho,
Surprised her reticences by flinging mine
Into the wind. This tossing off of garments
Which cloud the soul is none too easy doing
With us to-day. But still I think with Sapho
One might accomplish it, were she in the mood
To bare her loveliness of words and tell
The reasons, as she possibly conceived them,
Of why they are so lovely. Just to know
How she came at them, just to watch
The crisp sea sunshine playing on her hair,
And listen, thinking all the while 'twas she
Who spoke and that we two were sisters
Of a strange, isolated little family.
And she is Sapho—Sapho—not Miss or Mrs.,
A leaping fire we call so for convenience;

But Mrs. Browning—who would ever think
Of such presumption as to call her "Ba."
Which draws the perfect line between sea-cliffs
And a close-shuttered room in Wimpole Street.
Sapho could fly her impulses like bright
Balloons tip-tilting to a morning air
And write about it. Mrs. Browning's heart
Was squeezed in stiff conventions. So she lay
Stretched out upon a sofa, reading Greek
And speculating, as I must suppose,
In just this way on Sapho; all the need,
The huge, imperious need of loving, crushed
Within the body she believed so sick.
And it was sick, poor lady, because words
Are merely simulacra after deeds
Have wrought a pattern; when they take the place
Of actions they breed a poisonous miasma
Which, though it leave the brain, eats up the body.
So Mrs. Browning, aloof and delicate,
Lay still upon her sofa, all her strength
Going to uphold her over-topping brain.
It seems miraculous, but she escaped
To freedom and another motherhood
Than that of poems. She was a very woman
And needed both.

        If I had gone to call,
Would Wimpole Street have been the kindlier place,
Or Casa Guidi, in which to have met her?
I am a little doubtful of that meeting,
For Queen Victoria was very young and strong
And all-pervading in her apogee
At just that time. If we had stuck to poetry,
Sternly refusing to be drawn off by mesmerism
Or Roman revolutions, it might have done.
For, after all, she is another sister,
But always, I rather think, an older sister
And not herself so curious a technician
As to admit newfangled modes of writing—
"Except, of course, in Robert, and that is neither

41

Here nor there for Robert is a genius."
I do not like the turn this dream is taking,
Since I am very fond of Mrs. Browning
And very much indeed should like to hear her
Graciously asking me to call her "Ba."
But then the Devil of Verisimilitude
Creeps in and forces me to know she wouldn't.
Convention again, and how it chafes my nerves,
For we are such a little family
Of singing sisters, and as if I didn't know
What those years felt like tied down to the sofa.
Confound Victoria, and the slimy inhibitions
She loosed on all us Anglo-Saxon creatures!
Suppose there hadn't been a Robert Browning,
No "Sonnets from the Portuguese" would have been written.
They are the first of all her poems to be,
One might say, fertilized. For, after all,
A poet is flesh and blood as well as brain
And Mrs. Browning, as I said before,
Was very, very woman. Well, there are two
Of us, and vastly unlike that's for certain.
Unlike at least until we tear the veils
Away which commonly gird souls. I scarcely think
Mrs. Browning would have approved the process
In spite of what had surely been relief;
For speaking souls must always want to speak
Even when bat-eyed, narrow-minded Queens
Set prudishness to keep the keys of impulse.
Then do the frowning Gods invent new banes
And make the need of sofas. But Sapho was dead
And I, and others, not yet peeped above
The edge of possibility. So that's an end
To speculating over tea-time talks
Beyond the movement of pentameters
With Mrs. Browning.
                         But I go dreaming on,
In love with these my spiritual relations.
I rather think I see myself walk up
A flight of wooden steps and ring a bell

And send a card in to Miss Dickinson.
Yet that's a very silly way to do.
I should have taken the dream twist-ends about
And climbed over the fence and found her deep
Engrossed in the doings of a humming-bird
Among nasturtiums. Not having expected strangers,
She might forget to think me one, and holding up
A finger say quite casually: "Take care.
Don't frighten him, he's only just begun."
"Now this," I well believe I should have thought,
"Is even better than Sapho. With Emily
You're really here, or never anywhere at all
In range of mind." Wherefore, having begun
In the strict centre, we could slowly progress
To various circumferences, as we pleased.
We could, but should we? That would quite depend
On Emily. I think she'd be exacting,
Without intention possibly, and ask
A thousand tight-rope tricks of understanding.
But, bless you, I would somersault all day
If by so doing I might stay with her.
I hardly think that we should mention souls
Although they might just round the corner from us
In some half-quizzical, half-wistful metaphor.
I'm very sure that I should never seek
To turn her parables to stated fact.
Sapho would speak, I think, quite openly,
And Mrs. Browning guard a careful silence,
But Emily would set doors ajar and slam them
And love you for your speed of observation.

Strange trio of my sisters, most diverse,
And how extraordinarily unlike
Each is to me, and which way shall I go?
Sapho spent and gained; and Mrs. Browning,
After a miser girlhood, cut the strings
Which tied her money-bags and let them run;
But Emily hoarded—hoarded—only giving
Herself to cold, white paper. Starved and tortured,

She cheated her despair with games of patience
And fooled herself by winning. Frail little elf,
The lonely brain-child of a gaunt maturity,
She hung her womanhood upon a bough
And played ball with the stars—too long—too long—
The garment of herself hung on a tree
Until at last she lost even the desire
To take it down. Whose fault? Why let us say,
To be consistent, Queen Victoria's.
But really, not to over-rate the queen,
I feel obliged to mention Martin Luther,
And behind him the long line of Church Fathers
Who draped their prurience like a dirty cloth
About the naked majesty of God.
Good-bye, my sisters, all of you are great,
And all of you are marvellously strange,
And none of you has any word for me.
I cannot write like you, I cannot think
In terms of Pagan or of Christian now.
I only hope that possibly some day
Some other woman with an itch for writing
May turn to me as I have turned to you
And chat with me a brief few minutes. How
We lie, we poets! It is three good hours
I have been dreaming. Has it seemed so long
To you? And yet I thank you for the time
Although you leave me sad and self-distrustful,
For older sisters are very sobering things.
Put on your cloaks, my dears, the motor's waiting.
No, you have not seemed strange to me, but near,
Frightfully near, and rather terrifying.
I understand you all, for in myself—
Is that presumption? Yet indeed it's true—
We are one family. And still my answer
Will not be any one of yours, I see.
Well, never mind that now. Good night! Good night!

[1925]

# A Petticoat

A light white, a disgrace, an ink spot, a rosy charm.

[1914]

# A Waist

A star glide, a single frantic sullenness, a single financial grass greediness.

Object that is in wood. Hold the pine, hold the dark, hold in the rush, make the bottom.

A piece of crystal. A change, in a change that is remarkable there is no reason to say that there was a time.

A woolen object gilded. A country climb is the best disgrace, a couple of practices any of them in order is so left.

[1914]

# A Time to Eat

A pleasant simple habitual and tyrannical and authorised and educated and resumed and articulate separation. This is not tardy.

[1914]

# From *Before the Flowers of Friendship Faded Friendship Faded*

### XVIII

When I sleep I sleep and do not dream because it is as well that I am what I seem when I am in my bed and dream.

### XXII

He likes to be with her so he says does he like to be with her so he says.

### XXIX

I love my love with a v
Because it is like that
I love myself with a b
Because I am beside that
A king.
I love my love with an a
Because she is a queen
I love my love and a a is the best of then
Think well and be a king,
Think more and think again
I love my love with a dress and a hat
I love my love and not with this or with that
I love my love with a y because she is my bride
I love her with a d because she is my love beside
Thank you for being there
Nobody has to care
Thank you for being here
Because you are not there.
    And with and without me which is and without she she can be
late and then and how and all around we think and found that it is
time to cry she and I.

[1931]

ELINOR WYLIE

## The Puritan's Ballad

My love came up from Barnegat,
  The sea was in his eyes;
He trod as softly as a cat
  And told me terrible lies.

His hair was yellow as new-cut pine
  In shavings curled and feathered;
I thought how silver it would shine
  By cruel winters weathered.

But he was in his twentieth year,
  This time I'm speaking of;
We were head over heels in love with fear
  And half a-feared of love.

His feet were used to treading a gale
  And balancing thereon;
His face was brown as a foreign sail
  Threadbare against the sun.

His arms were thick as hickory logs
  Whittled to little wrists;
Strong as the teeth of terrier dogs
  Were the fingers of his fists.

Within his arms I feared to sink
  Where lions shook their manes,
And dragons drawn in azure ink
  Leapt quickened by his veins.

Dreadful his strength and length of limb
  As the sea to foundering ships;
I dipped my hands in love for him
  No deeper than their tips.

But our palms were welded by a flame
　　The moment we came to part,
And on his knuckles I read my name
　　Enscrolled within a heart.

And something made our wills to bend
　　As wild as trees blown over;
We were no longer friend and friend,
　　But only lover and lover.

"In seven weeks or seventy years—
　　God grant it may be sooner!—
I'll make a handkerchief for your tears
　　From the sails of my captain's schooner.

"We'll wear our loves like wedding rings
　　Long polished to our touch;
We shall be busy with other things
　　And they cannot bother us much.

"When you are skimming the wrinkled cream
　　And your ring clinks on the pan,
You'll say to yourself in a pensive dream,
　　'How wonderful a man!'

"When I am slitting a fish's head
　　And my ring clanks on the knife,
I'll say with thanks, as a prayer is said,
　　'How beautiful a wife!'

"And I shall fold my decorous paws
　　In velvet smooth and deep,
Like a kitten that covers up its claws
　　To sleep and sleep and sleep.

"Like a little blue pigeon you shall bow
　　Your bright alarming crest;
In the crook of my arm you'll lay your brow
　　To rest and rest and rest."

*Will he never come back from Barnegat*
*With thunder in his eyes,*
*Treading as soft as a tiger cat,*
*To tell me terrible lies?*

[1928]

## Little Eclogue

Poor Loneliness and lovely Solitude
Were sisters who inhabited a wood;
And one was fair as cressets in the skies,
The other freckle-faced, and full of sighs.
And Solitude had builded them a bower
Set round with bergamot and gillyflower;
Wide windows, and a door without a latch,
Below the brier and the woodbine thatch.
They lived like birds, on rustic crusts and crumbs,
Mushrooms, and blackberries, and honey-combs,
Cream in a bowl and butter in a crock;
The moon for lantern, and the sun for clock.
Decorum did simplicity enrich;
A Parian Diana in a niche
Over the windows, and a harp between
With strings like gilded rain against the green;
Trifles their parents, Austerity and Peace,
Had bought in Paris, or picked up in Greece.
An infant's skull, which Loneliness had found
Without the churchyard, in unhallowed ground,
Under a little cross of blackthorn sticks;
For Solitude an ivory crucifix
Carved in a dream perversely Byzantine;
A silver mirror of a chaste design,
And Plato in white vellum; in levant
Shelley and Donne, presented by her aunt
(Who might have been a Muse, had she been got
By Jupiter, but unluckily was not.)

And Solitude was grave and beautiful
As the evening star, but Loneliness was dull;
And one was wild and holy, one was tame;
About their appointed tasks they went and came
One like a moth, the other like a mouse.
Like a new pin the cool and ordered house;
For lightly its divided burden fell;
But one did worse, the other very well.
For whatsoever Solitude had touched
Was clean, and not a finger of her smutched;
But oft the milk had soured in the pan
To see poor Loneliness morose and wan;
And when she polished copper she became
Listless as smoke against the augmented flame;
And when she walked below the lucent sun
Her freckled face was dust, her hair was dun;
And still with meek affection she pursued
Her lovelier twin, her sister Solitude,
Who, while that she was pitiful and kind,
Preferred the forest, and her private mind.
One day this nymph escaped into the dawn
And fled away, contemptuous as a fawn;
And through the hours she ran like fire and steel;
Imagination followed her at heel;
And what delights she tasted as she roved
Are metaphysical, and remain unproved.
Then Loneliness fell to weeping like a fool;
And wandered forth, because the wind was cool,
To dry her tears beneath a bracken fan;
And found a sleeping demigod or man;
And gazed entranced upon the creature's face,
Which was adorable and commonplace.
And when she saw him laid upon the leaves
Her hair was silver-gold as barley sheaves;
And when she saw his eyelids folded thin
Her eyes were amber, and with stars therein;
And when she saw his eyelashes unclose
Her freckles were the dew upon a rose;
Yea, all her freckles melted with her heart

To sun and dew, which drew his lids apart
As though the sun were shining in his eyes;
And she was fair as cressets in the skies;
And when she left the shadow of the wood
She was far lovelier than Solitude.
Let you believe, let me unsurely guess
This wonder wrought upon poor Loneliness;
But what was done, to what intrinsic end,
And whether by a brother or a friend,
And whether by a lover or a foe,
Let men inquire, and gods obscurely know.

[1932]

# Helen

All Greece hates
the still eyes in the white face,
the lustre as of olives
where she stands,
and the white hands.

All Greece reviles
the wan face when she smiles,
hating it deeper still
when it grows wan and white,
remembering past enchantments
and past ills.

Greece sees unmoved,
God's daughter, born of love,
the beauty of cool feet
and slenderest knees,
could love indeed the maid,
only if she were laid,
white ash amid funereal cypresses.

[1924]


# From *Tribute to the Angels*

XXIX

We have seen her
the world over,

Our Lady of the Goldfinch,
Our Lady of the Candelabra,

Our Lady of the Pomegranate,
Our Lady of the Chair;

we have seen her, an empress,
magnificent in pomp and grace,

and we have seen her
with a single flower

or a cluster of garden-pinks
in a glass beside her;

we have seen her snood
drawn over her face,

or her face set in profile
with the blue hood and stars;

we have seen her head bowed down
with the weight of a domed crown,

or we have seen her, a wisp of a girl
trapped in a golden halo;

we have seen her with arrow, with doves
and a heart like a valentine;

we have seen her in fine silks imported
from all over the Levant,

and hung with pearls brought
from the city of Constantine;

we have seen her sleeve
of every imaginable shade

of damask and figured brocade;
it is true,

the painters did very well by her;
it is true, they missed never a line

of the suave turn of the head
or subtle shade of lowered eye-lid

or eye-lids half-raised; you find
her everywhere (or did find),

in cathedral, museum, cloister,
at the turn of the palace stair.

xxx

We see her hand in her lap,
smoothing the apple-green

or the apple-russet silk;
we see her hand at her throat,

fingering a talisman
brought by a crusader from Jerusalem;

we see her hand unknot a Syrian veil
or lay down a Venetian shawl

on a polished table that reflects
half a miniature broken column;

we see her stare past a mirror
through an open window,

where boat follows slow boat on the lagoon;
there are white flowers on the water.

xxxi

But none of these, none of these
suggest her as I saw her,

though we approach possibly
something of her cool beneficence

in the gracious friendliness
of the marble sea-maids in Venice,

who climb the altar-stair
at *Santa Maria dei Miracoli*,

or we acclaim her in the name
of another in Vienna,

*Maria von dem Schnee,*
Our Lady of the Snow.


XXXII

For I can say truthfully,
her veils were *white as snow,*

*so as no fuller on earth
can white them;* I can say

she looked beautiful, she looked lovely,
she was *clothed with a garment*

*down to the foot,* but it was not
*girt about with a golden girdle,*

there was no gold, no colour,
there was no gleam in the stuff

nor shadow of hem or seam,
as it fell to the floor; she bore

none of her usual attributes;
the Child was not with her.

[1945]

MARIANNE MOORE

# Marriage

This institution,
perhaps one should say enterprise
out of respect for which
one says one need not change one's mind
about a thing one has believed in,
requiring public promises
of one's intention
to fulfil a private obligation:
I wonder what Adam and Eve
think of it by this time,
this fire-gilt steel
alive with goldenness;
how bright it shows—
"of circular traditions and impostures,
committing many spoils,"
requiring all one's criminal ingenuity
to avoid!
Pschology which explains everything
explains nothing,
and we are still in doubt.
Eve: beautiful woman—
I have seen her
when she was so handsome
she gave me a start,
able to write simultaneously
in three languages—
English, German, and French—
and talk in the meantime;
equally positive in demanding a commotion
and in stipulating quiet:
"I should like to be alone";
to which the visitor replies,
"*I* should like to be alone;
why not be alone together?"

Below the incandescent stars
below the incandescent fruit,
the strange experience of beauty;
its existence is too much;
it tears one to pieces
and each fresh wave of consciousness
is poison.
"See her, see her in this common world,"
the central flaw
in that first crystal-fine experiment,
this amalgamation which can never be more
than an interesting impossibility,
describing it
as "that strange paradise
unlike flesh, stones,
gold or stately buildings,
the choicest piece of my life:
the heart rising
in its estate of peace
as a boat rises
with the rising of the water";
constrained in speaking of the serpent—
shed snakeskin in the history of politeness
not to be returned to again—
that invaluable accident
exonerating Adam.
And he has beauty also;
it's distressing—the O thou
to whom from whom,
without whom nothing—Adam;
"something feline,
something colubrine"—how true!
a crouching mythological monster
in that Persian miniature of emerald mines,
raw silk—ivory white, snow white,
oyster white and six others—
that paddock full of leopards and giraffes—
long lemon-yellow bodies
sown with trapezoids of blue.

Alive with words,
vibrating like a cymbal
touched before it has been struck,
he has prophesied correctly—
the industrious waterfall,
"the speedy stream
which violently bears all before it,
at one time silent as the air
and now as powerful as the wind."
"Treading chasms
on the uncertain footing of a spear,"
forgetting that there is in woman
a quality of mind
which as an instinctive manifestation
is unsafe,
he goes on speaking
in a formal customary strain,
of "past states, the present state,
seals, promises,
the evil one suffered,
the good one enjoys,
hell, heaven,
everything convenient
to promote one's joy."
In him a state of mind
perceives what it was not
intended that he should;
"he experiences a solemn joy
in seeing that he has become an idol."
Plagued by the nightingale
in the new leaves,
with its silence—
not its silence but its silences,
he says of it:
"It clothes me with a shirt of fire."
"He dares not clap his hands
to make it go on
lest it fly off;
if he does nothing, it will sleep;

if he cries out, it will not understand."
Unnerved by the nightingale
and dazzled by the apple,
impelled by "the illusion of a fire
effectual to extinguish fire,"
compared with which
the shining of the earth
is but deformity—a fire
"as high as deep
as bright as broad
as long as life itself,"
he stumbles over marriage,
"a very trivial object indeed"
to have destroyed the attitude
in which he stood—
the ease of the philosopher
unfathered by a woman.
Unhelpful Hymen!
a kind of overgrown cupid
reduced to insignificance
by the mechanical advertising
parading as involuntary comment,
by that experiment of Adam's
with ways out but no way in—
the ritual of marriage,
augmenting all its lavishness;
its fiddle-head ferns,
lotus flowers, opuntias, white dromedaries,
its hippopotamus—
nose and mouth combined
in one magnificent hopper—
its snake and the potent apple.
He tells us
that "for love that will
gaze an eagle blind,
that is with Hercules
climbing the trees
in the garden of the Hesperides,
from forty-five to seventy

is the best age,"
commending it
as a fine art, as an experiment,
a duty or as merely recreation.
One must not call him ruffian
nor friction a calamity—
the fight to be affectionate:
"no truth can be fully known
until it has been tried
by the tooth of disputation."
The blue panther with black eyes,
the basalt panther with blue eyes,
entirely graceful—
one must give them the path—
the black obsidian Diana
who "darkeneth her countenance
as a bear doth,"
the spiked hand
that has an affection for one
and proves it to the bone,
impatient to assure you
that impatience is the mark of independence,
not of bondage.
"Married people often look that way"—
"seldom and cold, up and down,
mixed and malarial
with a good day and a bad."
"When do we feed?"
We occidentals are so unemotional,
we quarrel as we feed;
self lost, the irony preserved
in "the Ahasuerus *tête-à-tête* banquet"
with its small orchids like snakes' tongues,
with its "good monster, lead the way,"
with little laughter
and munificence of humor
in that quixotic atmosphere of frankness
in which, "four o'clock does not exist,
but at five o'clock

the ladies in their imperious humility
are ready to receive you";
in which experience attests
that men have power
and sometimes one is made to feel it.
He says, " 'What monarch would not blush
to have a wife
with hair like a shaving-brush?'
The fact of woman
is 'not the sound of the flute
but very poison.' "
She says, "Men are monopolists
of 'stars, garters, buttons
and other shining baubles'—
unfit to be the guardians
of another person's happiness."
He says, "These mummies
must be handled carefully—
'the crumbs from a lion's meal,
a couple of shins and the bit of an ear';
turn to the letter M
and you will find
that a 'wife is a coffin,'
that severe object
with the pleasing geometry
stipulating space not people,
refusing to be buried
and uniquely disappointing,
revengefully wrought in the attitude
of an adoring child
to a distinguished parent."
She says, "This butterfly,
this waterfly, this nomad
that has 'proposed
to settle on my hand for life.'—
What can one do with it?
There must have been more time
in Shakespeare's day
to sit and watch a play.

You know so many artists who are fools."
He says, "You know so many fools
who are not artists."
The fact forgot
that 'some have merely rights
while some have obligations,'
he loves himself so much,
he can permit himself
no rival in that love.
She loves herself so much,
she cannot see herself enough—
a statuette of ivory on ivory,
the logical last touch
to an expansive splendor
earned as wages for work done:
one is not rich but poor
when one can always seem so right.
What can one do for them—
these savages
condemned to disaffect
all those who are not visionaries
alert to undertake the silly task
of making people noble?
This model of petrine fidelity
who "leaves her peaceful husband
only because she has seen enough of him"—
that orator reminding you,
"I am yours to command."
"Everything to do with love is mystery;
it is more than a day's work
to investigate this science."
One sees that it is rare—
that striking grasp of opposites
opposed each to the other, not to unity,
which in cycloid inclusiveness
has dwarfed the demonstration
of Columbus with the egg—
a triumph of simplicity—
that charitive Euroclydon

of frightening disinterestedness
which the world hates,
admitting:

> "I am such a cow,
> if I had a sorrow
> I should feel it a long time;
> I am not one of those
> who have a great sorrow
> in the morning
> and a great joy at noon;"

which says: "I have encountered it
among those unpretentious
protégés of wisdom,
where seeming to parade
as the debater and the Roman,
the statesmanship
of an archaic Daniel Webster
persists to their simplicity of temper
as the essence of the matter:

> 'Liberty and union
> now and forever';

the Book on the writing-table;
the hand in the breast-pocket."

[1923]


# O To Be A Dragon

> If I, like Solomon, . . .
> could have my wish—

my wish . . . O to be a dragon,
a symbol of the power of Heaven—of silkworm
size or immense; at times invisible.
Felicitous phenomenon!

[1959]

EDNA ST. VINCENT MILLAY

# From "Sonnets from an Ungrafted Tree"

Sonnet XVII

Gazing upon him now, severe and dead,
It seemed a curious thing that she had lain
Beside him many a night in that cold bed,
And that had been which would not be again.
From his desirous body the great heat
Was gone at last, it seemed, and the taut nerves
Loosened forever. Formally the sheet
Set forth for her today those heavy curves
And lengths familiar as the bedroom door.
She was as one who enters, sly, and proud,
To where her husband speaks before a crowd,
And sees a man she never saw before—
The man who eats his victuals at her side,
Small, and absurd, and hers: for once, not hers, unclassified.

[1923]

# Menses

(*He speaks, but to himself, being aware how it is with her*)

Think not I have not heard.
Well-fanged the double word
And well-directed flew.

I felt it. Down my side
Innocent as oil I see the ugly venom slide:
Poison enough to stiffen us both, and all our friends;
But I am not pierced, so there the mischief ends.

There is more to be said; I see it coiling;
The impact will be pain.
Yet coil; yet strike again.
You cannot riddle the stout mail I wove
Long since, of wit and love.

As for my answer . . . stupid in the sun
He lies, his fangs drawn:
I will not war with you.

You know how wild you are. You are willing to be turned
To other matters; you would be grateful, even.
You watch me shyly. I (for I have learned
More things than one in our few years together)
Chafe at the churlish wind, the unseasonable weather.

"Unseasonable?" you cry, with harsher scorn
Than the theme warrants; "Every year it is the same!
'Unseasonable!' they whine, these stupid peasants!—and never since
    they were born
Have they known a spring less wintry! Lord, the shame,
The crying shame of seeing a man no wiser than the beasts he feeds—
His skull as empty as a shell!"
        ("Go to. You are unwell.")

Such is my thought, but such are not my words.

"What is the name," I ask, "of those big birds
With yellow breast and low and heavy flight,
That make such mournful whistling?"

                                        "Meadowlarks,"
You answer primly, not a little cheered.
"Some people shoot them." Suddenly your eyes are wet
And your chin trembles. On my breast you lean,
And sob most pitifully for all the lovely things that are not and have
    been.

"How silly I am!—and I *know* how silly I am!"
You say; "You are very patient. You are very kind.
I shall be better soon. Just Heaven consign and damn
To tedious Hell this body with its muddy feet in my mind!"

                                        [1928; 1939]

# Rendezvous

Not for these lovely blooms that prank your chambers did I come.
    Indeed,
I could have loved you better in the dark;
That is to say, in rooms less bright with roses, rooms more casual, less
    aware
Of History in the wings about to enter with benevolent air
On ponderous tiptoe, at the cue "Proceed."
Not that I like the ash-trays over-crowded and the place in a mess,
Or the monastic cubicle too unctuously austere and stark,
But partly that these formal garlands for our Eighth Street Aphrodite
    are a bit too Greek,
And partly that to make the poor walls rich with our unaided
    loveliness
Would have been more *chic*.

Yet here I am, having told you of my quarrel with the taxi-driver over
    a line of Milton, and you laugh; and you are you, none other.
Your laughter pelts my skin with small delicious blows.

But I am perverse: I wish you had not scrubbed—with pumice, I
    suppose—
The tobacco stains from your beautiful fingers. And I wish I did not
    feel like your mother.

[1939]

67

# An Ancient Gesture

I thought, as I wiped my eyes on the corner of my apron:
Penelope did this too.
And more than once: you can't keep weaving all day
And undoing it all through the night;
Your arms get tired, and the back of your neck gets tight;
And along towards morning, when you think it will never be light,
And your husband has been gone, and you don't know where, for
    years,
Suddenly you burst into tears;
There is simply nothing else to do.

And I thought, as I wiped my eyes on the corner of my apron:
This is an ancient gesture, authentic, antique,
In the very best tradition, classic, Greek;
Ulysses did this too.
But only as a gesture,—a gesture which implied
To the assembled throng that he was much too moved to speak.
He learned it from Penelope . . .
Penelope, who really cried.

[1949]

## Medusa

I had come to the house, in a cave of trees,
Facing a sheer sky.
Everything moved,—a bell hung ready to strike,
Sun and reflection wheeled by.

When the bare eyes were before me
And the hissing hair,
Held up at a window, seen through a door.
The stiff bald eyes, the serpents on the forehead
Formed in the air.

This is a dead scene forever now.
Nothing will ever stir.
The end will never brighten it more than this,
Nor the rain blur.

The water will always fall, and will not fall,
And the tipped bell make no sound.
The grass will always be growing for hay
Deep on the ground.

And I shall stand here like a shadow
Under the great balanced day,
My eyes on the yellow dust, that was lifting in the wind,
And does not drift away.

[1923]

# The Crows

The woman who has grown old
And knows desire must die,
Yet turns to love again,
Hears the crows' cry.

She is a stem long hardened,
A weed that no scythe mows.
The heart's laughter will be to her
The crying of the crows,

Who slide in the air with the same voice
Over what yields not, and what yields,
Alike in spring, and when there is only bitter
Winter-burning in the fields.

[1923]

# Women

Women have no wilderness in them,
They are provident instead,
Content in the tight hot cell of their hearts
To eat dusty bread.

They do not see cattle cropping red winter grass,
They do not hear
Snow water going down under culverts
Shallow and clear.

They wait, when they should turn to journeys,
They stiffen, when they should bend.
They use against themselves that benevolence
To which no man is friend.

They cannot think of so many crops to a field
Or of clean wood cleft by an axe.
Their love is an eager meaninglessness
Too tense, or too lax.

They hear in every whisper that speaks to them
A shout and a cry.
As like as not, when they take life over their door-sills
They should let it go by.

[1923]

# Betrothed

You have put your two hands upon me, and your mouth,
You have said my name as a prayer.
Here where trees are planted by the water
I have watched your eyes, cleansed from regret,
And your lips, closed over all that love cannot say.

My mother remembers the agony of her womb
And long years that seemed to promise more than this.
She says, "You do not love me,
You do not want me,
You will go away."

In the country whereto I go
I shall not see the face of my friend
Nor her hair the color of sunburnt grasses;
Together we shall not find
The land on whose hills bends the new moon
In air traversed of birds.

What have I thought of love?
I have said, "It is beauty and sorrow."
I have thought that it would bring me lost delights, and splendor
As a wind out of old time. . . .

But there is only the evening here,
And the sound of willows
Now and again dipping their long oval leaves in the water.

[1923]

# Masked Woman's Song

Before I saw the tall man
Few women should see,
Beautiful and imposing
Was marble to me.

And virtue had its place
And evil its alarms,
But not for that worn face,
And not in those roped arms.

[1967]

# A communication to Nancy Cunard

These are not words set down for the rejected
Nor for outcasts cast by the mind's pity
Beyond the aid of lip or hand or from the speech
Of fires lighted in the wilderness by lost men
Reaching in fright and passion to each other.
This is not for the abandoned to hear.

It begins in the dark on a boxcar floor, the groaning timber
Stretched from bolt to bolt above the freight-train wheels
That grind and cry aloud like hounds upon the trail, the breathing
     weaving
Unseen within the dark from mouth to nostril, nostril to speaking
     mouth.
This is the theme of it, stated by one girl in a boxcar saying:
"Christ, what they pay you don't keep body and soul together."
"Where was you working?" "Working in a mill town."
The other girl in the corner saying: "Working the men when we could
     get them."
"Christ, what they pay you," wove the sound of breathing, "don't keep
     shoes on your feet.
Don't feed you. That's why we're shoving on."

(This is not for Virginia Price or Ruby Bates, the white girls dressed
like boys to go; not for Ozie Powell, six years in a cell playing the little
harp he played tap-dancing on the boxcar boards; not for Olen
Montgomery, the blind boy traveling towards Memphis that night,
hopping a ride to find a doctor who could cure his eyes; not for
Eugene Williams or Charlie Weems, not for Willie Robertson nor for
Leroy and Andy Wright, thirteen years old the time in March they
took him off the train in Paint Rock, Alabama; this is not for Clarence
Norris or Haywood Patterson, sentenced three times to die.)

This is for the sheriff with a gold lodge pin
And for the jury venireman who said: "Now, mos' folk don't go
     on

And think things out. The Bible never speaks
Of sexual intercourses. It jus' says a man knows a woman.
So after Cain killed Abel he went off and knew a woman
In the land of Nod. But the Bible tells as how
There couldn't be no human folk there then.
Now, jus' put two and two together. Cain had offspring
In the land of Nod so he musta had him a female baboon
Or chimpanzee or somethin' like it.
And that's how the nigger race begun."

This is for the Sunday-school teacher with the tobacco plug
Who addressed the jury, the juice splattering on the wall,
Pleading: "Whether in overalls or furs a woman is protected by the
    Alabama law
Against the vilest crime the human species knows. Now, even dogs
    choose their mates,
But these nine boys are lower than the birds of the air,
Lower than the fish in the sea, lower than the beasts of the fields.
There is a law reaching down from the mountaintops to the swamps
    and caves—
It's the wisdom of the ages, there to protect the sacred parts of the
    female species
Without them having to buckle around their middles
Six-shooters or some other method of defense."

This is set down for the others: people who go and come,
Open a door and pass through it, walk in the streets
With the shops lit, loitering, lingering, gazing.
This is for two men riding, Deputy Sheriff Sandlin, Deputy
    Sheriff Blacock,
With Ozie Powell, handcuffed. Twelve miles out of Cullman
They shot him through the head.

THE TESTIMONY

*Haywood Patterson:*                    *Victoria Price*

"So here goes an I shell try
Faitfully an I possibly can

| | |
|---|---|
| Reference to myself in | "I |
| particularly | cain't |
| And concerning the other boys | remember." |
| personal pride | |
| And life time up to now. | |
| You must be patiene with me | |
| and remember | |
| Most of my English is not of | "I |
| much interest | cain't |
| And that I am continually | remember." |
| Stopping and searching for the | |
| word." | |

So here goes and I shall try faithfully as possible to tell you as I understand if not mistaken that Olen Montgomery, who was part blind then, kept saying because of the dark there was inside the boxcar and outside it: "It sure don't seem to me we're getting any-wheres. It sure don't seem like it to me." I and my three comrades whom were with me, namely Roy Wright and his brother Andy and Eugene Williams, and about my character I have always been a good natural sort of boy, but as far as I am personally concerned about those pictures of me in the papers, why they are more or less un-doubtedly not having the full likeness of me for I am a sight better-looking than those pictures make me out. Why all my life I spent in and around working for Jews in their stores and so on and I have quite a few Jew friends whom can and always have gave me a good reputation as having regards for those whom have regards for me. The depression ran me away from home, I was off on my way to try my very best to find some work some elsewhere but misfortune befalled me without a moving cause. For it is events and misfortune which happens to people and how some must whom are less fortunate have their lives taken from them and how people die in chair for what they do not do.

THE SPIRITUAL FOR NINE VOICES

I went last night to a turkey feast (Oh, God, don't fail your children
    now!)
My people were sitting there the way they'll sit in heaven

With their wings spread out and their hearts all singing
Their mouths full of food and the table set with glass
(Oh, God, don't fail your children now!)
There were poor men sitting with their fingers dripping honey
All the ugly sisters were fair. I saw my brother who never had a penny
With a silk shirt on and a pair of golden braces
And gems strewn through his hair.

(Were you looking, Father, when the sheriffs came in?
Was your face turned towards us when they had their say?)

    There was baked sweet potato and fried corn pone
    There was eating galore, there was plenty in the horn.
(Were you there when Victoria Price took the stand?
Did you see the state attorney with her drawers in his hand?
Did you hear him asking for me to burn?)

    There were oysters cooked in amplitude
    There was sauce in every mouth.
    There was ham done slow in spice and clove
    And chicken enough for the young and the old.
(Was it you stilled the water on horse-swapping day
When the mob came to the jail? Was it you come out in a long tail
    coat
Come dancing high with the word in your mouth?)

    I saw my sister who never had a cent
    Come shaking and shuffling between the seats.
    Her hair was straight and her nails were pointed
    Her breasts were high and her legs double-jointed.

(Oh, God, don't fail your children now!)

### THE SENTENCE

Hear how it goes, the wheels of it traveling fast on the rails
    The boxcars, the gondolas running drunk through the night.
Hear the long high wail as it flashes through stations unlit
    Past signals ungiven, running wild through a country

A time when sleepers rouse in their beds and listen
    And cannot sleep again.
Hear it passing in no direction, to no destination
Carrying people caught in the boxcars, trapped on the coupled chert
    cars
(Hear the rattle of gravel as it rides whistling through the day and
    night.)
Not the old or the young on it, nor people with any difference in their
    color or shape,
Not girls or men, Negroes or white, but people with this in common:
People that no one had use for, had nothing to give to, no place to
    offer
But the cars of a freight train careening through Paint Rock, through
    Memphis,
    Through town after town without halting.
    The loose hands hang down, and swing with the swing of the
        train in the darkness,
    Holding nothing but poverty, syphilis white as a handful of dust,
        taking nothing as baggage
    But the sound of the harp Ozie Powell is playing or the voice of
        Montgomery
    Half-blind in oblivion saying: "It sure don't seem to me like
        we're getting anywheres.
    It don't seem to me like we're getting anywheres at all."

[1937]

# The Invitation in It, from *American Citizen*

Carson, turn your coat collar up, throw the cigarette from your hand
And dance with me. The mazurka of women is easy to learn.
It is danced by the young, the high-heeled, and the doll-faced
Who swing on the bar stools, their soft drinks before them.
The polka of war brides is easy to follow. They dance down the streets
With their legs bare, their coats hanging open. In their pockets
Are letters written from home to be opened
Not to be read, but ripped wide by the fingernail (varnished
The color of blood), to be shaken for the check or the money order,
The dollar bill folded. These are the honeymooners
In one-room shacks, in overnight cabins, in trailer camps, dancing
The *pas seul* in shoes that strap fast at the ankle, talking
G.I. talk as if they had learned it not this year,
Not here, but months at the breast, years learning to spell still.
"Sweating out three weeks of maneuvers, or sweating the week-end
        pass,
Or sweating him out night after night," they'll say, sweet-tongued as
        thrushes.
"Say, who's fighting this war, the M.P.'s or our husbands?" they'll ask
As they swing on the bar stools. Their voices may say:
"Up on Kiska last year, he lost eighty bucks in a crap game
And twelve playing cards, two weeks before Christmas,"
While the music plays on for the dancers; or say:
"This is my ring. How do you like it? We didn't have diamonds
Put in this year. We can get them cheaper back home.
We were going to have something engraved inside. We wanted
        'forever'
Engraved, but we didn't have time yet," or saying:
"The night I had fever he wanted to go over the hill,"
But where is the hill that is high enough, wild enough, lost enough
Leading away? (Carson, dance with me.) This is the waltz
Of the wives whose men are in khaki. Their faces are painted
As flawless as children's, their hearts each the flame of a candle
That his breath can extinguish at will.

[1944]

# For Marianne Moore's birthday

NOVEMBER 15, 1967

I wish you triumphs that are yours already,
And also wish to say whatever I have done
Has been in admiration (imitation even)
Of all you marvelously proliferate. Once someone
Turned to me and said in lowered voice (because you too were in
    the room)
That William Carlos Williams gave to you at sight that
Singular esteem known by no other name save love. These words
    were
Spoken perhaps a half century ago
(In Monroe Wheeler's Eastside flat) when you
Wore amber braids around your head. And now,
As then, I cannot write this book or that
Without you. You have always been
Nightingale, baseball fan, librarian of my visions,
Poised on a moving ladder in the sun.

[1970]

# For James Baldwin

Black cat, sweet brother,
Walk into the room
On cat's feet where I lie dying
And I'll start breathing regularly again.
Witch doctor for the dispossessed,
Saint tipping your halo to the evicted,
The world starts remembering its postponed loyalties
When I call out your name. I knew you hot nights
When you kept stepping
The light fantastic to music only the wretched
Of the earth could hear; blizzards
In New Hampshire when you wore
A foxskin cap, its tail red as autumn
On your shoulder. In the waters of the Sound
You jumped the ripples, knees knocking,
Flesh blue with brine, your fingers
Cold as a dead child's holding mine.


You said it all, everything
A long time ago before anyone else knew
How to say it. This country was about to be
Transformed, you said; not by an act of God,
Nothing like that, but by us,
You and me. Young blacks saw Africa emerging
And knew for the first time, you said,
That they were related to kings and
To princes. It could be seen
In the way they walked, tall as cypresses,
Strong as bridges across the thundering falls.


                    In the question period once
A lady asked isn't integration a two-way
Street, Mr. Baldwin, and you said

You mean you'll go back to Scarsdale tonight
And I'll go back to Harlem, is that the two ways
You mean?

We are a race in ourselves, you and I,
Sweet preacher. I talked with our ancestors
One night in dreams about it
And they bade me wear trappings of gold
And speak of it everywhere; speak of it on
The exultant mountain by day, and at night
On river banks where the stars touch fingers.
They said it might just save the world.

[1970]

# Why, Some of My Best Friends Are Women

I learned in my credulous youth
   That women are shallow as fountains.
Women make lies out of truth
   And out of a molehill their mountains.
Women are giddy and vain,
   Cold-hearted or tiresomely tender;
Yet, nevertheless, I maintain
   I dote on the feminine gender.


*For the female of the species may be deadlier than the male*
*But she can make herself a cup of coffee without reducing*
*The entire kitchen to a shambles.*


Perverse though their taste in cravats
   Is deemed by their lords and their betters,
They know the importance of hats
   And they write you the news in their letters.
Their minds may be lighter than foam,
   Or altered in haste and in hurry,
But they seldom bring company home
   When you're warming up yesterday's curry.


*And when lovely woman stoops to folly,*
*She does not invariably come in at four A.M.*
*Singing "Sweet Adeline."*


Oh, women are frail and they weep.
   They are recklessly given to scions.
But, wakened unduly from sleep,
   They are milder than tigers or lions.
Women hang clothes on their pegs
   Nor groan at the toil and the trouble.
Women have rather nice legs

And chins that are guiltless of stubble.
Women are restless, uneasy to handle,
But when they are burning both ends of the scandal,
They do not insist with a vow that is votive,
How high are their minds and how noble the motive.

As shopping companions they're heroes and saints;
They meet you in tearooms nor murmur complaints;
They listen, entranced, to a list of your vapors;
At breakfast they sometimes emerge from the papers;
A Brave Little Widow's not apt to sob-story 'em,
And they keep a cool head in a grocery emporium.
Yes, I rise to defend
    The quite possible She.
For the feminine gend-
    Er is O.K. by me.


*Besides, everybody admits it's a Man's World.*
*And just look what they've done to it!*

[1932]

# The 5:32

She said, If tomorrow my world were torn in two,
Blacked out, dissolved, I think I would remember
(As if transfixed in unsurrendering amber)
This hour best of all the hours I knew:
When cars came backing into the shabby station,
Children scuffing the seats, and the women driving
With ribbons around their hair, and the trains arriving,
And the men getting off with tired but practiced motion.

Yes, I would remember my life like this, she said:
Autumn, the platform red with Virginia creeper,
And a man coming toward me, smiling, the evening paper
Under his arm, and his hat pushed back on his head;
And wood smoke lying like haze on the quiet town,
And dinner waiting, and the sun not yet gone down.

[1932]

# I Love My Love

*"In the dark of the moon the hair rules."*—ROBERT DUNCAN

There was a man who married a maid. She laughed as he led her
    home.
The living fleece of her long bright hair she combed with a golden
    comb.
He led her home through his barley fields where the saffron poppies
    grew.
She combed, and whispered, "I love my love." Her voice like a
    plaintive coo.
Ha! Ha!
Her voice like a plaintive coo.

He lived alone with his chosen bride, at first their life was sweet.
Sweet was the touch of her playful hair binding his hands and feet.
When first she murmured adoring words her words did not appall.
"I love my love with a capital A. To my love I give my All.
Ah, Ha!
To my love I give my All."

She circled him with the secret web she wove as her strong hair
    grew.
Like a golden spider she wove and sang, "My love is tender and
    true."
She combed her hair with a golden comb and shackled him to a
    tree.
She shackled him close to the Tree of Life. "My love I'll never set
    free.
No, No.
My love I'll never set free."

Whenever he broke her golden bonds he was held with bonds of
    gold.
"Oh! cannot a man escape from love, from Love's hot smothering
    hold?"

He roared with fury. He broke her bonds. He ran in the light of the
    sun.
Her soft hair rippled and trapped his feet, as fast as his feet could
    run,
Ha! Ha!
As fast as his feet could run.

He dug a grave, and he dug it wide. He strangled her in her sleep.
He strangled his love with a strand of hair, and then he buried her
    deep.
He buried her deep when the sun was hid by a purple thunder cloud.
Her helpless hair sprawled over the corpse in a pale resplendent
    shroud.
Ha! Ha!
A pale resplendent shroud.

Morning and night of thunder rain, and then it came to pass
That the hair sprang up through the earth of the grave, and it grew
    like golden grass.
It grew and glittered along her grave alive in the light of the sun.
Every hair had a plaintive voice, the voice of his lovely one.

"I love my love with a capital T. My love is Tender and True.
I'll love my love in the barley fields when the thunder cloud is blue.
My body crumbles beneath the ground but the hairs of my head will
    grow.
I'll love my love with the hairs of my head. I'll never, never let go.
Ha! Ha!
I'll never, never let go."

The hair sang soft, and the hair sang high, singing of loves that
    drown,
Till he took his scythe by the light of the moon, and he scythed that
    singing hair down.
Every hair laughed a lilting laugh, and shrilled as his scythe swept
    through.
"I love my love with a capital T. My love is Tender and True.
Ha! Ha!
Tender, Tender, and True."

All through the night he wept and prayed, but before the first bird
    woke
Around the house in the barley fields blew the hair like billowing
    smoke.
Her hair blew over the barley fields where the slothful poppies gape.
All day long all its voices cooed, "My love can never escape,
No, No!
My love can never escape."

"Be still, be still, you devilish hair. Glide back to the grave and sleep.
Glide back to the grave and wrap her bones down where I buried her
    deep.
I am the man who escaped from love, though love was my fate and
    doom.
Can no man ever escape from love who breaks from a woman's
    womb?"

Over his house, when the sun stood high, her hair was a dazzling
    storm,
Rolling, lashing o'er walls and roof, heavy, and soft, and warm.
It thumped on the roof, it hissed and glowed over every window pane.
The smell of the hair was in the house. It smelled like a lion's mane,
Ha! Ha!
It smelled like a lion's mane.

Three times round the bed of their love, and his heart lurched with
    despair.
In through the keyhole, elvish bright, came creeping a single hair.
Softly, softly, it stroked his lips, on his eyelids traced a sign.
"I love my love with a capital Z. I mark him Zero and mine.
Ha! Ha!
I mark him Zero and mine."

The hair rushed in. He struggled and tore, but whenever he tore a
    tress,
"I love my love with a capital Z," sang the hair of the sorceress.
It swarmed upon him, it swaddled him fast, it muffled his every
    groan.
Like a golden monster it seized his flesh, and then it sought the bone,

Ha! Ha!
And then it sought the bone.

It smothered his flesh and sought the bones. Until his bones were bare
There was no sound but the joyful hiss of the sweet insatiable hair.
"I love my love," it laughed as it ran back to the grave, its home.
Then the living fleece of her long bright hair, she combed with a
    golden comb.

[1960]


## The House o' the Mirror

Upon the hill my lover stands.
A burning branch is in his hands.
He stamps impatient on the stane,
And calls, and claims me for his ain.

I bolt my door. I hood my light.
I rin tae slam the shutters tight.
I tug my curtains claise and thick.
I stop my clock lest it should tick.

My house is dark. My house is still.
He shines and thunders on the hill.
I pace the rooms, and as I pass
My een glint sidelang towards the glass.

The tarnished mirror ten feet tall,
There floats my image safe from all,
Though soon my love will loup the brae
And wreck my house e'er break o' day.

At his approach I'm like tae dee
Sae hard my hert belabors me.
My house o' stane shows frail as straw,
For at a clap its wa's doun fa'.

But wae's my hert, for weel I ken
He seeks a love ne'er found by men.
Through body's stour he seeks the lass
Wha haunts the darkness o' the glass.

The ghaist that in the mirror gleams,
Floating aloof, like one wha dreams.
For her he rages mad and blind,
And plunders a' my flesh tae find.

He dives within my body's deeps
Tae fathom whaur the phantom sleeps.
He shrieks because he canna clutch
What lies beyond the grief o' touch.

Aye, though we strauchle breast tae breast,
And kiss sae hard we cry for rest,
And daur a' pleasures till they cloy,
We find nae peace and little joy.

For still between us moves the shade
That ne'er will lie beneath his plaid.
A' but my ghaist tae him I give.
My ghaist nae man may touch and live.

Oh! mirror like the mid-night sky,
Sae high and dark, sae dark and high!
There bides my wraith remote frae men,
In warlds nae earthly lovers ken.

My flesh is starvit morn and night
For a' love's horror and delight.
My ghaist apart frae passion stands.
It is my ghaist that love demands.

While blood dunts loud agin mine ear,
And banes grow week wi' blissful fear,
Upon the hill my lover manes
For what has neither blood nor banes.

[1964]

PAULI MURRAY

## Ruth

Brown girl chanting Te Deums on Sunday
Rust-colored peasant with strength of granite,
Bronze girl welding ship hulls on Monday,
Let nothing smirch you, let no one crush you.

Queen of ghetto, sturdy hill-climber,
Walk with the lilt of ballet dancer,
Walk like a strong down-East wind blowing,
Walk with the majesty of the First Woman.

Gallant challenger, millioned-hope bearer,
The stars are your beacons, earth your inheritance,
Meet blaze and cannon with your own heart's passion,
Surrender to none the fire of your soul.

[1970]

## More of a Corpse Than a Woman

Give them my regards when you go to the school reunion;
and at the marriage-supper, say that I'm thinking about them.
They'll remember my name;   I went to the movies with that one;
feeling the weight of their death where she sat at my elbow;
              she never said a word
              but all of them were heard.

All of them alike, expensive girls, the leaden friends:
one used to play the piano, one of them once wrote a sonnet,
one even seemed awakened enough to photograph wheatfields—
the dull girls with the educated minds and technical passions—
              pure love was their employment,
              they tried it for enjoyment.

Meet them at the boat   :   they've brought the souvenirs of boredom,
a seashell from the faltering monarchy;
the nose of a marble saint;   and from the battlefield,
an empty shell divulged from a flower-bed.
              The lady's wealthy breath
              perfumes the air with death.

The leaden lady faces the fine, voluptuous woman,
faces a rising world bearing its gifts in its hands.
Kisses her casual dreams upon the lips she kisses,
risen, she moves away;   takes others;   moves away.
              Inadequate to love,
              supposes she's enough.

Give my regards to the well-protected woman,
I knew the ice-cream girl, we went to school together.
There's something to bury, people, when you begin to bury.
When your women are ready and rich in their wish for the world,
              destroy the leaden heart,
              we've a new race to start.

[1935]

# Night Feeding

Deeper than sleep but not so deep as death
I lay there sleeping and my magic head
remembered and forgot.   On first cry I
remembered and forgot and did believe.
I knew love and I knew evil:
woke to the burning song and the tree burning blind,
despair of our days and the calm milk-giver who
knows sleep, knows growth, the sex of fire and grass,
and the black snake with gold bones.

Black sleeps, gold burns;   on second cry I woke
fully and gave to feed and fed on feeding.
Gold seed, green pain, my wizards in the earth
walked through the house, black in the morning dark.
Shadows grew in my veins, my bright belief,
my head of dreams deeper than night and sleep.
Voices of all black animals crying to drink,
cries of all birth arise, simple as we,
found in the leaves, in clouds and dark, in dream,
deep as this hour, ready again to sleep.

[1935]

# Poem Out of Childhood

**I**

Breathe in experience, breathe out poetry—
Not Angles, angels—and the magnificent past
shot deep illuminations into high-school.
I opened the door into the concert-hall
and a rush of triumphant violins answered me
while the syphilitic woman turned her mouldered face
intruding upon Brahms. Suddenly, in an accident
the girl's brother was killed, but her father had just died:
she stood against the wall, leaning her cheek,
dumbly her arms fell, "What will become of me?" and
I went into the corridor for a drink of water.
These bandages of image wrap my head,
when I put my hand up I hardly feel the wounds.
We sat on the steps of the unrented house
raining blood down on Loeb and Leopold
creating again how they removed his glasses
and philosophically slit his throat.

> They who manipulated and misused our youth
> smearing those centuries upon our hands,
> trapping us in a welter of dead names,
> snuffing and shaking heads at patent truth . . .

We were ready to go the long descent with Virgil
the bough's gold shade advancing forever with us,
entering the populated cold of drawing-rooms;
Sappho, with her drowned hair trailing along Greek waters,
weed binding it, a fillet of kelp enclosing
the temples' ardent fruit—
        Not Sappho, Sacco.
Rebellion, pioneered among our lives,
viewing from far-off many-branching deltas,
innumerable seas.

## II

In adolescence I knew travellers
speakers digressing from the ink-pocked rooms,
bearing the unequivocal sunny word.

    Prinzip's year bore us: see us turning at breast
    quietly while the air throbs over Sarajevo
    after the mechanic laugh of that bullet.
    How could they know what sinister knowledge finds
    its way among the brain's wet palpitance
    what words would nudge and giggle at the spine
    what murders dance?
    These horrors have approached the growing child;
    now that the factory is sealed-up brick
    the kids throw stones, smashing the windows
    membranes of uselessness in desolation.

We grew older quickly, watching the father shave
and the splatter of lather harden on the glass,
playing in sand-boxes to escape paralysis,
being victimized by fataller sly things.
"Oh, and you," he said, scraping his jaw, "What will you be?"
"Maybe—something—like—Joan—of—Arc . . ."
Allies Advance, we see,
Six Miles South to Soissons. And we beat the drums,
Watchsprings snap in the mind, uncoil, relax,
the leafy years all somber with foreign war.
How could we know what exposed guts resembled?

A wave, shocked to motion, babbles margins
from Asia to Far Rockaway, spiralling
among clocks in its four-dimensional circles.
Disturbed by war, we pedalled bicycles
breakneck down the decline, until the treads
conquered our speed, and pulled our feet behind them,
and pulled our heads.
We never knew the war, standing so small
looking at eye-level toward the puttees, searching
the picture-books for sceptres, pennants for truth;
see Galahad unaided by puberty.

Rat-tat a drum upon the armistice,
Kodak As You Go—photo: they danced late,
and we were a generation of grim children
leaning over the bedroom sills, watching
the music and the shoulders and how the war was over,
laughing until the blow on the mouth broke night
wide out from cover.
The child's curls blow in a forgotten wind,
immortal ivy trembles on the wall:
the sun has crystallized these scenes, and tall
shadows remember time cannot rescind.

### III

Organize the full results of that rich past,
open the windows—potent catalyst,
harsh theory of knowledge, running down the aisles,
crying out in the classrooms, March ravening on the plain,
inexorable sun and wind and natural thought.

Dialectically our youth unfolds:
the pale child walking to the river, passional
in ignorance, in loneliness, demanding
its habitations for the leaping dream, kissing
quick air, the vibrations of transient light,
not knowing substance or reserve, walking
in valvular air, each person in the street
conceived surrounded by his life and pain,
fixed against time, subtly by these impaled:
death and that shapeless war. Listening at dead doors,
our youth assumes a thousand differing fleshes
summoning fact from abandoned machines of trade,
knocking on the wall of the nailed-up power-plant,
telephoning hello, the deserted factory, ready
for the affirmative clap of truth
ricochetting from thought to thought among
the childhood, the gestures, the rigid travellers.

.                          [1936]

# Mrs. Walpurga

In wet green midspring, midnight and the wind
floodladen and ground-wet, and the immense dry moon.
Mrs. Walpurga under neon saw
the fluid airs stream over fluid evening,
ground, memory, give way and rivers run
into her sticky obsessive kiss of branches,
kiss of a real and visionary mouth,
the moon, the mountain, the round breast's sleepless eye.

Shapes of her fantasy in music from the bars,
swarming like juke-box lights the avenues;
no longer parked in the forest, from these cars,
these velvet rooms and wooden tourist camps,
sheetless under the naked white of the moon.
Wet gaze of eye, plum-color shadow and young
streams of these mouths, the streaming surface of earth
flowing alive with water, the egg and its becoming.

Coming in silence.     The shapes of every dread
seducing the isolated will.      They do not care.
They are not tortured, not tired, not alone.
They break to an arm, a leg, half of a mouth,
kissing disintegrate, flow whole, couple again;
she is changed along, she is a stream in a stream.

These are her endless years, woman and child, in dream
molded and wet, a bowl growing on a wheel,
not mud, not bowl, not clay, but this *becoming,*
winter and split of darkness, years of wish.
To want these couples, want these coupling pairs,
emblems of many parents, of the bed,
of love divided by dream, love with his dead wife,
love with her husband dead, love with his living love.

Mrs. Walpurga cries out  :  "It is not true!"
The light shifts, flowing away.      "It was never like—"
She stops, but nothing stops.     It moves.     It moves.
And not like anything.      And it is true.
The shapes disfigure.      Here is the feature man,
not whole, he is detail, he gleams and goes.
Here is the woman all cloth, black velvet face,
black, head to ground, close black fit to the skin,
slashed at the mouth and eyes, slashed at the breasts,
slashed at the triangle, showing rose everywhere.

Nights are disturbed, here is a crying river
running through years, here is the flight among
all the Objects of Love.      This wish, this gesture
irresisted, immortal seduction!      The young sea
streams over the land of dream, and there
the mountain like a mist-flower, the dark upright peak.
And over the sheet-flood Mrs. Walpurga
in whitened cycles of her changing moon.

The silence and the music change;      this song
rises and sharps, and never quite can scream—
but this is laughter harsher than nakedness
can take  —  in the shady shady grove the leaves
move over, the men and women move and part,
the river braids and unfolds in mingling song;
and here is the rain of summer from the moon,
relenting, wet, and giving life at last,
and Mrs. Walpurga and we may wake.

[1945]

# This Morning

Waking this morning,
a violent woman in the violent day
laughing.

           Past the line of memory
along the long body of your life
in which move childhood, youth, your lifetime of touch,
eyes, lips, chest, belly, sex, legs, to the waves of the sheet.
I look past the little plant
on the city windowsill
to the tall towers bookshapes, crushed together in greed,
the river flashing flowing corroded,
the intricate harbor and the sea, the wars, the moon the planets
                all who people space
in the sun visible invisible.
African violets in the light
breathing, in a breathing universe. I want strong peace, and delight,
the wild good.
I want to make my touch poems:
to find my morning, to find you entire
alive moving among the anti-touch people.


        I say across the waves of the air to you:
today once more
I will try to be non-violent
one more day
this morning, waking the world away
in the violent day

                          [1970]

# Käthe Kollwitz

## I

Held between wars
my lifetime
              among wars, the big hands of the world of death
my lifetime
listens to yours.

The faces of the sufferers
in the street, in dailiness,
their lives showing
through their bodies
a look as of music
the revolutionary look
that says   I am in the world
to change the world
my lifetime
is to love to endure to suffer the music
to set its portrait
up as a sheet of the world
the most moving the most alive
Easter and bone
and Faust walking among the flowers of the world
and the child alive within the living woman, music of man,
and death holding my lifetime between great hands
the hands of enduring life
that suffers the gifts and madness of full life, on earth, in our time,
and through my life, through my eyes, through my arms and hands
may give the face of this music in portrait waiting for
the unknown person
held in the two hands, you.

## II

Woman as gates, saying :
"The process is after all like music,

like the development of a piece of music.
The fugues come back and

                                again and again
interweave.
A theme may seem to have been put aside,
but it keeps returning—
the same thing modulated,
somewhat changed in form.
Usually richer.
And it is very good that this is so."

A woman pouring her opposites.
"After all there are happy things in life too.
Why do you show only the dark side?"
"I could not answer this. But I know—
in the beginning my impulse to know
the working life

                        had little to do with
pity or sympathy.

                        I simply felt
that the life of the workers was beautiful."

She said, "I am groping in the dark."

She said, "When the door opens, of sensuality,
then you will understand it too. The struggle begins.
Never again to be free of it,
often you will feel it to be your enemy.
Sometimes
you will almost suffocate,
such joy it brings."

Saying of her husband  :  "My wish
is to die after Karl.
I know no person who can love as he can,
with his whole soul.
Often this love has oppressed me;
I wanted to be free.
But often too it has made me
so terribly happy."

101

She said : "We rowed over to Carrara at dawn,
climbed up to the marble quarries
and rowed back at night. The drops of water
fell like glittering stars
from our oars."

She said : "As a matter of fact,
I believe
            that bisexuality
is almost   a necessary factor
in artistic production; at any rate,
the tinge of masculinity within me
helped me
            in my work."

She said : "The only technique I can still manage.
It's hardly a technique at all, lithography.
In it
        only the essentials count."

A tight-lipped man in a restaurant last night
            saying to me :
"Kollwitz?   She's too black-and-white."


III

Held among wars, watching
    all of them
    all these people
    weavers,
    Carmagnole

Looking at
    all of them
    death, the children
    patients in waiting-rooms
    famine
    the street
    the corpse with the baby
    floating, on the dark river

102

A woman seeing
  the violent, inexorable
  movement of nakedness
  and the confession of No
  the confession of great weakness, war,
  all streaming to one son killed, Peter;
  even the son left living; repeated,
  the father, the mother; the grandson
  another Peter killed in another war; firestorm;
  dark, light, as two hands,
  this pole and that pole as the gates.

What would happen if one woman told the truth about her life?
The world would split open

## IV  SONG : THE CALLING-UP

Rumor, stir of ripeness
rising within this girl
sensual blossoming
of meaning, its light and form.

The birth-cry summoning
out of the male, the father
from the warm woman
a mother in response.

The word of death
calls up the fight with stone
wrestle with grief with time
from the material make
an art harder than bronze.

## V  SELF-PORTRAIT

Mouth looking directly at you
eyes in their inwardness looking
directly at you
half light   half darkness
woman, strong, German, young artist

103

flows into
wide sensual mouth meditating
looking right at you
eyes shadowed with brave hand
looking deep at you
flows into
wounded brave mouth
grieving and hooded eyes
alive, German, in her first War
flows into
strength of the worn face
a skein of lines
broods, flows into
mothers among the war graves
bent over death
facing the father
stubborn upon the field
flows into
the marks of her knowing—
*Nie Wieder Krieg*
repeated in the eyes
flows into
"Seedcorn must not be ground"
and the grooved cheek
lips drawn fine
the down-drawn grief
face of our age
flows into
*Pieta,* mother and
between her knees
life as her son in death
pouring from the sky of
one more war
flows into
face almost obliterated
hand over the mouth forever
hand over one eye now
the other great eye
 closed

[1971]

104

# Despisals

In the human cities, never again to
despise the backside of the city, the ghetto,
or build it again as we build the despised
backsides of houses. Look at your own building.
You are the city.

Among our secrecies, not to despise our Jews
(that is, ourselves) or our darkness, our blacks,
or in our sexuality      wherever it takes us
and we now know we are productive
too productive, too reproductive
for our present invention—never to despise
the homosexual who goes building another

with touch    with touch    (not to despise any touch)
each like himself, like herself each.
You are this.
                    In the body's ghetto
never to go despising the asshole
nor the useful shit that is our clean clue
to what we need.      Never to despise
the clitoris in her least speech.

Never to despise in myself what I have been taught
to despise.      Not to despise the other.
Not to despise the *it*. To make this relation
with the it   :    to know that I am it.

[1973]

## Advice

My hazard wouldn't be yours, not ever;
But every doom, like a hazelnut, comes down
To its own worm. So I am rocking here
Like any granny with her apron over her head
Saying, lordy me. It's my trouble.
There's nothing to be learned this way.
If I heard a girl crying help
I would go to save her;
But you hardly ever hear those words.
Dear children, you must try to say
Something when you are in need.
Don't confuse hunger with greed;
And don't wait until you are dead.

[1970]

# I Have Three Daughters

I have three daughters
Like greengage plums.
They sat all day
Sucking their thumbs.
And more's the pity,
They cried all day,
Why doesn't our mother's brown hair
Turn gray?

I have three daughters
Like three cherries.
They sat at the window
The boys to please.
And they couldn't wait
For their mother to grow old.
Why doesn't our mother's brown hair
Turn to snow?

I have three daughters
In the apple tree
Singing Mama send Daddy
With three young lovers
To take them away from me.

I have three daughters
Like greengage plums,
Sitting all day
And sighing all day
And sucking their thumbs;
Singing, Mama won't you fetch and carry,
And Daddy, won't you let us marry,
Singing, sprinkle snow down on Mama's hair
And lordy, give us our share.

[1970]

# Salt

In the bell toll of a clang,
My feet in no snare,
My hand in no hand,
I went to the land of nowhere.

And it came to pass
The live grass spoke to me,
No woman is fair sang the grass,
They eat up the men, sang the grass
And the mist of the hanging tree
Smiled in the beard of Jehovah,
Pass on said the teeth and tongue,
I mean you no harm,
Take care to be strong,
Admit you are wrong.

Farther on by and by
I began to spy
The earth in the eye of a rock,
Then another eye
And another eye,
They ringed me round like a clock.

Weep, was what I thought they implied,
But my eyes were dry as salt.
Nothing would make my tears unlock.
You must pay the penalty, they cried,
If you insist on being a bride
It's all your fault.

And I saw the dark hair roots,
The long arms and the boots
Of despair.
And all the words of the air

Hissed in my ear,
Share!
Take off your flesh and share,
And we'll let you look in
At the sorcerer's virginal house of skin,
Where no woman goes,
For women are nothing but clothes.
And I peeped through the curtain and saw
A houseful of beautiful men.

And then did the boot
And the arm and hair
Come down from the tree
And measure my length with me standing there.
She's too long said the boot,
Too fat said the arm,
The hair sprang to my chin
And my lip like a swarm.
And down with a thud of earth went my form.

In the hourglass
It came to pass
I returned from where I died,
With my funeral veil
And my fairy tale
And the tears I never cried,
And the story's grown stale,
Female and Male,
Where the stars fly,
And we all die
On the down side.

[1970]

109

## Lineage

My grandmothers were strong.
They followed plows and bent to toil.
They moved through fields sowing seed.
They touched earth and grain grew.
They were full of sturdiness and singing.
My grandmothers were strong.

My grandmothers are full of memories
Smelling of soap and onions and wet clay
With veins rolling roughly over quick hands
They have many clean words to say.
My grandmothers were strong.
Why am I not as they?

[1942]

# Molly Means

Old Molly Means was a hag and a witch;
Chile of the devil, the dark, and sitch.
Her heavy hair hung thick in ropes
And her blazing eyes was black as pitch.
Imp at three and wench at 'leben
She counted her husbands to the number seben.
 O Molly, Molly,  Molly Means
 There goes the ghost of Molly Means.

Some say she was born with a veil on her face
So she could look through unnatchal space
Through the future and through the past
And charm a body or an evil place
And every man could well despise
The evil look in her coal black eyes.
 Old Molly, Molly, Molly Means
 Dark is the ghost of Molly Means.

And when the tale begun to spread
Of evil and of holy dread:
Her black-hand arts and her evil powers
How she cast her spells and called the dead,
The younguns was afraid at night
And the farmers feared their crops would blight.
 Old Molly, Molly, Molly Means
 Cold is the ghost of Molly Means.

Then one dark day she put a spell
On a young gal-bride just come to dwell
In the lane just down from Molly's shack
And when her husband come riding back
His wife was barking like a dog
And on all fours like a common hog.
 O Molly, Molly, Molly Means
 Where is the ghost of Molly Means?

The neighbors come and they went away
And said she'd die before break of day
But her husband held her in his arms
And swore he'd break the wicked charms,
He'd search all up and down the land
And turn the spell on Molly's hand.
     O Molly, Molly, Molly Means
     Sharp is the ghost of Molly Means.

So he rode all day and he rode all night
And at the dawn he come in sight
Of a man who said he could move the spell
And cause the awful thing to dwell
On Molly Means, to bark and bleed
Till she died at the hands of her evil deed.
     Old Molly, Molly, Molly Means
     This is the ghost of Molly Means.

Sometimes at night through the shadowy trees
She rides along on a winter breeze.
You can hear her holler and whine and cry.
Her voice is thin and her moan is high,
And her cackling laugh or her barking cold
Bring terror to the young and old.
     O Molly, Molly, Molly Means
     Lean is the ghost of Molly Means.

[1942]

# Kissie Lee

Toughest gal I ever did see
Was a gal by the name of Kissie Lee;
The toughest gal God ever made
And she drew a dirty, wicked blade.

Now this here gal warn't always tough
Nobody dreamed she'd turn out rough
But her Grammaw Mamie had the name
Of being the town's sin and shame.

When Kissie Lee was young and good
Didn't nobody treat her like they should
Allus gettin' beat by a no-good shine
An' allus quick to cry and whine.

Till her Grammaw said, "Now listen to me,
I'm tiahed of yoah whinin', Kissie Lee.
People don't never treat you right,
An' you allus scrappin' or in a fight.

"Whin I was a gal wasn't no soul
Could do me wrong an' still stay whole.
Ah got me a razor to talk for me
An' aftah that they let me be."

Well Kissie Lee took her advice
And after that she didn't speak twice
'Cause when she learned to stab and run
She got herself a little gun.

And from that time that gal was mean,
Meanest mama you ever seen.
She could hold her likker and hold her man
And she went thoo life jus' raisin' san'.

113

One night she walked in Jim's saloon
And seen a guy what spoke too soon;
He done her dirt long time ago
When she was good and feeling low.

Kissie bought her drink and she paid her dime
Watchin' this guy what beat her time
And he was making for the outside door
When Kissie shot him to the floor.

Not a word she spoke but she switched her blade
And flashing that lil ole baby paid:
Evvy livin' guy got out of her way
Because Kissie Lee was drawin' her pay.

She could shoot glass doors offa the hinges,
She could take herself on the wildest binges.
And she died with her boots on switching blades
On Talladega Mountain in the likker raids.

[1942]

EVE MERRIAM

# Tryst

When we were married eight years,
we saved up enough money
for my husband to buy me
an engagement ring.
I wear it to the office
to take dictation from the boss,
but then when I go to type
I take it off and
hide it in my cosmetic bag,
you never know with the
messengers or temporaries
the agencies send around.
Then when I finish up
at the end of the day,
I go to the ladies' room and
hang it on a chain
around my neck,
that way I don't have to
worry in the subway.
Cooking or doing the dishes,
I hide it in the candy jar
mixed in with the mints,
nobody would ever look there
and sometimes I find new places
like in the plaid stamp books,
it's hard even for me
to know all the nooks where
I put it.
Sometimes I think
when I take off my nightgown
for us to make love
I ought to
put it on
its really beautiful,
but there's enough
to worry about then
on my mind,
I don't want
more responsibility.

[1971]

115

## The Mother

Abortions will not let you forget.
You remember the children you got that you did not get,
The damp small pulps with a little or with no hair,
The singers and workers that never handled the air.
You will never neglect or beat
Them, or silence or buy with a sweet.
You will never wind up the sucking-thumb
Or scuttle off ghosts that come.
You will never leave them, controlling your luscious sigh,
Return for a snack of them, with gobbling mother-eye.

I have heard in the voices of the wind the voices of my dim killed
        children.
I have contracted. I have eased
My dim dears at the breasts they could never suck.
I have said, Sweets, if I sinned, if I seized
Your luck
And your lives from your unfinished reach,
If I stole your births and your names,
Your straight baby tears and your games,
Your stilted or lovely loves, your tumults, your marriages, aches, and
        your deaths,
If I poisoned the beginnings of your breaths,
Believe that even in my deliberateness I was not deliberate.
Though why should I whine,
Whine that the crime was other than mine?—
Since anyhow you are dead.
Or rather, or instead,
You were never made.
But that too, I am afraid,
Is faulty: oh, what shall I say, how is the truth to be said?

You were born, you had body, you died.
It is just that you never giggled or planned or cried.

Believe me, I loved you all.
Believe me, I knew you, though faintly, and I loved, I loved you
All.

[1944]


## Jessie Mitchell's Mother

Into her mother's bedroom to wash the ballooning body.
"My mother is jelly-hearted and she has a brain of jelly:
Sweet, quiver-soft, irrelevant. Not essential.
Only a habit would cry if she should die.
A pleasant sort of fool without the least iron. . . .
Are you better, mother, do you think it will come today?"
The stretched yellow rag that was Jessie Mitchell's mother
Reviewed her. Young, and so thin, and so straight.
So straight! as if nothing could ever bend her.
But poor men would bend her, and doing things with poor men,
Being much in bed, and babies would bend her over,
And the rest of things in life that were for poor women,
Coming to them grinning and pretty with intent to bend and to kill.
Comparisons shattered her heart, ate at her bulwarks:
The shabby and the bright: she, almost hating her daughter,
Crept into an old sly refuge: "Jessie's black
And her way will be black, and jerkier even than mine.
Mine, in fact, because I was lovely, had flowers
Tucked in the jerks, flowers were here and there. . . ."
She revived for the moment settled and dried-up triumphs,
Forced perfume into old petals, pulled up the droop,
Refueled
Triumphant long-exhaled breaths.
Her exquisite yellow youth. . . .

[1950]

117

## Housing Shortage

I tried to live small.
I took a narrow bed.
I held my elbows to my sides.
I tried to step carefully
And to think softly
And to breathe shallowly
In my portion of air
And to disturb no one.

Yet see how I spread out and I cannot help it.
I take to myself more and more, and I take nothing
That I do not need, but my needs grow like weeds,
All over and invading; I clutter this place
With all the apparatus of living.
You stumble over it daily.

And then my lungs take their fill.
And then you gasp for air.

Excuse me for living,
But, since I am living,
Given inches, I take yards,
Taking yards, dream of miles,
And a landscape, unbounded
And vast in abandon.

You too dreaming the same.

[1952]

## Two Women

There is a woman climbing a glass hill
Of clothes and dishes on a dusty floor;
Today surmounted, tomorrow towers still.

There is a woman opening like a door.
Many come in, but only she is bitch.
Empty, is filled, then empty as before.

There are two women, standing, and on each
Is smiled salvation or is howled damnation,
And, saved or damned, must still stay within reach.

Until the end,
When all are served, the sermons and the omens,
The preachers served, the children and the elders,
And still they come,
And still demand,
And still stand on her floor and ask for more.

And still the clipped wing leans against
Her eagle of experience.

[1952]

MADELINE DEFREES

## Letter to an Absent Son

It's right to call you son. That cursing alcoholic
is the god I married early before I really knew him:
spiked to his crossbeam bed, I've lasted thirty years.
Nails are my habit now. Without them I'm afraid.

At night I spider up the wall to hide in crevices
deeper than guilt. His hot breath smokes me out.
I fall and fall into the arms I bargained for,
sifting them cool as rain. A flower touch could tame me.
Bring me down that giant beam to lie submissive
in his fumbling clutch. One touch. Bad weather
moves indoors: a cyclone takes me.

How shall I find a shelter in the clouds, driven by
gods, gold breaking out of them everywhere?
Nothing is what it pretends. It gathers to a loss
of leaves and graves. Winter in the breath.
Your father looked like you, his dying proportioned
oddly to my breast. I boxed him in my plain pine
arms and let him take his ease just for a minute.

[1968]

# Pendant Watch

In Missoula, Montana, where the townsfolk water
the sidewalks, and the Clark Fork River barely interrupts
the usual flow of traffic on Higgins Avenue, I pass,
outside a furniture store, the world's largest
captain's chair. In it sits the world's largest captain,
native to Montana, foursquare and friendly,
with a timeless eye trained on the University
while the mountain flashes holding heaven
in a mist the rest of us steer clear of.

Still agile at forty-odd, I could shinny up
that walnut leg to lie in the lap of the god,
call him husband or lover, warm as any woman in a clockwork
swoon. Except that some more concentrated fire balanced
the cogs, married gut to metal. Today's AP wire
ticks off: Nun Burns Self to Death, and in eight-point type
from Saigon, a Buddhist virgin goes out in sheer fire
while I splutter cold a spark at a time.

Time hangs golden at my breast, a decoration in disrepair
that may not run much longer. Still, I am there beside
that well-regulated throne or bed, not altogether dead.
And the captain knows. And I know. We have it timed to the second.

[1969]

## The Centaur

The summer that I was ten—
Can it be there was only one
summer that I was ten? It must

have been a long one then—
each day I'd go out to choose
a fresh horse from my stable

which was a willow grove
down by the old canal.
I'd go on my two bare feet.

But when, with my brother's jack-knife,
I had cut me a long limber horse
with a good thick knob for a head,

and peeled him slick and clean
except a few leaves for the tail,
and cinched my brother's belt

around his head for a rein,
I'd straddle and canter him fast
up the grass bank to the path,

trot along in the lovely dust
that talcumed over his hoofs,
hiding my toes, and turning

his feet to swift half-moons.
The willow knob with the strap
jouncing between my thighs

was the pommel and yet the poll
of my nickering pony's head.
My head and my neck were mine,

yet they were shaped like a horse.
My hair flopped to the side
like the mane of a horse in the wind.

My forelock swung in my eyes,
my neck arched and I snorted.
I shied and skittered and reared,

stopped and raised my knees,
pawed at the ground and quivered.
My teeth bared as we wheeled

and swished through the dust again.
I was the horse and the rider,
and the leather I slapped to his rump

spanked my own behind.
Doubled, my two hoofs beat
a gallop along the bank,

the wind twanged in my mane,
my mouth squared to the bit.
And yet I sat on my steed

quiet, negligent riding,
my toes standing the stirrups,
my thighs hugging his ribs.

At a walk we drew up to the porch.
I tethered him to a paling.
Dismounting, I smoothed my skirt

and entered the dusky hall.
My feet on the clean linoleum
left ghostly toes in the hall.


*Where have you been?* said my mother.
*Been riding,* I said from the sink,
and filled me a glass of water.


*What's that in your pocket?* she said.
*Just my knife.* It weighted my pocket
and stretched my dress awry.


*Go tie back your hair,* said my mother,
and *Why is your mouth all green?*
*Rob Roy, he pulled some clover
as we crossed the field,* I told her.

[1956]

# Women

Women
  should be
    pedestals
      moving
        pedestals
          moving
            to the
              motions
                of men

Or they
  should be
    little horses
      those wooden
        sweet
          oldfashioned
            painted
              rocking
                horses

the gladdest things in the toyroom

      The
     pegs
    of their
   ears
  so familiar
 and dear
to the trusting
fists
To be chafed

feelingly
and then
unfeelingly
To be
joyfully
ridden
rockingly
ridden until
the restored

egos dismount and the legs stride away

Immobile
  sweetlipped
    sturdy
      and smiling
        women
          should always
            be waiting

willing
to be set
into motion
Women
  should be
    pedestals
      to men

[1968]

## PART TWO

*The Will to Change*—ADRIENNE RICH

MONA VAN DUYN

# Leda

> *"Did she put on his knowledge with his power*
> *Before the indifferent beak could let her drop?"*

Not even for a moment. He knew, for one thing, what he was.
When he saw the swan in her eyes he could let her drop.
In the first look of love men find their great disguise,
and collecting these rare pictures of himself was his life.

Her body became the consequence of his juice,
while her mind closed on a bird and went to sleep.
Later, with the children in school, she opened her eyes
and saw her own openness, and felt relief.

In men's stories her life ended with his loss.
She stiffened under the storm of his wings to a glassy shape,
stricken and mysterious and immortal. But the fact is,
she was not, for such an ending, abstract enough.

She tried for a while to understand what it was
that had happened, and then decided to let it drop.
She married a smaller man with a beaky nose,
and melted away in the storm of everyday life.

[1964]

# Leda Reconsidered

She had a little time to think
as he stepped out of water
that paled from the loss of his whiteness
and came toward her.
A certain wit in the way he

129

handled his webbed feet,
the modesty of the light that lay on him,
a perfectly clear, and unforgiveable,
irony in the cock of his head
told her more than he knew.
She sat there in the sunshine,
naked as a new-hatched bird,
watching him come,
trying to put herself
in the place of the cob, and see
what he saw:

flesh comfortable, used,
but still neatly following the bones,
a posture relaxed,
almost unseemly, expressing
(for the imagination,
unlike the poor body it strips and stirs,
is never assaulted)
openness, complicity even,
the look of a woman
with a context in which she can put
what comes next
(no chance of maiden's hysteria
if his beak pinched hold of her neck-skin,
yet the strangeness of the thing
could still startle her
into new gestures,)
and something—a heaviness,
as if she could bear things,
or as if, when he fertilized her,
he were seeding the bank she sat on,
the earth in its aspect of
quiescence.
She saw, with mortal eyes
that stung at the sight,
the pain of his transformations,
which, beautiful or comic,
came to the world

with the risk of the whole self.
She saw what he had to work through
as he took, over and over,
the risk of love,
the risk of being held,
and saw to the bare heart
of his soaring, his journeying,
his wish for the world
whose arms he could enter in the image
of what is brave or golden.

To love with the whole imagination—
she had never tried.
Was there a form for that?
Deep, in her inmost, grubby
female center
(how could he know that,
in his airiness?)
lay the joy of being used,
and its heavy peace, perhaps,
would keep her down.
To give: women and gods
are alike in enjoying that ceremony,
find its smoke filling and sweet.
But to give up was an offering
only she could savor,
simply by covering
her eyes.
And now, how much would she try
to see, to take,
of what was not hers, of what
was not going to be offered?
There was that old story
of matching him change for change,
pursuing, and at the solstice
devouring him.
A man's story.
No, she was not that hungry
for experience. She had her loves.

To re-imagine her life—
as if the effort were muscular
she lifted herself a little
and felt the pull at neck
and shoulderblade, back
to the usual.
And suppose she reached with practiced arms
past the bird, short of the god,
for a vulnerable mid-point,
and held on,
just how short-sighted would that
be? Would the heavens in a flurry record
a major injustice to the world's
possibilities?

He took his time,
pausing to shake out a wing.
The arrogance of that gesture!
And yet she saw him
as the true god.
He was close to some uncommitted
part of her.
Her thoughts dissolved and
fell out of her body like dew
onto the grass of the bank,
the small wild flowers,
as his shadow,
the first chill of his ghostliness,
fell on her skin.
She waited for him so quietly that
he came on her quietly,
almost with tenderness,
not treading her.
Her hand moved into the dense plumes
on his breast to touch
the utter stranger.

[1964]

# The Fear of Flying

*". . . shall it be given us to speak in the spiritual,*
  *unearthly voice of a bat or a jet?"*

At the airport, ready to leave on my little trip,
I tell you goodbye and start
to get in line at the door, our relationship
so old we don't kiss, when my heart

goes crazy with pain and fear, jumps in my throat,
my stomach heaves, I want
to get out of this frozen skin and run for the heat
of your body and yet I can't.

Every time I'm about to get on a plane it's the same
sick terror. I've got to know what
brings on such hysteria, what in God's name
is the matter with me. It's not

the fear of death. You've rehearsed me so often in that,
with your false springs, your icy
changes of heart and face, I'm bored at the thought
of there being no more me

to see and feel them. It's not as if we were young
and couldn't bear to part—
far from it. We've been yoked together so long
it doesn't even hurt

that we both forget every anniversary.
There were good years together,
one has to remember that towards the end, surely—
moondazzle, peach weather,

brilliant noons, eloquent storms, sweet
new spears of tenderness,

all the lovely things, natural and trite,
one has to believe, I guess,

make life worth living, made it worth our while
to have come to middle age
with such brutal knowledge of one another. How well
I know each clever image

you present in public, the four parts you play
(none of them now for me) :
The cool, brittle disillusioned roué,
handsome as a fall tree,

with secret softnesses beneath, to be found
and nursed into late bloom,
much rarer of course than of April's callow ground,
by someone in the room.

Or, your hair redyed, the hand-holder,
fresh buds in your buttonhole,
the whole green youth bit again, the breezy,
twittery, dancing, boy-girl

approach. (How you pull that bright illusion out
of the hat at your age
over and over, I'll never know. It's what,
watching it from offstage,

can hurt me most, whose one-and-only springtime
in one of yours is over.)
Or, with faintly snow-streaked hair, you mime
the quiet, fatherly lover,

all passion spent, not at all dangerous—
yes, that appeals to some.
How often you used to fool me with that face
of pure, restful welcome—

then, if I leaned against you, I'd feel the sleet
of your look, go numb at your blast

of contempt, turn to a snow-wife of hate.
And we know, don't we, the last

of your roles? Remember, my dear, I played it with you
for long, bountiful seasons?
We bathed, we melted down to the bone in the blue
air, the ripe suns

of ourselves, stretched and vined together all over,
it seemed, sweltered, grew
lush undergrowth, weeds, flowers, groundcover.
I played and played with you,

day after burning day, the part of our lives
truest, perhaps, best,
and still can play it briefly if someone believes
I can: the sensualist.

Your cheek used to cool first and then rewarm,
but now our hot coinciding
is rare. Is this wordy drizzle a late-summer storm
or an autumnal? I'm hiding

something that wants to scream out, "Wait! Not yet!
It's too soon for me
to go away into thin air," a thing that
I can't say or see.

I see it, foolish and clear, and say it. Sometimes,
our minds are so used to whirling,
it's hard to believe the simple meters and rhymes
and explanations. Darling,

my world, my senses' home, familiar monster,
it would seem that I still love you,
and, like a schoolgirl deep in her first despair,
I hate to go above you.

[1969]

# The Women in Vietnam

This is about the women of that country
sometimes they spoke in slogans
They said
   We patch the roads as we patch our sweetheart's trousers
   The heart will stop but not the transport
They said
   We have ensured production even near bomb craters
   Children let your voices sing higher than the explosions of the bombs
They said
   We have important tasks to teach the children
   that the people are the collective masters
   to bear hardship
   to instill love in the family
   to guide for good health of the children (they must
   wear clothing according to climate)
They said
   once men beat their wives
   now they may not
   once a poor family sold its daughter to a rich old man
   now the young may love one another
They said
   once we planted our rice any old way
   now we plant the young shoots in straight rows
   so the imperialist pilot can see how steady our
   hands are

In the evening we walked along the shores of the Lake of the Restored
                    Sword
I said is it true? we are sisters?
They said, Yes, we are of one family

[1973]

One day when I was a child, long ago
Mr. Long Ago spoke up in school.
He said
Oh children you must roll your r's
no no not on your tongue little girl
IN YOUR THROAT
there is nothing so beautiful as r rolled in the throat
                    of a French woman
no woman more beautiful
he said looking back
                back
                    at beauty.

[1973]

SHIRLEY KAUFMAN

# Watts

for Sabatino (Sam) Rodia, builder of the Towers,
who died in Martinez, California July 16, 1965, before the riots


I

My friend who married the girl I
introduced him to after he felt
my breasts under the steering wheel
of his parents' borrowed DeSoto,
and swims in a big jar
in the San Fernando Valley,

my friend who plucks tonsils
with manicured tweezers, and gave me
a Barlach woodcut of two agonized
women for my last birthday,
                              tells me
he's learning to shoot
with his children, teaching them how
with a gun, and last week
he hit the bull's eye at fifty feet
twenty times out of twenty.

The son who sings in the choir
wins prizes. The youngest, a girl,
plays the flute and the cello.
The middle one studies hard.

      Why?
I ask
wanting to start over.
      Why?

      We all need a gun

in the house. Learn
to use one. The first time
I fired it, they jumped.
Now they love it. And Watts,
he says.
Think about Watts.


2

Monday morning and the red garbage
truck shifts up the hill, jerking
like bones, like California
sliding in the sea.
                    Bent,
with the big can strapped to his shoulder,
cigar in his teeth, tattoo on his arm,
and two flat boxes of slimy lettuce,
chicken bones, sardine cans,
used-up carbon stuck to his hands,
he climbs the path to the street
and heaves the dreck in.
                              What
do we keep?
                    Eyes, lips, heavy
drops on the neck, my friend
with his pool in his fists.

        Sensibility,
he says,
        I don't know what that means.

Scatters the water
from his wrists.


3

I went to Watts to see
the Towers. To see the sky
come at me

in thin frames, bleached
by the bluer glass.
                    The Towers.
Flying like ladders, testing
a coolness that we never
reach.
            As if I raised
myself into that breach, as if
I climbed on coiled springs
                        into air.


(Taylor over the keyboard
                        lifting
the sound so fast his hands
are spaces that the wind
pours through.)


                Broken mirrors
and my face in parts,
the shapes of corn ears,
baskets, one thin shoe.
Thirty-three years, Rodia,
card number 6719 in the International
Hod Carriers, Building and Common
Laborers' Union, his blunt
trowel slapping the wet cement,
twisting the hoops to let
the light come in, lifting
the junk, the junk
                to spires!


The way trees grow and slowly,
ring over ring.
                Plates,
abalone shells, bottles,
lengths of pipe.


                Against
his death.

## 4

Guns in warm houses.
Rifles. Knives.

        Glass
in the streets and burned-out
doors.

      I'm saving
finger nails, cut-off hair,
nothing that sticks or stays
the same, but still
it's there. Shape of my lap
turned into something different
when I stand.

       It grows.
Dead leaves and babies,
cancelled maps,
         even
my shadows, reflections in water,
loose skin over each
knuckle of my hand.

               [1969]


# Room

O this is the creature that does not exist.—Rilke

      **I**

The sky can't get in.
Or sun where you enter
the core of the wood.
Extravagant, burned-out
trees. There is no
provision for darkness.

141

Shadows flow smooth
down your skin, and the skin
of the tree thickens.
You stretch to his face,
and the flesh of your ribs
grows into his arms.
You give whatever is
possible. After so many
forests. And you are
slowly what you are
in any light.
        It happens
only when you give it
room. That milky beast.
Fed on the chance
that it might be,
it is. Destructible
as anything that lasts.

### 2

Lights hum at the window
like hives opened out.
They swarm through your head.
They move in the dark
of his fingers finding
your breasts.
        And laurel.
Changed back to woman,
more lavish than she
ever was. Who is he
sliding in your arms? What
will become of you?

### 3

Is it because he
told you what he dreamed?
Drawing a boat through
the fountain. Carefully.

142

Fontainebleau's opulent
gardens. Or does it
grow to more than you
can manage as a game?
Every château in France.
Your belly is warm
and feathered. His mouth
is tasting your shoulder.
And the duck goes after
her babies in the pond.
Waking and waking and
waking, you breathe
the light from his skin.
A swimmer whose arms lift
heavy, suddenly.

4

You are behind the surface
of yourselves. His hand
strokes the outside
of your hand. Your colder
skin. Why does it
cry each time
at the tense bone until
the flesh gives in?
The sun is over
the great park. He has
gone out of you.

[1969]

# Mothers, Daughters

Through every night we hate,
preparing the next day's
war. She bangs the door.
Her face laps up my own

despair, the sour, brown eyes,
the heavy hair she won't
tie back. She's cruel,
as if my private meanness
found a way to punish us.
We gnaw at each other's
skulls. Give me what's mine.
I'd haul her back, choking
myself in her, herself
in me. There is a book
called *Poisons* on her shelf.
Her room stinks with incense,
animal turds, hamsters
she strokes like silk. They
exercise on the bathroom
floor, and two drop through
the furnace vent. The whole
house smells of the accident,
the hot skins, the small
flesh rotting. Six days
we turn the gas up then
to fry the dead. I'd fry
her head if I could until
she cried love, love me!

All she won't let me do.
Her stringy figure in
the windowed room shares
its thin bones with no one.
Only her shadow on the glass
waits like an older sister.
Now she stalks, leans forward,
concentrates merely on getting
from here to there. Her feet
are bare. I hear her breathe
where I can't get in. If I
break through to her, she will
drive nails into my tongue.

[1969]

144

# Apples

No use waiting for it to stop
raining in my face like a wet towel,
having to catch a plane,
to pick the apples from her tree
and bring them home.

The safest place to be
is under the branches. She
in her bed and her mouth
dry in the dry room.
Don't go out in the rain.

I stretch my arms for apples
anyway, feel how the ripe ones
slide in my hands like cups
that want to be perfect. Juices
locked up in the skin.

She used to slice them in quarters,
cut through the core,
open the inside out. Fingers
steady on the knife, expert
at stripping things.

Sometimes she split them sideways
into halves to let a star break
from the center with tight seeds,
because I wanted that,
six petals in the flesh.

Flavor of apples inhaled as flowers,
not even biting them.
Apples at lunch or after school
like soup, a fragrance rising
in the steam, eat and be well.

I bring the peeled fruit to her
where she lies, carve it
in narrow sections, celery white,
place them between her fingers,
Mother, eat. And be well.

Sit where her brown eyes
empty out the light, watching
her mind slip backwards
on the pillow, swallowing
apples, swallowing her life.

[1970]

## To the Snake

Green Snake, when I hung you round my neck
and stroked your cold, pulsing throat
            as you hissed to me, glinting
arrowy gold scales, and I felt
            the weight of you on my shoulders,
and the whispering silver of your dryness
            sounded close at my ears—

Green Snake—I swore to my companions that certainly
            you were harmless! But truly
I had no certainty, and no hope, only desiring
            to hold you, for that joy,
                              which left
a long wake of pleasure, as the leaves moved
and you faded into the pattern
of grass and shadows, and I returned
smiling and haunted, to a dark morning.

                                        [1958]

# Song for Ishtar

The moon is a sow
and grunts in my throat
Her great shining shines through me
so the mud of my hollow gleams
and breaks in silver bubbles

She is a sow
and I a pig and a poet

When she opens her white
lips to devour me I bite back
and laughter rocks the moon

In the black of desire
we rock and grunt, grunt and
shine

[1962]

# Hypocrite Women

Hypocrite women, how seldom we speak
of our own doubts, while dubiously
we mother man in his doubt!

And if at Mill Valley perched in the trees
the sweet rain drifting through western air
a white sweating bull of a poet told us

our cunts are ugly—why didn't we
admit we have thought so too? (And
what shame? They are not for the eye!)

No, they are dark and wrinkled and hairy,
caves of the Moon . . .     And when a
dark humming fills us, a

coldness towards life,
we are too much women to
own to such unwomanliness.

Whorishly with the psychopomp
we play and plead—and say
nothing of this later.     And our dreams,

with what frivolity we have pared them
like toenails, clipped them like ends of
split hair.

[1962]

149

# In Mind

There's in my mind a woman
of innocence, unadorned but

fair-featured, and smelling of
apples or grass. She wears

a utopian smock or shift, her hair
is light brown and smooth, and she

is kind and very clean without
ostentation—
              but she has
no imagination.
                And there's a
turbulent moon-ridden girl

or old woman, or both,
dressed in opals and rags, feathers

and torn taffeta,
who knows strange songs—

but she is not kind.

[1962]

# About Marriage

Don't lock me in wedlock, I want
marriage, an
encounter—

I told you about the
green light of
May

> (a veil of quiet befallen
> the downtown park,
> late
>
> Saturday after
> noon, long
> shadows and cool.
>
> air, scent of
> new grass,
> fresh leaves,
>
> blossom on the threshold of
> abundance—
>
> and the birds I met there,
> birds of passage breaking their journey,
> three birds each of a different species:
>
> the azalea-breasted with round poll, dark,
> the brindled, merry, mousegliding one,
> and the smallest, golden as gorse and wearing
> a black Venetian mask
>
> and with them the three douce hen-birds
> feathered in tender, lively brown—
> I stood

a half-hour under the enchantment,
no-one passed near,
the birds saw me and


let me be
near them.)

It's not
irrelevant:
I would be
met

and meet you
so,
in a green

airy space, not
locked in.

[1962]


# Stepping Westward

What is green in me
darkens, muscadine.

If woman is inconstant,
good, I am faithful to

ebb and flow, I fall
in season and now

is a time of ripening.
If her part

is to be true,
a north star,

good, I hold steady
in the black sky

and vanish by day,
yet burn there

in blue or above
quilts of cloud.

There is no savor
more sweet, more salt

than to be glad to be
what, woman,

and who, myself,
I am, a shadow

that grows longer as the sun
moves, drawn out

on a thread of wonder.
If I bear burdens

they begin to be remembered
as gifts, goods, a basket

of bread that hurts
my shoulders but closes me

in fragrance. I can
eat as I go.

[1966]

# Life at War

The disasters numb within us
caught in the chest, rolling
in the brain like pebbles. The feeling
resembles lumps of raw dough

weighing down a child's stomach on baking day.
Or Rilke said it, 'My heart . . .
Could I say of it, it overflows
with bitterness . . . but no, as though

its contents were simply balled into
formless lumps, thus
do I carry it about.'
The same war

continues.
We have breathed the grits of it in, all our lives,
our lungs are pocked with it,
the mucous membrane of our dreams
coated with it, the imagination
filmed over with the gray filth of it:

the knowledge that humankind,

delicate Man, whose flesh
responds to a caress, whose eyes
are flowers that perceive the stars,

whose music excels the music of birds,
whose laughter matches the laughter of dogs,
whose understanding manifests designs
fairer than the spider's most intricate web,

still turns without surprise, with mere regret
to the scheduled breaking open of breasts whose milk
runs out over the entrails of still-alive babies,
transformation of witnessing eyes to pulp-fragments,
implosion of skinned penises into carcass-gulleys.

We are the humans, men who can make;
whose language imagines *mercy,*
*lovingkindness;* we have believed one another
mirrored forms of a God we felt as good—

who do these acts, who convince ourselves
it is necessary; these acts are done
to our own flesh; burned human flesh
is smelling in Viet Nam as I write.

Yes, this is the knowledge that jostles for space
in our bodies along with all we
go on knowing of joy, of love;

our nerve filaments twitch with its presence
day and night,
nothing we say has not the husky phlegm of it in the saying,
nothing we do has the quickness, the sureness,
the deep intelligence living at peace would have.

[1968]

# An Embroidery (I)

Rose Red's hair is brown as fur
and shines in firelight as she prepares
supper of honey and apples, curds and whey,
for the bear, and leaves it ready
on the hearth-stone.

Rose White's grey eyes
look into the dark forest.

Rose Red's cheeks are burning,
sign of her ardent, joyful
compassionate heart.
Rose White is pale,
turning away when she hears
the bear's paw on the latch.

When he enters, there is
frost on his fur,
he draws near to the fire
giving off sparks.

Rose White catches the scent of the forest,
of mushrooms, of rosin.

Together Rose Red and Rose White
sing to the bear;
it is a cradle song, a loom song,
a song about marriage, about
a pilgrimage to the mountains
long ago.
            Raised on an elbow,
the bear stretched on the hearth
nods and hums; soon he sighs
and puts down his head.

He sleeps; the Roses
bank the fire.
Sunk in the clouds of their feather bed
they prepare to dream.

Rose Red in a cave that smells of honey
dreams she is combing the fur of her cubs
with a golden comb.
Rose White is lying awake.

Rose White shall marry the bear's brother.
Shall he too
when the time is ripe,
step from the bear's hide?
Is that other, her bridegroom,
here in the room?

[1971]

# To William Wordsworth from Virginia

I think, old bone, the world's not with us much.
I think it is too difficult to see,
But easy to discuss. Behold the bush.
His seasons out-maneuver Proteus.
This year, because of the drought, the barberry
Is all goldflakes in August, but I'll still say
To the First Grade next month, "*Now* it is Fall.
You see the leaves go bright, and then go small.
You see October's greatcoat. It is gold.
It will lie on the earth to keep the seed's foot warm.
Then, Andrew Obenchain, what happens in June?"
And Andrew, being mountain-bred, will know
Catawba runs too deep for the bus to get
Across the ford—at least it did last May,
And school was out, and the laundry wouldn't dry,
And when the creek went down, the bluebells lay
In Hancock's pasture-border, thick as hay.

What do they tell the First Grade in Peru,
I wonder? All the story: God is good,
He counts the children, and the sparrow's wing.
God loved William Wordsworth in the spring.
William Wordsworth had enough to eat.
Wye was his broth, Helvellyn was his meat,
And English was his cookstove. And where did words
Come from, Carlyle Rucker? Words that slide
The world together. Words that split the tide
Apart for Moses (not for Mahon's bus),
Words that say, the bushes burn for us—
Lilac, forsythia, orange, Sharon rose—
For us the seasons wheel, the lovers wait,
All things become the flesh of our delight,
The evidence of our wishes.

## Witch, so might

I stand beside the barberry and dream
Wisdom to babes, and health to beggar men,
And help to David hunting in the hills
The Appalachian fox. By words, I might.
But, sir, I am tired of living in a lake
Among the watery weeds and weedy blue
Shadows of flowers that Hancock never grew.
I am tired of my wet wishes, of running away
Like all the nymphs, from the droughty eye of day.
Run, Daphne. Run, Europa, Io, run!
There is not a god left underneath the sun
To balk, to ride, to suffer, to obey.
Here is the unseasonable barberry.
Here is the black face of a child in need.
Here is the bloody figure of a man.
Run, Great Excursioner. Run if you can.

[1961]

# For a Homecoming

I wish you were not flying, and I wish
Women were not fond, and men were not foolish.
Who'd ever invent
Wings out of wax, that had godsent
Patience-plumes to plumb her element?
Safe in my space, and surfeited, I stare
At the new violence in the air,
And think of little boys who screw the tops
Off the cleaning fluid, and knot the heads of mops,
And peel the bark off trees, and kick the stones
When there's no one around to pester with questions.
Oh, I know,
I'd be content in a cave, and I know that some
Incredibly curious germ of evolution
Lets you conceive a rafter and a beam
And a plastic tablecloth. A single name
Is all my woe, whatever was first on the tongue
In the beginning. Disaster and joy came then
Honestly: a banana was not a storm,
Absent was over, present was, possibly, warm.
But oh the daisy-petal words: is not,
Is or is not, is safe, tired, hungry, sick,
Unfaithful, lost, laughing, will not come home,
Will come home late. I will not sleep all night,
Preparing the news, hearing the morning break
In the trees, and the wings unfold that cannot make
Any but natural journeys while they wake.

[1961]

JANE COOPER

# The Knowledge That Comes Through Experience*

I feel my face being bitten by the tides
Of knowledge as sea-tides bite at a beach;
Love leaves its implications, wars encroach
On the flat white square between my ear and jaw
Picking it as the sea hollows out sand. . . .
I might as well stick my head in the maw

Of the ocean as live this generously:
Feelings aside I never know my face.
I comb my hair and what I see is timeless,
Not a face at all but (besides the hair)
Lips and a pair of eyes, two hands, a body
Pale as a fish imprisoned in the mirror.

When shall I rest, when shall I find myself
The way I'll be, iced in a shop window?
Maybe I'll wake tonight in the undertow
Of sleep and lie adrift, gutted helpless
By the salt at my blue eyes—then the gulfs
Of looks and desire will shine clean at last.

Meanwhile I use myself. I am useful
Rather foolishly, like a fish who yearns
Dimly towards daylight. There is much to learn
And curiosity riddles our rewards.
It seems to me I may be capable
Once I'm a skeleton, of love and wars.

[1950; 1973]

# My Young Mother

My young mother, her face narrow
and dark with unresolved wishes
under a hatbrim of the twenties,
stood by my middleaged bed.

Still as a child pretending sleep
to a grownup watchful or calling,
I lay in a corner of my dream
staring at the mole above her lip.

Familiar mole! but that girlish look
as if I had nothing to give her—
Eyes blue—brim dark—
calling me from sleep after decades.

[1957]

# In the House of the Dying

So once again, hearing the tired aunts
whisper together under the kitchen globe,
I turn away; I am not one of them.

At the sink I watch the water cover my hands
in a sheath of light. Upstairs she lies alone
dreaming of autumn nights when her children were born.

On the steps between us grows in a hush of waiting
the impossible silence between two generations.
The aunts buzz on like flies around a bulb.

I am dressed like them. Standing with my back turned
I wash the dishes in the same easy way.
Only at birth and death do I utterly fail.

For death is my old friend who waits on the stairs.
Whenever I pass I nod to him like the newsman
who is there every day; for them he is the priest.

While the birth of love is so terrible to me
I feel unworthy of the commonest marriage.
Upstairs she lies, washed through by the two miracles.

[1957]

# Rock Climbing

Higher than gulls' nests, higher than children go,
Scrambling and dangling to survey the sea,
   We crest the last outcropping strewn
      East of this island.


Now pell-mell, now stopping to pinch a finger
In an open fissure down which no sun glints,
   Where water gnaws and subsides, we comb
      As the tide rises


Each rock that locks us in a partial vision
Of the expanding, curved and eye-reflecting blue
   Which liberates but still hangs over
      Our minds' breathing.


As yet the gleams are steep and unexpected:
We study lichens like a dying scale,
   Silver as fishes; here crisp moss
      Moist in a crevice;


Then even lichens powder, and the rocks
Give way to sunny tables, dry escarpments,
   Each with its different texture, pocked
      Or smoothly sloping


Down to the pitch where barnacles or stain
Dark as a rust line show the heaving power
   Of water's shoulders, raised at night,
      Then wrested over.


And now the last rock! piled hugely up
And shoved to end a sprinkle like a jetty

Of little boulders in the green-brown
        Irregular surface

Where seaweed shaped like coral swimming, kelp,
Pebbles and broken shells of clam or crab
    All shine or flicker up as down-watching
        We kneel and wonder.

Now balancing, laughing, brisk as children who
Spread out their arms and toe along a pole
    We skip from top to top, lift knees,
        Come out at angles

Until we have scaled it! stand aloft at last
With all the ocean for our freedom and
    Our meditation, all the swing
        Of limbs for glitter.

Warmed by the sun, tingling, with tired calves
And eyes of exultation we address
    The father of our knowledge, shrouded
        Faintly beyond us

At the lost line where wind is turned to water
And all is turned to light, dissolved or rinsed
    To silver where our eyes fish (gulls
        Sailing and falling

Out, out. . . .) And now the seabirds call
Far off, recalled by memories like hunger,
    Screech and return, flying the tides
        Of pure air inwards

To where their nests are, intimate and cold;
While standing on those cliffs we slowly rest
    And looking back to hillsides build
        Imaginary houses.

[1957]

VASSAR MILLER

## Spinster's Lullaby

For Jeff

Clinging to my breast, no stronger
Than a small snail snugly curled,
Safe a moment from the world,
Lullaby a little longer.

Wondering how one tiny human
Resting so, on toothpick knees
In my scraggly lap, gets ease,
I rejoice, no less a woman

With my nipples pinched and dumb
To your need whose one word's sucking.
Never mind, though. To my rocking
Nap a minute, find your thumb

While I gnaw a dream and nod
To the gracious sway that settles
Both our hearts, imperiled petals
Trembling on the pulse of God.

[1960]

# Trimming the Sails

I move among my pots and pans
That have no life except my own,
Nor warmth save from my flesh and bone,
That serve my tastes and not a man's.

I'm jealous of each plate and cup,
Frail symbol of my womanhood.
Creator-like, I call it good
And vow I will not give it up.

I move among my things and think
Of Woolman, who, for loving care
He had for slaves, used wooden ware,
And wash my silver in the sink,

Wishing my knives and forks were finer.
Though Lady Poverty won heart
Of Francis, her male counterpart
Would find in me a sad decliner.

Sometimes regret's old dogs will hound me
With feeble barks, yet my true love
Is Brother Fire and Sister Stove
And walls and friends and books around me.

Yet to renounce your high romances
Being part pain—may so to do
Prove half humility that you
May bless, good Woolman and sweet Francis!

[1960]

# On Approaching My Birthday

My mother bore me in the heat of summer
when the grass blanched under sun's hammer stroke
and the birds sang off key, panting between notes,
and the pear trees once all winged with whiteness
sagged, breaking with fruit, and only the zinnias,
like harlots, bloomed out vulgar and audacious,
and when the cicadas played all day long
their hidden harpsichords accompanying
her grief, my mother bore me, as I say,
then died shortly thereafter, no doubt
of her disgust and left me her disease
when I grew up to wither into truth.

[1968]

CAROLYN KIZER

# Hera, Hung from the Sky

I hang by my heels from the sky.
The sun, exploded at last,
Hammered his wrath to chains
Forged for my lightest bones.
Once I was warmed to my ears,
Kept close; now blind with fire!
What a child, taking heat for delight
So simply! Scorched within,
I still burn as I swing,
A pendulum kicking the night,
An alarum at dawn, I deflect
The passage of birds, ring down
The bannering rain. I indict
This body, its ruses, games,
Its plot to unseat the sun.
I pitted my feminine weight
Against God, his terrible throne.
From the great dome of despair,
I groan, I swing, I swing
In unconstellated air.

I had shared a sovereign cloud:
The lesser, the shadowy twin
To my lord. All woman and weight
Of connubial love that sings
Within the cabinet's close
And embracing intimacy.
I threw it all to the skies
In an instant of power, poise—
Arrogant, flushed with his love,
His condescending praise;
From envy of shine and blaze,
Mad, but beautifully mad,
Hypnotized by the gaze

169

Of self into self, the dream
That woman was great as man—
As humid, as blown with fame,
So great I seemed to be!
I threw myself to the skies
And the sky has cast me down.
I have lost the war of the air:
Half-strangled in my hair,
I dangle, drowned in fire.

[1961]


# A Muse of Water

We who must act as handmaidens
To our own goddess, turn too fast,
Trip on our hems, to glimpse the muse
Gliding below her lake or sea,
Are left, long-staring after her,
Narcissists by necessity;

Or water-carriers of our young
Till waters burst, and white streams flow
Artesian, from the lifted breast:
Cup-bearers then, to tiny gods,
Imperious table-pounders, who
Are final arbiters of thirst.

Fasten the blouse, and mount the steps
From kitchen taps to Royal Barge,
Assume the trident, don the crown,
Command the Water Music now
That men bestow on Virgin Queens;
Or, goddessing above the waist,

Appear as swan on Thames or Charles
Where iridescent foam conceals

The paddle-stroke beneath the glide:
Immortal feathers preened in poems!
Not our true, intimate nature, stained
By labor, and the casual tide.

Masters of civilization, you
Who moved to river bank from cave,
Putting up tents, and deities,
Though every rivulet wander through
The final, unpolluted glades
To cinder-bank and culvert-lip,

And all the pretty chatterers
Still round the pebbles as they pass
Lightly over their watercourse,
And even the calm rivers flow,
We have, while springs and skies renew,
Dry wells, dead seas, and lingering drouth.

Water itself is not enough.
Harness her turbulence to work
For man: fill his reflecting pools.
Drained for his cofferdams, or stored
In reservoirs for his personal use:
Turn switches! Let the fountains play!

And yet these buccaneers still kneel
Trembling at the water's verge:
"Cool River-Goddess, sweet ravine,
Spirit of pool and shade, inspire!"
So he needs poultice for his flesh.
So he needs water for his fire.

We rose in mists and died in clouds
Or sank below the trammeled soil
To silent conduits underground,
Joining the blind-fish, and the mole.
A gleam of silver in the shale:
Lost murmur! Subterranean moan!

So flows in dark caves, dries away,
What would have brimmed from bank to bank,
Kissing the fields you turned to stone,
Under the boughs your axes broke.
And you blame streams for thinning out,
Plundered by man's insatiate want?

Rejoice when a faint music rises
Out of a brackish clump of weeds,
Out of the marsh at ocean-side,
Out of the oil-stained river's gleam,
By the long causeways and grey piers
Your civilizing lusts have made.

Discover the deserted beach
Where ghosts of curlews safely wade:
Here the warm shallows lave your feet
Like tawny hair of magdalens.
Here, if you care, and lie full-length,
Is water deep enough to drown.

[1961]

## One

From Sappho to myself, consider the fate of women.
How unwomanly to discuss it! Like a noose or an albatross necktie
The clinical sobriquet hangs us: cod-piece coveters.
Never mind these epithets; I myself have collected some honeys.
Juvenal set us apart in denouncing our vices
Which had grown, in part, from having been set apart:
Women abused their spouses, cuckolded them, even plotted
To poison them. Sensing, behind the violence of his manner—
"Think I'm crazy or drunk?"—his emotional stake in us,
As we forgive Strindberg and Nietzsche, we forgive all those
Who cannot forget us. We *are* hyenas. Yes, we admit it.

While men have politely debated free will, we have howled for it,
Howl still, pacing the centuries, tragedy heroines.
Some who sat quietly in the corner with their embroidery
Were Defarges, stabbing the wool with the names of their ancient
Oppressors, who ruled by the divine right of the male—
I'm impatient of interruptions! I'm aware there were millions
Of mutes for every Saint Joan or sainted Jane Austen,
Who, vague-eyed and acquiescent, worshiped God as a man.
I'm not concerned with those cabbageheads, not truly feminine
But neutered by labor. I mean real women, like *you* and like *me*.

Freed in fact, not in custom, lifted from furrow and scullery,
Not obliged, now, to be the pot for the annual chicken,
*Have we begun to arrive in time?* With out well-known
Respect for life because it hurts so much to come out with it;
Disdainful of "sovereignty," "national honor" and other abstractions;
We can say, like the ancient Chinese to successive waves of invaders,
"Relax, and let us absorb you. You can learn temperance
In a more temperate climate." Give us just a few decades
Of grace, to encourage the fine art of acquiescence
And we might save the race. Meanwhile, observe our creative chaos,
Flux, efflorescence—whatever you care to call it!

# Two

I take as my theme, "The Independent Woman,"
Independent but maimed: observe the exigent neckties
Choking violet writers; the sad slacks of stipple-faced matrons;
Indigo intellectuals, crop-haired and callous-toed,
Cute spectacles, chewed cuticles, aced out by full-time beauties
In the race for a male. Retreating to drabness, bad manners
And sleeping with manuscripts. Forgive our transgressions
Of old gallantries as we hitch in chairs, light our own cigarettes,
Not expecting your care, having forfeited it by trying to get even.

But we need dependency, cosseting and well-treatment.
So do men sometimes. Why don't they admit it?
We will be cows for a while, because babies howl for us,
Be kittens or bitches, who want to eat grass now and then
For the sake of our health. But the role of pastoral heroine
Is not permanent, Jack. We want to get back to the meeting.

Knitting booties and brows, tartars or termagants, ancient
Fertility symbols, chained to our cycle, released
Only in part by devices of hygiene and personal daintiness,
Strapped into our girdles, held down, yet uplifted by man's
Ingenious constructions, holding coiffures in a breeze,
Hobbled and swathed in whimsey, tripping on feminine
Shoes with fool heels, losing our lipsticks, you, me,
In ephemeral stockings, clutching our handbags and packages.

Our masks, always in peril of smearing or cracking,
In need of continuous check in the mirror or silverware,
Keep us in thrall to ourselves, concerned with our surfaces.
Look at man's uniform drabness, his impersonal envelope!
Over chicken wrists or meek shoulders, a formal, hard-fibered
    assurance.
The drape of the male is designed to achieve self-forgetfulness.

So, sister, forget yourself a few times and see where it gets you:

Up the creek, alone with your talent, sans everything else.
You can wait for the menopause, and catch up on your reading.
So primp, preen, prink, pluck and prize your flesh,
All posturings! All ravishment! All sensibility!
Meanwhile, have you used your mind today?
What pomegranate raised you from the dead,
Springing, full-grown, from your own head, Athena?


## Three

I will speak about women of letters, for I'm in the racket.
Our biggest successes to date? Old maids to a woman.
And our saddest conspicuous failures? The married spinsters
On loan to the husbands they treated like surrogate fathers.
Think of that crew of self-pitiers, not-very-distant,
Who carried the torch for themselves and got first-degree burns.
Or the sad sonneteers, toast-and-teasdales we loved at thirteen;
Middle-aged virgins seducing the purile anthologists
Through lust-of-the-mind; barbiturate-drenched Camilles
With continuous periods, murmuring softly on sofas
When poetry wasn't a craft but a sickly effluvium,
The air thick with incense, musk, and emotional blackmail.

I suppose they reacted from an earlier womanly modesty
When too many girls were scabs to their stricken sisterhood,
Impugning our sex to stay in good with the men,
Commencing their insecure bluster. How they must have swaggered
When women themselves indorsed their own inferiority!
Vestals, vassals and vessels, rolled into several,
They took notes in rolling syllabics, in careful journals,
Aiming to please a posterity that despises them.
But we'll always have traitors who swear that a woman surrenders
Her Supreme Function, by equating Art with aggression
And failure with Femininity. Still, it's just as unfair
To equate Art with Femininity, like a prettily-packaged commodity
When we are the custodians of the world's best-kept secret:
Merely the private lives of one-half of humanity.

But even with masculine dominance, we mares and mistresses
Produced some sleek saboteuses, making their cracks
Which the porridge-brained males of the day were too thick to
    perceive,
Mistaking young hornets for perfectly harmless bumblebees.
Being thought innocuous rouses some women to frenzy;
They try to be ugly by aping the ways of the men
And succeed. Swearing, sucking cigars and scorching the bedspread,
Slopping straight shots, eyes blotted, vanity-blown
In the expectation of glory: *she writes like a man!*
This drives other women mad in a mist of chiffon
(one poetess draped her gauze over red flannels, a practical feminist).

But we're emerging from all that, more or less,
Except for some lady-like laggards and Quarterly priestesses
Who flog men for fun, and kick women to maim competition.
Now, if we struggle abnormally, we may almost seem normal;
If we submerge our self-pity in disciplined industry;
If we stand up and be hated, and swear not to sleep with editors;
If we regard ourselves formally, respecting our true limitations
Without making an unseemly show of trying to unfreeze our assets;
Keeping our heads and our pride while remaining unmarried;
And if wedded, kill guilt in its tracks when we stack up the dishes
And defect to the typewriter. And if mothers, believe in the luck of
    our children,
Whom we forbid to devour us, whom we shall not devour,
And the luck of our husbands and lovers, who keep free women.

[1965]

176

MAXINE KUMIN

# A Voice from the Roses

*After Arachne*

Having confused me
with the nearest of her nine
nimble sisters—
the beautiful one
she witched into seizures
of drools and tremors
for picking away at her needlepoint—
my mother directed the craft
of her vengeance against me.

I have lain
on this thorn thirty years,
spinning out of my
pear-shaped belly,
my puffball pearl-gray belly
always perfectly damp,
intricate maps of my brainpan,
lines and ligatures
that catch the morning light
and carve it into prisms;
you might say, messages.

The furious barb
that I fed with my body's juices,
this nib of my babyhood
has softened, as even saliva
will eat away porcelain.
Tugged this way and that
by the force of my spinning,
the old thorn
now clasps me lightly.

Nevertheless
it is rooted. It is
raising a tree inside me.
The buds of my mother's arbor
grow ripe in my sex.
Mother, Queen of the roses,
wearer of forks and petals,
when may I be free of you?
When will I be done
with the force of your magic?

[1961]

## The Appointment

This is my wolf. He sits
at the foot of the bed
in the dark all night


breathing so evenly
I am almost deceived.
It is not the swollen


cat uncurling
restlessly, a house
of kittens knocking


against her flanks;
it isn't the hot fog
fingering the window locks


while the daffodils
wait in the wings
like spearholders;

not the children fisted
in three busy dreams
they will retell at breakfast;

and not you, clearly
not you fixed over me
all these good years

that he watches.
I lie to him nightlong.
I delay him with praises.

In the morning we wash
together chummily.
I rinse my toothbrush.

After that,
he puts his red eyes out
under the extra blanket.

[1961]


## Together

The water closing
over us and the
going down is all.
Gills are given.
We convert in a
town of broken hulls
and green doubloons.
O you dead pirates
hear us! There is
no salvage. All
you know is the color
of warm caramel. All
is salt. See how

our eyes have migrated
to the uphill side?
Now we are new round
mouths and no spines
letting the water cover.
It happens over
and over, me in
your body and you
in mine.

[1970]


## After Love

Afterwards, the compromise.
Bodies resume their boundaries.

These legs, for instance, mine.
Your arms take you back in.

Spoons of our fingers, lips
admit their ownership.

The bedding yawns, a door
blows aimlessly ajar

and overhead, a plane
singsongs coming down.

Nothing is changed, except
there was a moment when

the wolf, the mongering wolf
who stands outside the self

lay lightly down, and slept.

[1970]

ANNE HALLEY

## A Pride of Ladies

They wore light dresses and their arms were bare,
paddling backwater seasons, moonstruck, coy,
who cooled their necks with pale green spicy scents
and spread skirts stiff in petals as they sat
dazzled, waiting becalmed; and one might lift
hair bright as buglings on the wind.
All princesses.

And someone came, or would come soon enough
whose common words were stranger than the spell;
whose quick and faintly furry hand might not
fit those curved palms; would have been glad to stay
stretched flat, count polished pebbles, wait, and sun
a young brown back, pretending to be earth.

And not a prince. His breath was dark and sour.
He was not tall. But he was chosen. Chose,
and so must come, perhaps in the new moon.
Awkward himself, and shy, would learn to be
Mariner, Swineherd, King,
and set one free.

[1965]

# O Doctor Dear My Love

O doctor dear my love, admit
there are enough. Why should we need
justifiable worldwide fear,
whether the sneaky drug deforming
quietly, from inside out, or
the drizzle, firestorming doom
out there, invisible, swarming—
no scabrous ooze, secretive sore
and not the loosehung head
of what I saw led down the road,
an emptiness, a waste in bulging skin.
But this. Enough has not enough.

     Dear ministrant, dear doctor
exhume this blade of flesh with your bright steel.
Come succor me, believable monsters.

On the other side, no easy matter.
Think on the others, love, my doctor:
think the milked male, the humiliating
dash across a dawnwhite street,
the locked laboratory,
but the semen caught, deliverable,
hot from the press; think, lastex lady
inside whose whorly layers nothing takes.
Think those slitherings, bedpans, trickles,
salt tears to float fishes
smell on only—
Think so much hard, some human, work.

Enough and not enough makes less.
Monsters we suffer as we will,
Old Sawbones, sorcerer, we waste
in rubber skins, in little death:

     O dear my doctor, love, be still
Hush, surgeon, little friend, come fast.

[1965]

182

# Housewife's Letter: to Mary

If I could, I'd write
how glad I live and cultivate:
to put tomatoes in and squash,
green salad on a yellow cloth,
how especially the white and blue
plates please me then. Also, I do
ironing mornings, make my list,
go squeeze fruit, open corn husks, watch
the butcher while he cuts our meat
and tote up prices in my head.
Evenings, I shake the cloth and fold
clean sheets away, count socks, and read
desultorily, and then to bed.

All this, could I, I'd write to you
and—doctored—parts are almost true.
But this is so: some days I've seen
my neighbor in her curlers, frown-
ing intently, sweeping hard
her porch, her sidewalk, her paved yard.
Her serious eye, following broom,
penetrates to my scratchpad room
and so—on my good days—I sweep
the front porch hard, and hope to keep
a neighbor image in my eye,
good aproned neighbor, whom I'd try
to emulate, to mimic, be—
translate some certainties to me.

That mothers' meeting, visit, when
Elisabeth first felt her son
leap into life: Mother of God
and Prophet's Mother, forward bowed,
embracing secrets, each in each,
they celebrate each other's fruit—
cylindrical and gravid, plain,
I puzzle over what they mean;

what do they speak of, in what tone,
how calmly stand. If mortal men
could touch them thus—O sacred, grim
they look to me: this year, I'm thin
have cut my washerwoman hair—
yet they persist, so solid, there,
content to carry, bear this weight
and be as vines, initiate.

I have been fruitful, lucky, blessed
more ways than I can count, at rest—
or ought to be—and even thrive
efficiently: yet come alive
odd moments in surprise that I
should still expect, impossibly,
and at the same time wholly hate
my old expectancy. I wait
long past my time, like the old Saint,
but unlike her, I'll make complaint.

For when I stand here on the step
and sigh and nod my housewife's head
and wipe my hands and click my tongue
at dust, or rain, or noise, or sun,
though motion's right, I feel it wrong.
I can remember all my dolls'
tea-sets and washboards, cribs on wheels,
and the whole mess, the miniatures
of pie-tins, babies, plastic meals—
a dustblown attic full of wrapped-
up child's play. How begin, unpack,
through splintery crates and newsprint feel
the living child and make it real.

It's real enough. Inside my house,
uncustomed, unceremonious,
I seem to wade among the shards
proliferating, wrecked discards,
a whole decline of Western Man

in microcosm: who'd begin
to sort it out, make do, decide
to deal with this, to let that ride—
make love, patch plaster, choose your work,
your car, your party, and your church,
keep conscience, throw out sense of sin,
free impulse, but in discipline—
a ruptured rug, a beaten chair
stare at me, stupid as despair.

And I am full of anger, need
not words made flesh, nor wordless act,
nor cycles inarticulate,
have never felt a moral thrill
at choosing good against my will
and no orgasm, man or God's,
delivers long from my black thoughts—
Housewifely Guardians, sweeping yet,
sweep out their graves and ours: O let
those flourish surely on, who know
the laws in which they bear and grow,
let multiply, secure from ill,
vessels wellformed for grace to fill.

[1965]

## Against Dark's Harm

The baby at my breast
suckles me to rest.
Who lately rode my blood
finds me further flood,
pulls me to his dim
unimagined dream.

Amulet and charm
against dark's harm,
coiled in my side,
shelter me from fright
and the edged knife,
despair, distress
and all self-sickness.

[1965]

# Autograph Book / Prophecy

First comes love and then comes marriage
Then comes Annie with a baby carriage.

That's as dirty as kids got back in my fourth grade.
Lelia and Junie blushed and giggled
had to put their heads down      hysterical
run to the basement
Then all the way home

                    Yes you will
                    No I won't
                    Yes you will
                    Won't
                    Will
                    Won't

Won't what?

I can admit now.      I didn't get it
couldn't read between the lines.
Literal minded
repressed.

However

We all finally got it.

We're all hitched

And there's lots of carriages
typewriter, baby buggy, station wagon      you name it
pushing on between
the canned and the frozen
from living bra to winding sheet

There's a joke there somewhere.

Get it?

                        [1973]

ANNE SEXTON

## Housewife

Some women marry houses.
It's another kind of skin; it has a heart,
a mouth, a liver and bowel movements.
The walls are permanent and pink.
See how she sits on her knees all day,
faithfully washing herself down.
Men enter by force, drawn back like Jonah
into their fleshy mothers.
A woman *is* her mother.
That's the main thing.

[1961]

# The Abortion

*Somebody who should have been born*
*is gone.*

Just as the earth puckered its mouth,
each bud puffing out from its knot,
I changed my shoes, and then drove south.

Up past the Blue Mountains, where
Pennsylvania humps on endlessly,
wearing, like a crayoned cat, its green hair,

its roads sunken in like a gray washboard;
where, in truth, the ground cracks evilly,
a dark socket from which the coal has poured,

*Somebody who should have been born*
*is gone.*

the grass as bristly and stout as chives,
and me wondering when the ground would break,
and me wondering how anything fragile survives;

up in Pennsylvania, I met a little man,
not Rumpelstiltskin, at all, at all . . .
he took the fullness that love began.

Returning north, even the sky grew thin
like a high window looking nowhere.
The road was as flat as a sheet of tin.

*Somebody who should have been born*
*is gone.*

Yes, woman, such logic will lead
to loss without death. Or say what you meant,
you coward . . . this baby that I bleed.

[1961]

189

# Consorting with Angels

I was tired of being a woman,
tired of the spoons and the pots,
tired of my mouth and my breasts,
tired of the cosmetics and the silks.
There were still men who sat at my table,
circled around the bowl I offered up.
The bowl was filled with purple grapes
and the flies hovered in for the scent
and even my father came with his white bone.
But I was tired of the gender of things.

Last night I had a dream
and I said to it . . .
"You are the answer.
You will outlive my husband and my father."
In that dream there was a city made of chains
where Joan was put to death in man's clothes
and the nature of the angels went unexplained,
no two made in the same species,
one with a nose, one with an ear in its hand,
one chewing a star and recording its orbit,
each one like a poem obeying itself,
performing God's functions,
a people apart.

"You are the answer,"
I said, and entered,
lying down on the gates of the city.
Then the chains were fastened around me
and I lost my common gender and my final aspect.
Adam was on the left of me
and Eve was on the right of me,
both thoroughly inconsistent with the world of reason.
We wove our arms together
and rode under the sun.

I was not a woman anymore,
not one thing or the other.

O daughters of Jerusalem,
the king has brought me into his chamber.
I am black and I am beautiful.
I've been opened and undressed.
I have no arms or legs.
I'm all one skin like a fish.
I'm no more a woman
than Christ was a man.

[1966]

# For My Lover, Returning to His Wife

She is all there.
She was melted carefully down for you
and cast up from your childhood,
cast up from your one hundred favorite aggies.

She has always been there, my darling.
She is, in fact, exquisite.
Fireworks in the dull middle of February
and as real as a cast-iron pot.

Let's face it, I have been momentary.
A luxury. A bright red sloop in the harbor.
My hair rising like smoke from the car window.
Littleneck clams out of season.

She is more than that. She is your have to have,
has grown you your practical your tropical growth.
This is not an experiment. She is all harmony.
She sees to oars and oarlocks for the dinghy,

has placed wild flowers at the window at breakfast,
sat by the potter's wheel at midday,

set forth three children under the moon,
three cherubs drawn by Michelangelo,

done this with her legs spread out
in the terrible months in the chapel.
If you glance up, the children are there
like delicate balloons resting on the ceiling.

She has also carried each one down the hall
after supper, their heads privately bent,
two legs protesting, person to person,
her face flushed with a song and their little sleep.

I give you back your heart.
I give you permission—

for the fuse inside her, throbbing
angrily in the dirt, for the bitch in her
and the burying of her wound—
for the burying of her small red wound alive—

for the pale flickering flare under her ribs,
for the drunken sailor who waits in her left pulse,
for the mother's knee, for the stockings,
for the garter belt, for the call—

the curious call
when you will burrow in arms and breasts
and tug at the orange ribbon in her hair
and answer the call, the curious call.

She is so naked and singular.
She is the sum of yourself and your dream.
Climb her like a monument, step after step.
She is solid.

As for me, I am a watercolor.
I wash off.

[1967]

ADRIENNE RICH

# An Unsaid Word

She who has power to call her man
From that estranged intensity
Where his mind forages alone,
Yet keeps her peace and leaves him free,
And when his thoughts to her return
Stands where he left her, still his own,
Knows this the hardest thing to learn.

[1951]


# Snapshots of a Daughter-in-Law

1. You, once a belle in Shreveport,
   with henna-colored hair, skin like a peachbud,
   still have your dresses copied from that time,
   and play a Chopin prelude
   called by Cortot: *"Delicious recollections
   float like perfume through the memory."*

   Your mind now, mouldering like wedding-cake,
   heavy with useless experience, rich
   with suspicion, rumor, fantasy,
   crumbling to pieces under the knife-edge
   of mere fact. In the prime of your life.

   Nervy, glowering, your daughter
   wipes the teaspoons, grows another way.

2. Banging the coffee-pot into the sink
   she hears the angels chiding, and looks out
   past the raked gardens to the sloppy sky.
   Only a week since They said: *Have no patience.*

The next time it was: *Be insatiable.*
Then: *Save yourself; others you cannot save.*
Sometimes she's let the tapstream scald her arm,
a match burn to her thumbnail,

or held her hand above the kettle's snout
right in the woolly steam. They are probably angels,
since nothing hurts her any more, except
each morning's grit blowing into her eyes.

3. A thinking woman sleeps with monsters.
   The beak that grips her, she becomes. And Nature,
   that sprung-lidded, still commodious
   steamer-trunk of *tempora* and *mores*
   gets stuffed with it all:      the mildewed orange-flowers,
   the female pills, the terrible breasts
   of Boadicea beneath flat foxes' heads and orchids.

   Two handsome women, gripped in argument,
   each proud, acute, subtle, I hear scream
   across the cut glass and majolica
   like Furies cornered from their prey:
   The argument *ad feminem,* all the old knives
   that have rusted in my back, I drive in yours,
   *ma semblable, ma soeur!*

4. Knowing themselves too well in one another;
   their gifts no pure fruition, but a thorn,
   the prick filed sharp against a hint of scorn . . .
   Reading while waiting
   for the iron to heat,
   writing, *This is the gnat that mangles men,*
   in that Amherst pantry while the jellies boil and scum,
   or, more often,
   iron-eyed and beaked and purposed as a bird,
   dusting everything on the whatnot every day of life.

5. *Dulce ridentem, dulce loquentem,*
   she shaves her legs until they gleam
   like petrified mammoth-tusk.

6.  When to her lute Corinna sings
    neither words nor music are her own;
    only the long hair dipping
    over her cheek, only the song
    of silk against her knees
    and these
    adjusted in reflections of an eye.

    Poised, trembling and unsatisfied, before
    an unlocked door, that cage of cages,
    tell us, you bird, you tragical machine—
    is this *fertilisante douleur?* Pinned down
    by love, for you the only natural action,
    are you edged more keen
    to prise the secrets of the vault? has Nature shown
    her household books to you, daughter-in-law,
    that her sons never saw?

7.  *"To have in this uncertain world some stay*
    *which cannot be undermined, is*
    *of the utmost consequence."*
                                   Thus wrote
    a woman, partly brave and partly good,
    who fought with what she partly understood.
    Few men about her would or could do more,
    hence she was labelled harpy, shrew and whore.

8.  "You all die at fifteen," said Diderot,
    and turn part legend, part convention.
    Still, eyes inaccurately dream
    behind closed windows blankening with steam.
    Deliciously, all that we might have been,
    all that we were—fire, tears,
    wit, taste, martyred ambition—
    stirs like the memory of refused adultery
    the drained and flagging bosom of our middle years.

9.  *Not that it is done well, but*
    *that it is done at all?* Yes, think

of the odds! or shrug them off forever.
This luxury of the precocious child,
Time's precious chronic invalid,—
would we, darlings, resign it if we could?
Our blight has been our sinecure:
mere talent was enough for us—
glitter in fragments and rough drafts.

Sigh no more, ladies.
                Time is male
and in his cups drinks to the fair.
Bemused by gallantry, we hear
our mediocrities over-praised,
indolence read as abnegation,
slattern thought styled intuition,
every lapse forgiven, our crime
only to cast too bold a shadow
or smash the mould straight off.

For that, solitary confinement,
tear gas, attrition shelling.
Few applicants for that honor.

10.                        Well,
she's long about her coming, who must be
more merciless to herself than history.
Her mind full to the wind, I see her plunge
breasted and glancing through the currents,
taking the light upon her
at least as beautiful as any boy
or helicopter,
                poised, still coming,
her fine blades making the air wince
but her cargo
no promise then:
delivered
palpable
ours.

                                [1963]

# Women

(for C.R.G.)

My three sisters are sitting
on rocks of black obsidian.
For the first time, in this light, I can see who they are.

My first sister is sewing her costume for the procession.
She is going as the Transparent Lady
and all her nerves will be visible.

My second sister is also sewing,
at the seam over her heart which has never healed entirely.
At last, she hopes, this tightness in her chest will ease.

My third sister is gazing
at a dark-red crust spreading westward far out on the sea.
Her stockings are torn but she is beautiful.

[1969]

# 5:30 A.M.

Birds and periodic blood.
Old recapitulations.
The fox, panting, fire-eyed,
gone to earth in my chest.
How beautiful we are,
he and I, with our auburn
pelts, our trails of blood,
our miracle escapes,
our whiplash panic flogging us on
to new miracles!
They've supplied us with pills
for bleeding, pills for panic.
Wash them down the sink.
This is truth, then:
dull needle groping in the spinal fluid,
weak acid in the bottom of the cup,
foreboding, foreboding.
No one tells the truth about truth,
that it's what the fox
sees from his scuffled burrow:
dull-jawed, onrushing
killer, being that
inanely single-minded
will have our skins at last.

[1969]

# I Dream I'm the Death of Orpheus

I am walking rapidly through striations of light and dark thrown under
    an arcade.

I am a woman in the prime of life, with certain powers
and those powers severely limited
by authorities whose faces I rarely see.
I am a woman in the prime of life
driving her dead poet in a black Rolls-Royce
through a landscape of twilight and thorns.
A woman with a certain mission
which if obeyed to the letter will leave her intact.
A woman with the nerves of a panther
a woman with contacts among Hell's Angels
a woman feeling the fullness of her powers
at the precise moment when she must not use them
a woman sworn to lucidity
who sees through the mayhem, the smoky fires
of these underground streets
her dead poet learning to walk backward against the wind
on the wrong side of the mirror

[1971]

199

# November 1968

Stripped
you're beginning to float free
up through the smoke of brushfires
and incinerators
the unleafed branches won't hold you
nor the radar aerials

You're what the autumn knew would happen
after the last collapse
of primary color
once the last absolutes were torn to pieces
you could begin

How you broke open, what sheathed you
until this moment
I know nothing about it
my ignorance of you amazes me
now that I watch you
starting to give yourself away
to the wind

[1971]

# The Will to Change

1.                    (For L.D., dead 11/69.

That Chinese restaurant was a joke
with its repeating fountains

& chopsticks in tissue paper
The vodka was too sweet

the beancurd too hot
You came with your Egyptian hieroglyph

your angel's smile
Almost the next day

as surely as if shot
you were thin air

At the risk of appearing ridiculous—
we take back this halfworld for you

and all whose murders accrue
past your death


2.                    (For Sandra Levinson.

Knocked down in the canefield
by a clumsily swung machete

she is helped to her feet
by Fidel

and snapped by photographers
the blonde Yanqui in jeans

We're living through a time
that needs to be lived through us

(and in the morning papers
Bobby Seale, chalked

by the courtroom artist
defaced by the gag)

3.                        (For D.J.L.

Beardless again, phoning
from a storefront in Yorkville

. . . we need a typewriter, a crib
& Michael's number . . .

I swim to you thru dead
latitudes of fever

. . . accepting the discipline . . .
You mean your old freedom

to disappear—you miss that?
. . . but I can dig having lost it . . .

David, I could dig losing everything.
Knowing what you mean, to make that leap

bite into the fear, over & over
& survive. Hoarding my 'liberty'

like a compulsive—more
than I can use up in a lifetime—

two dozen oranges in the refrigerator
for one American weekend

4.                        (For A.H.C.

At the wings of the mirror, peacock plumes
from the Feast of San Gennaro

gaze thru the dark
All night the A-train forages

under our bedroom
All night I dream of a man

black, gagged, shackled, coffined
in a courtroom where I am

passive, white & silent
though my mouth is free

All night I see his eyes
iridescent under torture

and hear the shuddering of the earth
as the trains tear us apart


5.

The cabdriver from the Bronx
screaming: 'This city's GOTTA die!'

dynamiting it hourly from his soul
as surely as any terrorist

Burning the bodies of the scum on welfare
ejaculating into the flames

(*and*, said Freud,
*who welcomed it when it was done?*)

the professors of the fact
that someone has suffered

seeking truth in a mist of librium
the artists talking of freedom

in  their  chains                                    [1971]

203

## Sleep-Learning

All that I try to save him from
Is what he dreams about:
Abandonment, abandonment.
I watch his face
Each night emerging clearer,
Stern son who reads my dreams:
The dreams I had,
And those my brother had
And which my parents learned from theirs,
Moving behind mauve lids
That seal his eyes.

He dreams I want to leave him,
Roams through night-forests, desolate.
And I dream I've abandoned him,
Feel waxy pleasure of that sin,
Its subsequent atonement.
Next morning both our faces
Mark the change:
Mine with the guilty look of those
Who knowingly succumb to dreams,
And his the speculative gaze
Of someone learning.

[1968]

COLETTE INEZ

# The Woman Who Loved Worms
(From a Japanese Legend)

Disdaining butterflies
as frivolous,
she puttered with caterpillars,
and wore a coarse kimono,
crinkled and loose at the neck.

Refused to tweeze her brows
to crescents,
and scowled beneath dark bands
of caterpillar fur.

Even the stationery
on which she scrawled
unkempt calligraphy,
startled the jade-inlaid
indolent ladies,
whom she despised
like the butterflies
wafting kimono sleeves
through senseless poems
about moonsets and peonies;
popular rot of the times.
No, she loved worms,
blackening the moon of her nails
with mud and slugs,
root gnawing grubs,
and the wing case of beetles.

And crouched in the garden,
tugging at her unpinned hair,
weevils queuing across her bare
and unbound feet.

Swift as wasps, the years.
Midge tick and maggot words
crowded her haiku
and lines on her skin turned her old,
thin as a spinster cricket.

Noon in the snow pavilion,
gulping heated saki,
she recalled Lord Unamuro,
preposterous toad
squatting by the teatray,
proposing with conditions,
a suitable marriage.

Ha! She stoned imaginary butterflies,
and pinching dirt,
crawled to death's cocoon
dragging a moth to inspect
in the long afternoon.

[1969]

CYNTHIA MACDONALD

# Instruction from Bly

The poet told me if I was serious
I must isolate myself for at least a year—
Not become a hermit, but leave
My family, job, friends—so I did. My sister
Agreed to take over as mother though not
As wife. I wonder if she will become that too;
I've always thought maybe she didn't marry
Because she wanted Howard herself. So I
Have moved here to North Dakota where
I work in a gas station, the only woman s.s.
Attendant in N.D. Nowhere could be more isolated
And no job could: whistles and "baby
Pump some of that to me" crack in the cold
Or melt in the summer.

            try         try     try
         crycry      crycry  crycry              cry

I have been here seven months. Poetry should
Be flowing from my navel by now, if . . .
Out of the solitude, I expected I would erect
Something magnificent, the feminine analogue
Of Jeffer's tower. Maybe it would have gone
Into the ground instead of up.

        s                   k           y
                    high

I have discovered I drink when I am solitary. I
Have discovered I can read page ninety-two of
*Remembrance of Things Past* twenty times in solitary
Without ever reading it. If I don't die of alcoholism,
I will of cholesterol: solitary cooking.

      fryfryfry     fryfry     fryfryfryfry     frydie

Rhyme is important, my way of keeping
A grip on things. I wonder if the poet meant
It would all happen after I left, or if he is a sadist
Who wants to send all those stupid enough to sit
At his feet to N.D. or S.D. or West Va.,
Hazing before possible joining. I wonder if Jean
Is in the double bed.

tower
power

I cannot think about the children, but I
Do all the time. "Women artists fail
Because they have babies." The last thing I wrote
Was "The Children at the Beach" and that was over
A month ago. I am alone so I have to have company so
I turn on TV; at home
I only turned it off.

thumbtacks      processionals
north
red

It is time to go to work. First I need a drink. I consider
The Smirnoff bottle on the coffee table; a fly
Lands on it. And then it all happens: the life
Of that bottle flashes before me. Little by little,
Or quickly, it is used up; empty, as clear as it was
Full, it journeys to the dump; it rests upon the mounds of
Beautiful excess where what we are—
Sunflowers, grass, sand—
Is joined to what we make—
Cans, tires and it itself in every form of bottle.
I put on my s.s. coveralls, a saffron robe, knowing I have found
What I was sent to find. The sky speaks to me; the sound
Of the cars on Highway 2 is a song. Soon I will see the pumps,
Those curved rectangles shaped like the U.S. and smell the gas,
Our incense. O country, O moon, O stars,
O american rhyme is yours is mine is ours.

[1973]

# Objets d'Art

When I was seventeen, a man in the Dakar Station
Men's Room (I couldn't read the signs) said to me:
You're a real ball cutter. I thought about that
For months and finally decided
He was right. Once I knew that was my thing,
Or whatever we would have said in those days,
I began to perfect my methods. Until then
I had never thought of trophies. Preservation
Was at first a problem: pickling worked
But was a lot of trouble. Freezing
Proved to be the answer. I had to buy
A second freezer just last year; the first
Was filled with rows and rows of
Pink and purple lumps encased in Saran wrap.

I have more subjects than I can handle,
But only volunteers. It is an art like hypnosis
Which cannot be imposed on the unwilling victim.
If you desire further information about the process and
The benefits, please drop in any night from nine to twelve.
My place is east of Third on Fifty-sixth.
You'll know it by the three gold ones over the door.

[1973]

## The Disquieting Muses

Mother, mother, what illbred aunt
Or what disfigured and unsightly
Cousin did you so unwisely keep
Unasked to my christening, that she
Sent these ladies in her stead
With heads like darning-eggs to nod
And nod and nod at foot and head
And at the left side of my crib?

Mother, who made to order stories
Of Mixie Blackshort the heroic bear,
Mother, whose witches always, always
Got baked into gingerbread, I wonder
Whether you saw them, whether you said
Words to rid me of those three ladies
Nodding by night around my bed,
Mouthless, eyeless, with stitched bald head.

In the hurricane, when father's twelve
Study windows bellied in
Like bubbles about to break, you fed
My brother and me cookies and Ovaltine
And helped the two of us to choir:
"Thor is angry: boom boom boom!
Thor is angry: we don't care!"
But those ladies broke the panes.

When on tiptoe the schoolgirls danced,
Blinking flashlights like fireflies
And singing the glowworm song, I could
Not lift a foot in the twinkle-dress
But, heavy-footed, stood aside
In the shadow cast by my dismal-headed

Godmothers, and you cried and cried:
And the shadow stretched, the lights went out.

Mother, you sent me to piano lessons
And praised my arabesques and trills
Although each teacher found my touch
Oddly wooden in spite of scales
And the hours of practicing, my ear
Tone-deaf and yes, unteachable.
I learned, I learned, I learned elsewhere,
From muses unhired by you, dear mother,

I woke one day to see you, mother,
Floating above me in bluest air
On a green balloon bright with a million
Flowers and bluebirds that never were
Never, never, found anywhere.
But the little planet bobbed away
Like a soap-bubble as you called: Come here!
And I faced my traveling companions.

Day now, night now, at head, side, feet,
They stand their vigil in gowns of stone,
Faces blank as the day I was born,
Their shadows long in the setting sun
That never brightens or goes down.
And this is the kingdom you bore me to,
Mother, mother. But no frown of mine
Will betray the company I keep.

[1959]

# Candles

They are the last romantics, these candles:
Upside-down hearts of light tipping wax fingers,
And the fingers, taken in by their own haloes,
Grown milky, almost clear, like the bodies of saints.
It is touching, the way they'll ignore

A whole family of prominent objects
Simply to plumb the deeps of an eye
In its hollow of shadows, its fringe of reeds,
And the owner past thirty, no beauty at all.
Daylight would be more judicious,

Giving everybody a fair hearing.
They should have gone out with balloon flights and the stereopticon.
This is no time for the private point of view.
When I light them, my nostrils prickle.
Their pale, tentative yellows

Drag up false, Edwardian sentiments,
And I remember my maternal grandmother from Vienna.
As a schoolgirl she gave roses to Franz Josef.
The burghers sweated and wept. The children wore white.
And my grandfather moped in the Tyrol,

Imagining himself a headwaiter in America,
Floating in a high-church hush
Among ice buckets, frosty napkins.
These little globes of light are sweet as pears.
Kindly with invalids and mawkish women,

They mollify the bald moon.
Nun-souled, they burn heavenward and never marry.
The eyes of the child I nurse are scarcely open.
In twenty years I shall be retrograde
As these drafty ephemerids.

I watch their spilt tears cloud and dull to pearls.
How shall I tell anything at all
To this infant still in a birth-drowse?
Tonight, like a shawl, the mild light enfolds her,
The shadows stoop over like guests at a christening.

[1960]


# Daddy

You do not do, you do not do
Any more, black shoe
In which I have lived like a foot
For thirty years, poor and white,
Barely daring to breathe or Achoo.

Daddy, I have had to kill you.
You died before I had time——
Marble-heavy, a bag full of God,
Ghastly statue with one grey toe
Big as a Frisco seal

And a head in the freakish Atlantic
Where it pours bean green over blue
In the waters off beautiful Nauset.
I used to pray to recover you.
Ach, du.

In the German tongue, in the Polish town
Scraped flat by the roller
Of wars, wars, wars.
But the name of the town is common.
My Polack friend

Says there are a dozen or two.
So I never could tell where you
Put your foot, your root,

I never could talk to you.
The tongue stuck in my jaw.

It stuck in a barb wire snare.
Ich, ich, ich, ich,
I could hardly speak.
I thought every German was you.
And the language obscene

An engine, an engine
Chuffing me off like a Jew.
A Jew to Dachau, Auschwitz, Belsen.
I began to talk like a Jew.
I think I may well be a Jew.

The snows of the Tyrol, the clear beer of Vienna
Are not very pure or true.
With my gypsy ancestress and my weird luck
And my Taroc pack and my Taroc pack
I may be a bit of a Jew.

I have always been scared of *you*,
With your Luftwaffe, your gobbledygoo.
And your neat moustache
And your Aryan eye, bright blue.
Panzer-man, panzer-man, O You——

Not God but a swastika
So black no sky could squeak through.
Every woman adores a Fascist,
The boot in the face, the brute
Brute heart of a brute like you.

You stand at the blackboard, daddy,
In the picture I have of you,
A cleft in your chin instead of your foot
But no less a devil for that, no not
Any less the black man who

Bit my pretty red heart in two.
I was ten when they buried you.
At twenty I tried to die.
And get back, back, back to you.
I thought even the bones would do.

But they pulled me out of the sack,
And they stuck me together with glue.
And then I knew what to do.
I made a model of you,
A man in black with a Meinkampf look

And a love of the rack and the screw.
And I said I do, I do.
So daddy, I'm finally through.
The black telephone's off at the root,
The voices just can't worm through.

If I've killed one man, I've killed two——
The vampire who said he was you
And drank my blood for a year,
Seven years, if you want to know.
Daddy, you can lie back now.

There's a stake in your fat black heart
And the villagers never liked you.
They are dancing and stamping on you.
They always *knew* it was you.
Daddy, daddy, you bastard, I'm through.

[1963]

# The Applicant

First, are you our sort of a person?
Do you wear
A glass eye, false teeth or a crutch,
A brace or a hook,
Rubber breasts or a rubber crotch,

Stitches to show something's missing? No, no? Then
How can we give you a thing?
Stop crying.
Open your hand.
Empty? Empty. Here is a hand

To fill it and willing
To bring teacups and roll away headaches
And do whatever you tell it.
Will you marry it?
It is guaranteed

To thumb shut your eyes at the end
And dissolve of sorrow.
We make new stock from the salt.
I notice you are stark naked.
How about this suit——

Black and stiff, but not a bad fit.
Will you marry it?
It is waterproof, shatterproof, proof
Against fire and bombs through the roof.
Believe me, they'll bury you in it.

Now your head, excuse me, is empty.
I have the ticket for that.
Come here, sweetie, out of the closet.
Well, what do you think of *that?*
Naked as paper to start

But in twenty-five years she'll be silver,
In fifty, gold.
A living doll, everywhere you look.
It can sew, it can cook,
It can talk, talk, talk.

It works, there is nothing wrong with it.
You have a hole, it's a poultice.
You have an eye, it's an image.
My boy, it's your last resort.
Will you marry it, marry it, marry it.

[1963]

## Wintering

This is the easy time, there is nothing doing.
I have whirled the midwife's extractor,
I have my honey,
Six jars of it,
Six cat's eyes in the wine cellar,

Wintering in a dark without window
At the heart of the house
Next to the last tenant's rancid jam
And the bottles of empty glitters——
Sir So-and-so's gin.

This is the room I have never been in.
This is the room I could never breathe in.
The black bunched in there like a bat,
No light
But the torch and its faint

Chinese yellow on appalling objects——
Black asininity. Decay.
Possession.

217

It is they who own me.
Neither cruel nor indifferent,

Only ignorant.
This is the time of hanging on for the bees—the bees
So slow I hardly know them,
Filing like soldiers
To the syrup tin

To make up for the honey I've taken.
Tate and Lyle keeps them going,
The refined snow.
It is Tate and Lyle they live on, instead of flowers.
They take it. The cold sets in.

Now they ball in a mass,
Black
Mind against all that white.
The smile of the snow is white.
It spreads itself out, a mile-long body of Meissen,

Into which, on warm days,
They can only carry their dead.
The bees are all women,
Maids and the long royal lady.
They have got rid of the men,

The blunt, clumsy stumblers, the boors.
Winter is for women——
The woman, still at her knitting,
At the cradle of Spanish walnut,
Her body a bulb in the cold and too dumb to think.

Will the hive survive, will the gladiolas
Succeed in banking their fires
To enter another year?
What will they taste of, the Christmas roses?
The bees are flying. They taste the spring.

[1963]

# Winter Trees

The wet dawn inks are doing their blue dissolve.
On their blotter of fog the trees
Seem a botanical drawing—
Memories growing, ring on ring,
A series of weddings.

Knowing neither abortions nor bitchery,
Truer than women,
They seed so effortlessly!
Tasting the winds, that are footless,
Waist-deep in history—

Full of wings, otherworldliness.
In this, they are Ledas.
O mother of leaves and sweetness
Who are these pietas?
The shadows of ringdoves chanting, but easing nothing.

[1963]

ANNE STEVENSON

# The Suburb

No time, no time,
and with so many in line to be
born or fed or made love to, there is no
excuse for staring at it, though it's spring again
and the leaves have come out looking
limp and wet like little green new born babies.

The girls have come out in their new bought dresses,
carefully, carefully. They know they're in danger.
Already there are couples crumpled under the chestnuts.
The houses crowd closer, listening to each other's radios.
Weeds have got into the window boxes. The washing hangs,
helpless. Children are lusting for ice cream.

It is my lot each May to be hot and pregnant,
a long way away from the years when I slept by myself—
the white bed by the dressing table, pious with cherry blossoms,
the flatteries and punishments of photographs and mirrors.
We walked home by starlight and he touched my breasts.
"Please, please!" Then I let him anyway. Cars
droned and flashed, sucking at the cow parsley. Later
there were teas and the engagement party. The wedding
in the rain. The hotel where I slept in the bathroom.
The night when he slept on the floor.

The ache of remembering, bitterer than a birth. Better
to lie still and let the babies run through me.
To let them possess me. They will spare me
spring after spring. Their hungers deliver me.
I grow fat as they devour me. I give them my sleep
and they absolve me from waking. Who can accuse me?
I am beyond blame.

[1964]

AUDRE LORDE

# The Woman Thing

The hunters are back
From beating the winter's face
In search of a challenge or task
In search of food
Making fresh tracks for their children's hunger
They do not watch the sun
They cannot wear its heat for a sign
Of triumph or freedom
The hunters are treading heavily homeward
Through snow that is marked
With their own footprints
Emptyhanded the hunters return
Snow-maddened, sustained by their rages.

In the night, after food
They will seek
Young girls for their amusement.
Now the hunters are coming
And the unbaked girls flee from their angers.
All this day I have craved
Food for my child's hunger.
Emptyhanded the hunters come shouting
Injustices drip from their mouths
Like stale snow melted in sunlight.

And this womanthing my mother taught me
Bakes off its covering of snow
Like a rising blackening sun.

[1970]

# A Poem for a Poet

I always think of a coffin's quiet
When I sit in the world of my car
Observing
Particularly when the windows are closed and washed clean
By the rain. I like to sit there sometimes
And watch other worlds pass. Yesterday evening
Waiting Jennie, another chapter,
I sat in my car on Sheridan Square
Flat and broke and a little bit damp
Thinking about money and rain and how
The Village broads with their narrow hips
Rolled like drunken shovels down Christopher Street.

Then I saw you unmistakably
Darting out between a police car
And what used to be Atkins' all-night diner
On the corner of Fourth and Sheridan Square
Where we sat making bets the last time I saw you
On how many busts we could count through the plateglass windows
In those last skinny hours before dawn
With our light worded out but still burning
And the evening's promise dregs in our coffee cups—
And I saw you dash out and turn left at the corner
Your beard spiky with rain and refusing
Shelter under your chin.

I had thought you were dead Jarrell
Struck down by a car at sunset on a North Carolina Road
Or maybe you were the driver
Tricked into a fatal swerve by some twilit shadow
Or was that Frank O'Hara
Or Conrad Kent Rivers
And you were the lonesome spook in a Windy City motel
Draped in the secrets of your convulsive death
All alone

All poets all loved and dying alone
That final death less real than those deaths you lived
And for which I forgave you.

I watched you hurry down Fourth Street Jarrell
From the world of my car in the rain
Remembering Spring Festival night
At Women's College in North Carolina and
Wasn't that world a coffin
Retreat of spring whispers romance and rhetoric
Untouched by the winds buffeting up the road from Greenville
And nobody mentioned the Black Revolution or Sit-Ins
Or Freedom Rides or SNCC or cattle-prods in Jackson, Mississippi—
Where I was to find myself how many years later;
/You were mistaken that night and I told you so
In the letter that began—Dear Jarrell,
If you sit in one place long enough
The whole world will pass you by. . . .
You were wrong that night when you said
I took my living too seriously
Meaning—you were afraid I might take you too seriously,
And you shouldn't have worried, because
Although I always dug you too much to put you down
I never took you at all
Except as a good piece of my first journey South,
Except as I take you now gladly and separate
At a distance and wondering
As I have so often, how come
Being so cool, you weren't also a little bit
Black.

And also why you have returned to this dying city
And what piece of me is it then
Buried down in North Carolina.

[1970]

## The Quarrel

You know I said to Mark that I'm furious at you.

No he said are you bugged. He was drawing Brad who was asleep on the bed.

Yes I said I'm pretty god damned bugged. I sat down by the fire and stuck my feet out to warm them up.

Jesus I thought you think it's so easy. There you sit innocence personified. I didn't say anything else to him.

You know I thought I've got work to do too sometimes. In fact I probably have just as fucking much work to do as you do. A piece of wood fell out of the fire and I poked it back in with my toe.

I am sick I said to the woodpile of doing dishes. I am just as lazy as you. Maybe lazier. The toe of my shoe was scorched from the fire and I rubbed it where the suede was gone.

Just because I happen to be a chick I thought.

Mark finished one drawing and looked at it. Then he put it down and started another one.

It's damned arrogant of you I thought to assume that only you have things to do. Especially tonight.

And what a god damned concession it was for me to bother to tell you that I was bugged at all I said to the back of his neck. I didn't say it out loud.

I got up and went into the kitchen to do the dishes. And shit I thought I probably won't bother again. But I'll get bugged and not bother to tell you and after a while everything will be awful and I'll never say anything because it's so fucking uncool to talk about it. And that I thought will be that and what a shame.

Hey hon Mark yelled at me from the living room. It says here Picasso produces fourteen hours a day.

[1961]

## Moon Mattress

for the child
we didn't have

THE KILL

Pastel the flowers, the wreaths in the pastel gardens
we pluck them out of our hair to hang on trees
the snakes coil on the branches, the dead
put out new roots.
These things hold fast.

Somewhere green glass tinkles in the wind
a napkin arranges itself & wipes a mouth
my hands are clean.   you share this death
                w/me.   my hands are clean.

in the arbor
in the arbor
the little fishes swim.
                the green light glinting
sifting out of the water.

under yr hat what bloodred facts are creeping
crawling like lice on yr head.   What do the mountains
have to say about this.
How many times did they tell you
                to open yr eyes?
the laurel tree at the end of the path
bowed 3 times to the east.

in the act of murder we are interrupted.
what kind of feast is this?
where are the maidens?

a woman has slipped off her shoes, they dance by themselves
disconsolately, at the end of the path they dance


## THE SHIP

there are wolves near the cottage, the snow shifts
yr hands
busy themselves w/poking out the fire.
I am knitting a pale blue comforter
we have thrown out the garbage, no chance
to retrieve the bones for the soup.
the dog wd bark if he werent so tired, the wolves
are very near.

"The african violet
is dying"          I tell you
(you are reading the sunday times)
hailstones are falling w/messages written on them
a baby w/red knees coughs, holding onto a chair

you say "is that really
the time"          the wolves
surround the cottage
i hang a rosary around my neck
(rub it first w/garlic)
& start to paint a hungarian easter egg


## THE WAITING ROOM

the masterly act, the patchwork quilt
a conch
to be filled perhaps w/sputum
I dont know, my pillow
is red when I wake up, sometimes the blood

dries, and my face is stuck. I cant tell you
how often I've cut myself loose

nicely attired she stepped forward, the scales
in her hands.   but she wasnt blindfolded
or she peeked,                her eyes red
conjunctivitis. She said "you have something wrong
w/yr liver.   You are prone to fat
and melancholia"        We kissed her hands
slobbered over them in fact
she was twitching inside her robes

Every human skull
uncovered, is one more home
for the spirits of darkness.
I leave the dice at the rat hole every night
no one keeps score

The dogs in the courtyard know,
they howl a little.
If only her bracelets jangled as she did it
or if we saw her face

[1963]

E. N. SARGENT

# A Sailor at Midnight

A sailor at midnight came ashore
You know what he came looking for
But he found me instead
And he followed where I led.
I took him home through dark streets, glad
To have him. I took him home to bed.
He had kisses, it seems, in store
For man, woman or whore
And soft caresses and stories
Of wrecks and dead men and many more
Things I liked; it wasn't so much what he said
As how he said it—"Dead men floating all around!" he cried, and
    shoved the head
Of his thing into me (I bled
A little he was so large). A sort of dread
Struck him. "What are you, anyway," he whispered. "Are you a
    virgin?"
"No, I'm a poet," I said. "Fuck me again."

[1960]

## Miss Rosie

When I watch you
wrapped up like garbage
sitting, surrounded by the smell
of too old potato peels
or
when I watch you
in your old man's shoes
with the little toe cut out
sitting, waiting for your mind
like next week's grocery
I say
when I watch you
you wet brown bag of a woman
who used to be the best looking gal in Georgia
used to be called the Georgia Rose
I stand up
through your destruction
I stand up

[1969]

# Admonitions

boys
i don't promise you nothing
but this
what you pawn
i will redeem
what you steal
i will conceal
my private silence to
your public guilt
is all i got

girls
first time a white man
opens his fly
like a good thing
we'll just laugh
laugh real loud my
black women

children
when they ask you
why is your mama so funny
say
she is a poet
she don't have no sense

[1969]

SANDRA HOCHMAN

## The Eyes of Flesh

My
father
dreams
that I
shall be
a wife.

Setting me
up in weeds
outside a
house where
beds of flowers
plunge
into fertilizer (he
would plant
me there)
with greenish braids
veined on my
ivory neck
twisted above
blood-checked gingham
in a knot
of love.

All his tears
fall from
his glassy rimmed
spectacles
to awaken him.

Father, sleep
in Jerusalem.
I hate
the plastic

fixtures
in this place
where we
erase
my childhood. For
a house
is where
deep
purposes are
broken
off.

[1963]


## Postscript

I gave my life to learning how to live.
Now that I have organized it all, now that
I have finally found out how to keep my clothes
In order, when to wash and when to sew, how
To control my glands and sexual impulses,
How to raise a family, which friends to get
Rid of and which to be loyal to, who
Is phony and who is true, how to get rid of
Ambition and how to be thrifty, now that I have
Finally learned how to be closer to the nude
And secret silence, my life
Is just about over.

[1969]

# What Would I Do White?

What would I do white?
What would I do clearly full
of not exactly beans nor
pearls my nose a manicure
my eyes a picture of your wall?

I would disturb the streets by
passing by so pretty kids
on stolen petty cash would look
at me like foreign
writing in the sky

I would forget my furs on any chair.
I would ignore the doormen at the knob
the social sanskrit of my life
unwilling to disclose my cosmetology,
I would forget.

Over my wine I would acquire
I would inspire big returns to equity
the equity of capital I am
accustomed to accept

like wintertime.

I would do nothing.
That would be enough.

[1967]

# For My Mother

for my mother
I would write a list
of promises so solid
loafing fish and onions
okra palm tree coconut
and Khus-Khus paradise
would
hard among the mongoose
enemies delight
a neo-noon-night trick
prosperity

for my father
I would decorate a doorway
weaving women into the daytime
of his travel also
season the snow to rice and peas
to peppery pearls on a flowering
platter drunkards stilt
at breakfast bacchanalia
swaying swift or stubborn
coral rocks
regenerate

for my only love
I would stop the silence

one of these days

won't come too soon
when the blank
familias blank
will fold away

a highly inflammable
balloon eclipsed by seminal
and nubile

loving

[1967]


# The Reception

Doretha wore the short blue lace last night
and William watched her drinking so she fight
with him in flying collar slim-jim orange
tie and alligator belt below the navel pants uptight


"I flirt. You hear me? Yes I flirt.
Been on my pretty knees all week
to clean the rich white downtown dirt
the greedy garbage money reek.


I flirt. Damned right. You look at me."
But William watched her carefully
his mustache shaky she could see
him jealous, "which is how he always be


at parties." Clementine and Wilhelmina
looked at trouble in the light blue lace
and held to George while Roosevelt Senior
circled by the yella high and bitterly light blue face


he liked because she worked
the crowded room like clay like molding men
from dust to muscle jerked
and arms and shoulders moving when

she moved. The Lord Almighty Seagrams bless
Doretha in her short blue dress
and Roosevelt waiting for his chance:
a true gut-funky blues to make her really dance.

[1967]


## If you saw a Negro lady

If you saw a Negro lady
sitting on a Tuesday
near the whirl-sludge doors of
Horn & Hardart on the main drag
of downtown Brooklyn

solitary and conspicuous as plain
and neat as walls impossible to
fresco and you watched her self-
conscious features shape about
a Horn & Hardart teaspoon
with a pucker from a cartoon

she would not understand
with spine as straight and solid
as her years of bending over floors
allowed

skin cleared of interest by a ruthless
soap      nails square and yellowclean
from metal files

sitting in a forty-year-old flush
of solitude and prickling
from the new white cotton blouse
concealing nothing she had ever noticed
even when she bathed and never
hummed a bathtub tune nor knew one

If you saw her square
above the dirty
mopped-on antiseptic floors
before the rag-wiped table tops

little finger      broad and stiff
in heavy emulation of a cockney

mannerism

would you turn her treat
into surprise observing
happy birthday

[1970]

## Gracie

I mean, I'm a no shoes hillbilly an' home
is deeper in the map than Kentucky or Tennessee an'
all I been raised to do is walk the chicken
yard, spillin' grain from ma's
apron, maybe once a week wear a bonnet
into town. I have red hair an' white skin;

men lean on their elbows lookin' at me. Ma's
voice tells me, "Don't breathe so deep," an'
the preacher says how happy I'll be when I'm dead. Skin
touchin' skin is evil. I'm to keep inside the chicken
yard, no eye's to see beneath my bonnet.
Farm boys suck their cheeks an' call, "Come home

with me, I'll give you your own chicken
yard an' take you proudly once a week to town." Home
ain't enough. As I spill grain from ma's
apron, I see city streets hung with lights an'
a dark room with a window lookin' on the bonnet
of the sky. Voices stroke at my skin

through its walls. When the grain's gone from ma's
apron, I hang it on its hook by her bonnet.
I figure to be my own fare North an' leave home.
My legs are crossed under a counter. I smell chicken
fry. A man leans on his elbows; his eyes drink my skin.
In a dark room, my dress undoes my body an'

I lie with him. His hot mouth comes home
on mine. I expect to hear the preacher's or ma's
voice yellin' at me, but the only voices in the wall's skin
are strange an' soft. I have beer an' chicken
for breakfast. All day I wear his body like a bonnet.
My stockins are run. The streets are hung with lights an'
he sleeps. I stand by the window an'
look into the night's skin, fancy home an' the chicken
yard, ma's apron an' my head cool in its bonnet.

ROCHELLE OWENS

## Dance & Eye Me (Wicked)ly
## My Breath a Fixed Sphere

Would you believe some-
    one who said he
            fuck't
                    Pallas Athena
        7 times?     had a goddess?


                    so much
                for that fancy?
    I was struck last time by (moon) madness
            as I watched you
        dance & eye me (wicked)ly
                                my breath
                    a fixed sphere
                            my palms &
                joints
                        making 8 times 7 spins
            while you moved
                        (backwards &
        forwards)
                Around the sun!


    O BODIES LURE ME!


                        fire springs
                brightens from
                            (bodies)
            purest light     brilliant & ruddy
                so
                    favorable!


                        [1968]

239

## The Power of Love
## He Wants Shih
## (Everything)

First, I put my
hands on her—shou meng haou!
I'll show you.
I make my arms hard
against her softness—
she sighs . . .
her love for me
is my weapon . . .
the feeling ceases
in me . . .
& her feelings
increase . . .
her skin under
my fingers feels
like blood
not yet dry . . .
a star on fire!
& I feel wrath in me . . .
& melancholy . . . &
ice against my teeth & also
. . . a tiny joy.

If I said to her what
was inside me . . . the words
would be . . . I will punch you . . .
to pulpwood!
The sounds I would make
would be the screams of a
vulture against
her throat.
Her mouth & legs . . . are open
. . . but my mind is working.
It's heaven's will, shua hsi!

In my mind I smear the mucus
from my nose on her breasts . . .
& drop ants into her two mouths . . .
I fill up all her orifices—
I'm very generous . . .
& she calls me the divinity
of mountains & streams &
I think of how it would be
to piss on her! She calls
herself happy & blessed &
how she feels privileged
to love me & protect me
so that I will never feel
lonely or frightened again!
I'm thinking how it
would be to throw her
into a pig-trough—
the pig slop squashing
under her buttocks &
her breasts jiggling
like rabbits!
I made her brim over
like a dark pool . . .
with my tricks—my magic!
She kept her eyes always always
on my belly, it seemed to me
as if she expected nightingales
to fly out of my belly!
& I told her stories!
Stories that I felt she must
hear!

     I
       wandered
               along
      with her
            in her mind
         at my own sweet will!
   While
        I wandered with her

I minced her
into
meatballs!
I am a magician!
& an acrobat!
& that is enough for me!

She is a
mouse
with its
intestines
hanging
out
I think she wants
to seize me
& grab
& scratch
& tickle me
inside my head is an ax
& I cut off her head!

What is that?
the pigeons?

[1968]

## Noon of the sunbather

The sun struts over the asphalt world
arching his gaudy plumes till the streets smoke
and the city sweats oil under his metal feet.
A woman nude on a rooftop lifts her arms:

"Men have swarmed like ants over my thighs,
held their Sunday picnics of gripe and crumb,
the twitch and nip of all their gristle traffic.
When will my brain pitch like a burning tower?
Lion, come down! explode the city of my bones."

The god stands on the steel blue arch and listens.
Then he strides the hills of igniting air,
straight to the roof he hastens, wings outspread.
In his first breath she blackens and curls like paper.
The limp winds of noon disperse her ashes.

But the ashes dance. Each ashfleck leaps at the sun.

[1963]

# The friend

We sat across the table.
he said, cut off your hands.
they are always poking at things.
they might touch me.
I said yes.

Food grew cold on the table.
he said, burn your body.
it is not clean and smells like sex.
it rubs my mind sore.
I said yes.

I love you, I said.
that's very nice, he said
I like to be loved,
that makes me happy.
Have you cut off your hands yet?

[1964]

# Song of the Fucked Duck

In using there are always two.
the manipulator dances with a partner who cons herself.
There are lies that glow so brightly we consent
to give a finger and then an arm
to let them burn.
I was dazzled by the crowd where everyone called my name.
Now I stand outside the funhouse exit, down the slide
reading my guidebook of Marx in Esperanto
and if I don't know anymore which way means forward
down is where my head is, next to my feet
with a pocketful of words and plastic tokens.

Form follows function, says the organizer
and turns himself into a paperclip,
into a vacuum cleaner,
into a machinegun.
Function follows analysis
but the forebrain
is only an owl in the tree of self.
One third of life we prowl in the grottos of sleep
where neglected worms ripen into dragons
where the spoilt pencil swells into an oak
and the cows of our early sins are called home chewing their cuds
and turning the sad faces of our childhood upon us.
Come back and scrub the floor, the stain is still there,
come back with your brush and kneel down
scrub and scrub again
it will never be clean.
Fantasy unacted sours the brain.
Buried desires sprout like mushrooms on the chin of the morning.
The will to be totally rational
is the will to be made out of glass and steel:
and to use others as if they were glass and steel.
We can see clearly no farther
than our hands can touch.

The cockroach knows as much as you know about living.
We trust with our hands and our eyes and our bellies.
The cunt accepts.
The teeth and back reject.
What we have to give each other:
dumb and mysterious as water swirling.
Always in the long corridors of the psyche
doors are opening and doors are slamming shut.
We rise each day to give birth or to murder
selves that go through our hands like tiny fish.
You said: I am the organizer, and took and used.
You wrapped your head in theory like yards of gauze

and touched others only as tools that fit to your task
and if the tool broke you seized another.
Arrogance is not a revolutionary virtue.
The manipulator liberates only
the mad bulldozers of the ego to level the ground.
I was a tool that screamed in the hand.
I have been loving you so long and hard and mean
and the taste of you is part of my tongue
and your face is burnt into my eyelids
and I could build you with my fingers out of dust
and now it is over.
Whether we want or not
our roots go down to strange waters,
we are creatures of the seasons and the earth.
You always had a reason and you have them still
rattling like dried leaves on a stunted tree.

[1969]

246

# The Woman in the

The woman in the
ordinary pudgy graduate student girl
is crouching with eyes and muscles clenched.
Round and smooth as a pebble
you efface yourself
under ripples of conversation and debate.
The woman in the block of ivory soap
has massive thighs that neigh
and great breasts and strong arms that blare and trumpet.
The woman of the golden fleece
laughs from the belly uproariously
inside the girl who imitates
a Christmas card virgin with glued hands.
It is time to bust out of girlscout camp.
It is time to stop running
for most popular sweetheart of Campbell Soup.
You are still searching for yourself in others' eyes
and creeping so you wont be punished.
In you bottled up is a woman peppery as curry,
a yam of a woman of butter and brass,
compounded of acid and sweet like a pineapple,
like a handgrenade set to explode,
like goldenrod ready to bloom.

[1971]

# Night letter

Scalded cat,
claws, arched back and blistered pride:
my friend. You'd have cooked down
my ropey carcass in a kettle for soup.
I was honing my knife.
What is friendship
to the desperate?
Is it bigger than a meal?

Before any mirror or man we jostled.
Fought from angst to Zeno,
sucked the onion of suspicion,
poured lie on the telephone.
Always head on: one raw from divorce court
spitting toads and nailclippings,
the other fresh baked from a new final bed
with strawberry-cream-filled brain.
One cooing
while the other spat.
To the hunted
what is loyalty?
Is it deeper than an empty purse?
Wider than a borrowed bed?

Of my two best friends at school
I continued to love the first Marie better
because she died young
so I could always carry her along with me
a wizened embryo inside.
But you and I clawed at hardscrabble hill
willing to fight anyone
especially each other
to survive.

Couldn't we have made alliance?
We were each so sure
of the way out,
the way in.
Now they've burnt out your nerves, my lungs.
We are better fed
but no better understood,
scabby and gruff with battle.
Bits of our love are doubtless in the dossiers
of the appropriate organizations.
Bits of our love are mouldering
in the lost and found offices of bankrupt railroads.
Bits stick like broken glass
in the minds of our wellearned enemies.
Regret is a damp wind
off the used car lot
where most of our peers came to rest.
Now, years too late, my voice quavers:
Can I help?

[1973]

JANE STEMBRIDGE

## Loving

When we loved
we didn't love right.

The mornings weren't funny
and we lost too much sleep.

I wish we could do it all again,
with clown hats on.

[1966]


## City

Children walk
with one
hand
out

to feel
what they are
walking
past.

A
city

is a bumpy
thing.

[1966]

# Mrs. Hamer

The
revolutionary
element remained

intact.

They
simply

stood, she said

no sir.

                    (*for emphasis*)

We didn't come
for no two
seats

since

all of us
is tired.

                    [1966]

## Dresses

Twelve and ugly
always wearing hand-me-downs
(O beautiful dresses I cannot have you)
and Mrs. Brown
"went to town, with her panties hanging down,"
deaconess of my father's church in Tulsa.
Bringing boxes of old clothes,
she called them presents for me,
muddy bumpy ladies dresses,
the kind you pin brooches on
between the bosoms (or breasts
as it said in *Song of Solomon* that summer).
Mrs. Brown being Christian,
inviting me to milk her cows
in the country. Three days in the country.
Mrs. Brown saying "it is hot dear,
wouldn't you like to take off all your clothes
while the men are away?"
Afraid to say no,
I wore my underwear and hated her
lying wrinkled and naked in the sun on her bed.

Hurt that I wanted to go home,
she never sent presents after that.
But other boxes came. Other people's clothes—
faded, too tight in the hips or saggy on top.
"It looks lovely dear," they would say, dreaming
of their kindnesses, how Christ would forgive them if
he came to earth and found them sitting
in the movie house on Sunday.
(O beautiful dresses I cannot have you)
Ribbons pink and blue satin
streaming from the hair of Ginger Stinson who let boys
kiss her and was popular.

Maroon velvet curtains in the gymnasium
hiding games behind them—*Phantom of the Opera.*

When I was a child I spoke as a child
I thought as a child I understood
as a child.
But how can one put away childish things?
Mrs. Brown's dresses still button to my chin.

[1966]


## Poem in Which My Legs Are Accepted

Legs!
How we have suffered each other,
never meeting the standards of magazines
                              or official measurements.

I have hung you from trapezes,
          sat you on wooden rollers,
               pulled and pushed you
                              with the anxiety of taffy,
and still, you are yourselves!

Most obvious imperfection, blight on my fantasy life,
strong,
plump,
never to be skinny
or even hinting of the svelte beauties in history books
                              or Sears catalogues.
Here you are—solid, fleshy and
white as when I first noticed you, sitting on the toilet,
                              spread softly over the wooden seat,
having been with me only twelve years,
                              yet
as obvious as the legs of my thirty-year-old gym teacher.

Legs!
O that was the year we did acrobatics in the annual gym show.
How you split for me!
                        One-handed cartwheels
                        from this end of the gymnasium to the other,
                        ending in double splits,
legs you flashed in blue rayon slacks my mother bought for the
        occasion
and tho you were confidently swinging along,
the rest of me blushed at the sound of clapping.

Legs!
How I have worried about you, not able to hide you,
embarrassed at beaches, in highschool
                        when the cheerleaders' slim brown legs
                                        spread all over
                                        the sand
                                        with the perfection
                                        of bamboo.
I hated you, and still you have never given out on me.

With you
I have risen to the top of blue waves,
with you
I have carried food home as a loving gift
                                when my arms began
                                unjelling like madrilene.

Legs, you are a pillow,
white and plentiful with feathers for his wild head.
You are the endless scenery
behind the tense sinewy elegance of his two dark legs.
You welcome him joyfully
and dance.
And you will be the locks in a new canal between continents.
                        The ship of life will push out of you
                        and rejoice
                                in the whiteness,

                                in the first floating and rising of water.

[1966]

254

# Poem Wondering if I'm Pregnant

Is it you? Are you there,
thief I can't see,
    drinking,
     leaving me at the edge
     of breathing?
New mystery floating up my left arm,
clinging to the curtain.
     Uncontrollable.
Eyes on stalks, full of pollen,
stem juice, petals making ready to unfold,
to be set in a white window,
or an empty courtyard.
Fingers fresh. And cranium,
     a clean architecture
     with doors
     that swing open . . .
is it you, penny face?
Is it you?

[1969]

# Poems for the New

1—

we're connecting,
                foot under my rib.
I'm sore with life!
At night,
                your toes grow. Inches of the new!
The lion prowls the sky
and shakes his tail for you.
Pieces of moon
                fly by my kitchen window.
And your father comes
riding the lion's back
                in the dark,
to hold me,
                you,
                    in the perfect circle of him.


2—

Voluptuous against him, I am
nothing superfluous,
but all—
bones, bark of him, root of him take.
I am round
with his sprouting,
new thing new thing!
He wraps me.
The sheets are white.
My belly has tracks on it—
                hands and feet
are moving
under this taut skin.
In snow, in light,
we are about to become!

[1969]

# FayWray to the King

Dear Kong
Some have slurred our relationship
Some have called it unnatural;
Some have said I'm a tart;
Some have said you're an ape.
Dear Kong
Rumor, and rumormongers, old farts.
It's what you say that hurts.
It's when you criticize your little Fay that hurts.
Not rumor, rumormongers, and good taste.
When you speak of splitting, instead of loving,
When you talk of hating, instead of copulating,
When you rant of not relating, instead of knowing,
That's what hurts
Your little Fay,
Your own sweet flirt,
Your tiny Miss Wray.

They have been wrong—
As if miscegenetic pleasure was a freak of nature,
As if I was not easily satisfied or well supplied;
If only they could touch your hairy rump and tool—
They'd realize I wasn't such a fool.

Dear Kong
You are my beast;
Devour my nice white body if you please;
Don't act like a cowardly golliwog
Or use philosophical doublespeak;
Save me from the terrible pterodactyl;
I'm agog at your marvelous soul
And adore the hairs on your toes
And cylinder which towers above
The Empire State, though they say

You have torn four sexes to shreds
And had other women in bed.

Dear Kong
Save your adorable Fay;
Miss Wray who adores you
And loves you, is true to you.
                    Affectionately, YOUR QUEEN

[1970]

SONIA SANCHEZ

## poem at thirty

it is midnight
no magical bewitching
hour for me
i know only that
i am here waiting
remembering that
once as a child
i walked two
miles in my sleep.
did i know
then where i
was going?
traveling. i'm
always traveling.
i want to tell
you about me
about nights on a
brown couch when
i wrapped my
bones in lint and
refused to move.
no one touches
me anymore.
father do not
send me out
among strangers.
you you black man
stretching scraping
the mold from your body
here is my hand.
i am not afraid
of the night.

[1968]

LYNN SUKENICK

## Parting: A Game

Begin by parting your hair.
Put everything in boxes. Lift boxes from floor.
      Put boxes in different rooms.
Separate eggs from chickens, bread slices from
      butter, asparagus from tips.
Hum steam on the mirror; let it lie down under
      the mirror's horizon.
Peel one nail from one finger.
Put your hand between rocks and pry them apart,
      though you burn with eel bites.
See how the tide
dances on graves.
Watch mildew come.
Fall in love. Then
see how the bus disappears
around the corner.
Double
the empty spaces.

[1972]

HELEN CHASIN

## Looking Out

Mother, I am something more
than your girl; still our old quarrel
brings me up.
A Miss Universe parade of ex-wives,
marketers, secretaries, park ladies
with prams, mistresses,
fiancées, mysterious female lives
shimmer and ache against my sight
like migraine.

       The world
is half full of women, each
a face of our argument,
each with ex-husband,
dinner guest, boss, lover,
or no one. Sisters,
enemies: some might understand that
attached, varied, and secret,
they are my battle.

[1968]

# The Poetess Kō Ōgimi

her mouth an O
as if she's on to something
surprising
        or difficult, or doing
*the lady's complaint,* or first-naming
her grief

leans, an apostrophe.
Her thin carpets heap and scatter
like sheets of paper, they sail like a raft, oh
she rides them, a survivor, looks over
the beige sea slant-eyed.
                      **Where**
have the thirty-five others gotten to
or been left at? . . .
                  **Wherever**
now she's alone. Her kimono sleeve
gestures at her breast.
Maybe there's a marriage, children, but not

here, just her
scarves flying, skimming
the air's strata, and
her rugs snaking like ribbons of low water
and no

pen or worksheets:  pure process.  Oh oh
she squats like any woman in some anguish
on those various colorful stuffs
crooning out of her Japanese hair.
Will she never leave off? Unless
this *here* is a hereafter
death will get her to.

                          [1970]

The Poetess Kō Ōgimi: hanging scroll, formerly part of the Scrolls of the
Thirty-Six Poets, 13th century, ink and colors on paper, 14 × 23½ in. Attrib-
uted to Fujiwara Nobuzane.

# Photograph at the Cloisters: April 1972*

For C and H

This is where we're at the gate.
What a time we had getting here:
the sun's at half past, see the lines
in our faces, and our hands
are maps: what happened
and how we could go if we wanted to.

Think of being happy this way: long walks
and stone quiet, the colors
pure light, a cell
of your own *prière de ne pas déranger*
oh I know that voice.
And not having to pull the sun up, to plan
the evening.

Whenever it was when you were a girl
when you thought about being a nun
were you lovely? in black
in pain always more beautiful
than a dead lady, waiting.

Look at us, how long our hair is.
Imagine. You've just given your husband up
and those children over there have my smile
they're waving, *ciao*, my way
of saying goodbye. Think of a woman
burning the way days do.
The flowers are fireworks, they flare in their spaces
like stars for words for doing something terrible.

[1973]

# Mythmaking

Beauty is never satisfied
with beauty. Helen,
gazing in the glass,
framed by the lecherous curtains,
the enchanted bed,
knew herself beautiful. Yet she felt life pass
about her. Laughter had been hers
to breed alone. Now mute,
the humdrum pulse run down, she lay
a palpitation of her memory;
a deceitful body and a crumbling smile
where all that love and elixirs had bred.

Men knew her aging odor.
Ravished by the nosings of her fears,
she married. Her fastened gaiety became a jewel
decking a sot. Oh well, we do
with what we have and haven't got;
the pagan cried
against endurance, dressed
and went to dinner at the side
of Menelaus. What would she become, if not her men
would come inside her,
make her whole again!
Each night was Helen
on the reminiscent bed
waiting with spread heart and legs
and willing arch for willing arrowhead.

Sprung from the cracking bow of Troy
he could not notice Helen growing old,
but fitted as a flower, or a toy,
as use to pleasure, went to hold
the woman in his arms.

And were they satisfied, these two,
when afterwards Helen closed her eyes
and slept?
Helen, who turned the too-much heart
to a great dumb shrivelling, could do as much
to any lover.
So squandered Paris in her arms lay dry
and she lay lavish and methodical;
(who offers bread by night may offer mould)
beauty to beauty did not satisfy;
such meetings of perfections cut us, turn us cold
as aging Helen, bittering in her sleep,
and cheat us of desire
by too much hungering.

She must have been glad to wake, not to be satisfied,
to see her husband stir himself and raise a fleet,
and all the world fall shadow
to the crumpling of that sheet.

[1966]


## The Meeting

Susan, we meet in late fall
in the bitter wind.
But while I in my blue cape
grieve for my dead baby, you grow
in your purple cape a huddled
hidden living child.

And I am reminded
of the meeting of Mary
and Elizabeth, the mothers
of Jesus and John the Baptist,
with the Giotto hills rising, steep humps,
in the background. Each woman

has placed her hand
on the abdomen of the other: within each
a child leaps.

It is fall, perhaps November there.
For each, the birth date nears.
The skies are grey, though the Italian
hills break from shadow.
Their draperies glow;
Mary, of course,
in blue. And Eliza—

beth. What sweetness,
such a meeting of women!
Brief respite from the bitterness
of winter: they do not suspect
the suffering to follow.
It is said
the two children spoke to each other,
then, from within their wombs.

Now, standing on the flagstones
in our capes whose shapes
are gothic windows, we
are silent: deprivation
chokes me in the cold; you have
such secrets; you are
heavy with hope.

And as the snow flakes, salt
flakes fall, the world
grows large and vacant: I think
of those pale women, leaning inward,
and of how
their small sons, unborn John and Jesus,
recognized each other
and kicked
their mothers with joy and
evangelical fervor.

[1971]

# But you, my darling, should have married the prince

When we were children, clasping hands,
do you remember that moist circle, play?
How we were dancing and knew only the dandelions,
and the earth was livid with dandelions.
I see us now as in a photograph that never was:
hair like soapbubbles spun by nuns, the singing
raucous as starch. Our cries still echo
down the corridors of my ears: we,
rank and weedy, wanting to be old.

There were no secrets then
to prickle our knees.
No one hid in the closet.
Beards were friendly as forests of grass—
how we trembled, pretending to be lost,
caught in the chins of uncles.

We pared apples, made wishes,
and washed in the first dew of May.
Mother went through our laundry
and we didn't mind . . .
but how we wept when our cousin got married.
Home from the army, his six-month moustache
saluted both sides of his face.
Jealous as bridemaids we watched
as he married the girl. She had apricot hair
and a cameo ring.
*Look, now, how he takes her hand.*
Never was it like that, picking scabs!
Peaches and morning were right for those two,
not for us, little pickles, fevered in bed, yanking
knots from our furious hair in the dark
and begging to be blond.

Nights came. Net notching our chests,
thighs sticky, we went to the dances
and put up our hair.
You lost your virginity
in mother's garden
and finally I was kissed.

Now we are older. You are married.
Natashas both, we have grown up.
Those shivery wonderings lit from the street
are over; cousins put away in paper boxes.
Outside, the walnut trees
grow sticky as old tears
and I lie sweating in the dark.
The dusk comes swallow-winged;
the apples rot with wishes.
Where there is no magic, one stays a toad
and we who screamed to know it
know it, and grow old.

[1971]

MARGARET ATWOOD

# Against Still Life

Orange in the middle of a table:

It isn't enough
to walk around it
at a distance, saying
it's an orange:
nothing to do
with us, nothing
else: leave it alone

I want to pick it up
in my hand
I want to peel the
skin off; I want
more to be said to me
than just Orange:
want to be told
everything it has to say

And you, sitting across
the table, at a distance, with
your smile contained, and like the orange
in the sun: silent:

Your silence
isn't enough for me
now, no matter with what
contentment you fold
your hands together; I want
anything you can say
in the sunlight:

stories of your various
childhoods, aimless journeyings,

your loves; your articulate
skeleton; your posturings; your lies.
These orange silences
(sunlight and hidden smile)
make me want to
wrench you into saying;
now I'd crack your skull
like a walnut, split it like a pumpkin
to make you talk, or get
a look inside

But quietly:
if I take the orange
with care enough and hold it
gently

I may find
an egg
a sun
an orange moon
perhaps a skull; center
of all energy
resting in my hand

can change it to
whatever I desire
it to be

and you, man, orange afternoon
lover, wherever
you sit across from me
(tables, trains, buses)

if I watch
quietly enough
and long enough

at last, you will say
(maybe without speaking)

(there are mountains
inside your skull
garden and chaos, ocean
and hurricane; certain
corners of rooms, portraits
of great-grandmothers, curtains
of a particular shade;
your deserts; your private
dinosaurs; the first
woman)

all I need to know:
tell me
everything
just as it was
from the beginning.

[1966]

At first I was given centuries
to wait in caves, in leather
tents, knowing you would never come back

Then it speeded up: only
several years between
the day you jangled off
into the mountains, and the day (it was
spring again) I rose from the embroidery
frame at the messenger's entrance.

That happened twice, or was it
more; and there was once, not so
long ago, you failed,
and came back in a wheelchair

with a moustache and a sunburn
and were insufferable.

Time before last though, I remember
I had a good eight months between
running alongside the train, skirts hitched, handing
you violets in at the window
and opening the letter; I watched
your snapshot fade for twenty years.

And last time (I drove to the airport
still dressed in my factory
overalls, the wrench
I had forgotten sticking out of the back
pocket; there you were,
zippered and helmeted, it was zero
hour, you said Be
Brave) it was at least three weeks before
I got the telegram and could start regretting.

But recently, the bad evenings
there are only seconds
between the warning on the radio and the
explosion; my hands
don't reach you

and on quieter nights
you jump up from
your chair without even touching your dinner
and I can scarcely kiss you goodbye
before you run out into the street and they shoot

[1971]

The accident has occurred,
the ship has broken, the motor
of the car has failed, we have been
separated from the others,
we are alone in the sand, the ocean,
the frozen snow

I remember what I have to do
in order to stay alive,
I take stock of our belongings
most of them useless

I know I should be digging shelters,
killing seabirds and making
clothes from their feathers,
cutting the rinds from cacti, chewing
roots for water, scraping through
the ice for treebark, for moss

but I rest here without power
to save myself, tasting
salt in my mouth, the fact that
you won't save me

watching the mirage of us
hands locked, smiling,
as it fades into the white desert.

I touch you, straighten the sheet, you turn over
in the bed, tender
sun comes through the curtains

Which of us will survive
which of us will survive the other

[1971]

LYNN STRONGIN

## Emily Dickinson Postage Stamp

No saint on a disc of snow,
you came back, Emily. Whole,
into green:
Not that green which corrupts
the wave of the brain:
but a green greater than ocean:

On a stamp,
hands folded over flowers;
staring thru all you've lost:
one love? two love? O host,
to read a letter, first you'd close the door:
   Who wrote the world—then heard no more.

[1972]

MARI EVANS

# I Am a Black Woman

I am a black woman
the music of my song
some sweet arpeggio of tears
is written in a minor key
and I
can be heard humming in the night
Can be heard
                humming
in the night

I saw my mate leap screaming to the sea
and I/with these hands/cupped the lifebreath
from my issue in the canebrake
I lost Nat's swinging body in a rain of tears
and heard my son scream all the way from Anzio
for Peace he never knew. . . . I
learned Da Nang and Pork Chop Hill
in anguish
Now my nostrils know the gas
and these trigger tire/d fingers
seek the softness in my warrior's beard

I
am a black woman
tall as a cypress
strong
beyond all definition still
defying place
and time
and circumstance
   assailed

        impervious
            indestructible
Look
    on me and be
renewed

                                        [1970]

LENORE KANDEL

## Bus Ride

what savage beast would willfully consent to ride jammed haunch
     to haunch
with others of his kind
carried from spot to spot, glimpsing the passing world through
greasy rectangles of heavy glass
     oh god but we are civilized!
   observe the lady, matron-dominant by type
   she wears the uniform: mink coat, silk hat, a small corsage of pale
   Hawaiian blooms
       no use; old eve still wearing the skins of dead animals the genital
         organs of plants

I remember you, old lady, when you first decided you were such hot
     stuff,
prancing around on your hind legs with that phony apple in your
     teeth—
running on all fours when you thought no one was looking
       (I wonder, do you do that now—I can picture you in your
       bar-b-q back yard, stripped down to corset and falsies
       and whinnying at your neighbor's nubile sons with your
       finger up your flabby unsatisfied crotch while your
       de-balled houseman sits inside leafing through playboy
       and swallowing his spit)

again, you and your sisters do surround me, shining the plastic
seats with well-fed bottoms, your arms all crammed with
further goodies for your private delectation
were I that primal beast
I would have torn you joint by joint and saved your bones for
hard nights in the winter for my young to chew on
       but civilized
I sit in shame, guarding my own poor bones from such as you and
leaping from the bus to scurry home, intact
one time again                                            [1960]

277

# Blues for Sister Sally

I

    moon-faced baby with cocaine arms
                    nineteen summers
                    nineteen lovers

        novice of the junkie angel
        lay sister of mankind penitent
                    sister in marijuana
                    sister in hashish
                    sister in morphine

        against the bathroom grimy sink
        pumping her arms full of life
                    (holy holy)
    she bears the stigma (holy holy) of the raving christ
                    (holy holy)
                    holy needle
                    holy powder
                    holy vein

    dear miss lovelorn: my sister makes it with a hunk
    of glass do you think this is normal miss lovelorn

            I DEMAND AN ANSWER!

II

                    weep
        for my sister she walks with open veins
        leaving her blood in the sewers of your cities
                    from east coast
                    to west coast
                    to nowhere

278

how shall we canonize our sister who is not quite dead
    who fornicates with strangers
    who masturbates with needles
who is afraid of the dark and wears her long hair soft and black
    against her bloodless face


III

    midnight and the room dream-green and hazy
    we are all part of the collage

            brother and sister, she leans against the wall
            and he, slipping the needle in her painless arm

            pale fingers (with love) against the pale arm

IV

    children our afternoon is soft, we lean against each other

            our stash is in our elbows
            our fix is in our heads
    god is a junkie and he has sold salvation
            for a week's supply

                                        [1960]

Somedays now
I can squash a cockroach
under a clear glass and
watch the brown
and yellow juices
flattening out
around the crushed
shiny parts.
And if the front
of it is sticking
out from under the side,
I'll watch it wriggle
while the rest dies.

On the same days
I can ignore
every subway stare.
And if some old man
or sweaty kid decides
to feel for *me*, baby,
through *my* coat, baby,
I can look him
squarely in the face
and deal an even
"Fuck you."

But this one time
I was standing in the subway
and this boy came up
to me and asked me a question,
and I looked at him and
said, "what?"
And he said something
about Brooklyn
and showed me an address
on a piece of paper from his billfold.

I didn't know whether he wanted
to take me with him or
just didn't know how to get there.

I looked at his face,
but it went hard and soft
at the same time.
So I said:
        "I don't know,
          you'll have to ask someone else,"
and looked out onto the tracks.
Then a man on my other side
said to me:
          "Did you know that fellow?"
He didn't want me to
talk to strangers,
I suppose.
So I shook my head
and just didn't look around.

[1970]

PART THREE

*We are screaming,*
*we are flying,*
*laughing, and won't stop*—JEAN TEPPERMAN

## Asking for Ruthie

you know her hustle
you know her white legs
flicker among headlights
and her eyes pick up the wind
while the fast hassle of living
ticks off her days
you know her ways

you know her hustle
you know her lonely pockets
lined with tricks
turned and forgotten
the men like mice hide
under her mind
lumpy, bigeyed
you know her pride

you know her blonde arms cut
by broken nickels in
hotelrooms and by razors of
summer lightning on the road
but you know the wizard
highway, no resisting so
she moves, she is forever missing

get her a stopping place
before the night slides dirty
fingers under her eyelids and
the weight of much bad kissing
breaks that ricepaper face

sun cover her, earth
make love to Ruthie

stake her to hot lunches in the wheat fields
make bunches of purple ravens
fly out in formation, over her eyes
and let her newest lovers
be gentle as women
and longer lasting

[1970]


# From *The Common Woman*
## Ella, in a square apron, along Highway 80

She's a copperheaded waitress,
tired and sharp-worded, she hides
her bad brown tooth behind a wicked
smile, and flicks her ass
out of habit, to fend off the pass
that passes for affection.
She keeps her mind the way men
keep a knife—keen to strip the game
down to her size. She has a thin spine,
swallows her eggs cold, and tells lies.
She slaps a wet rag at the truck drivers
if they should complain. She understands
the necessity for pain, turns away
the smaller tips, out of pride, and
keeps a flask under the counter. Once,
she shot a lover who misused her child.
Before she got out of jail, the courts had pounced
and given the child away. Like some isolated lake,
her flat blue eyes take care of their own stark
bottoms. Her hands are nervous, curled, ready
to scrape.
The common woman is as common
as a rattlesnake.

[1970]

# Under Your Voice, Among Legends

1.

mama writes
"your papa's
dad is gone"

he is. they ride him from the farm
in Sunday socks
comb out his beard & bless
then let him down at last
by Grandma in the thick Nebraska sod

the tin spittoon is tossed
in trash by the cistern, orchard apples
rot, the new Ford bought
the morning I was born
ruts up in mud to the runningboard

I am not there
I dream it

; he does not care

2.

the summer I was ten
I climbed rust-ragged steps
of your granary, Grandpa

to the loft where your son
the boy my father
slept

& was met in the crusted silence
by strange smells, odor

of old dreams, corn
& rotting grain

        I remember
how the boards cried out
beneath me, how fear
hooked at the root of my tongue
& the cobweb ghosts descending

how my heart erupted
as the red-eyed raven rose
monstrous
mounting the shadows

& I was plunged sobbing
into the kerosene clasp
of my grandmother's kitchen

into the warm yeast smells of Bohemian baking
prunefilled kolaches, poppyseed rolls rising
under bleached sacks, the August apples foaming
in stone vats in the pantry


3.

that summer you shot
the black mad bull, & I felt
blood of the stuck pig, hot
dung of horses

saw small deer broken in the railbed
held dead snakes at sunset
followed green-faced pheasants
grazing near the field's edge

        under your voice, among legends
        I woke to my poems
        lonely at times, curious
        companionship with the bones

song of the Skidi maidens
blood spun at dawn, libation
to the morningstar Corn Mother
chanting the grown gold out

now twenty years have burned
your stories into glass
I drink from them by day, by night
I grapple the ancient bird

hung vast & enigmatic, haunter
of granary shadows, cold
totem of knowledge, guard
of the red-eyed past


4.

here the seasons go down
stifled
       clicker of heels in the night street
city of neon dancers, the electric
drunken blood

        & I am knotted with longing
        for the old earth-handed knowledge

for Indian-eyed watchers of seasons
storm-fearing farmers, snow
on the prairie shoulders rippling
like flexed muscles in wind

for my cornsilk Christmas dolls
necklace of dried corn
yucca smell, soapweed
the incense odor of sage

for my brothers, strongnosed
in the firelight, sunburned
with the earth smell on their ankles

my sisters bent over the piano
swaying like reapers
like weavers over the keys

for the long star-fallen nights
we sat like goatherds
tending our speech

wet mornings, wistful
repetitive
velvet afternoons among the wheat gold winter weeds

       o pioneers!

       o sweet grandfather Adam

I sit in the subways among metal faces raging
as the wars roar in on transistor tracks

I race under the world city crying
for my lost home, Nebraska, my grandfather's orchard

       I plant money in the asphalt

       ; I lunch on bitter apples

[1969]

CAROLE FREEMAN

## i saw them lynch

i saw them lynch festus whiteside and
all the limp white women with lymphatic greasy eyelids came
to watch silent silent in the dusty burning noon
shifting noiselessly from heavy foot to heavy
foot licking beast lips showing beast teeth in
anticipation of the feast
and they all plodded forward after the
lynching to grab and snatch the choice
pieces, rending them with their bloody teeth crunching on his
        hollow bones.

[1968]

# when my uncle willie saw

      when
my uncle willie saw
aunt mimmies new baby he
look at his big cracked black hands the thick
pink nails split then
he looked at black mimmie with her gold teeth flashing and
he look at the baby
      then
later on he brag to everybody how he
got indin blood from his grand mama
      thenwhen
my uncle willie and aunt tee mimmie had
nother baby he
look at auntee then he
look out the window he
look at the midwife who smiling a little
shaking her head a little
and he say it albinodentyall member us get albinirs on mah cudin
      Tim side?
Aunt tee she grinsome then she laugh then she say willie-sherrif
      merriweather
say of this a boy if ah names him merriweather he gon give you fi'
      dollars?
then!
i seen uncle willie cry some.

[1968]

ROBIN MORGAN

## The Invisible Woman

The invisible woman in the asylum corridor
sees others quite clearly,
including the doctor who patiently tells her
she isn't invisible,
and pities the doctor, who must be mad
to stand there in the asylum corridor,
talking and gesturing
to nothing at all.

The invisible woman has great compassion.
So, after a while, she pulls on her body
like a rumpled glove, and switches on her voice
to comfort the elated doctor with words.
Better to suffer this prominence
than for the poor young doctor to learn
he himself is insane.
Only the strong can know that.

[1970]

## Bitter Herbs

NATURAL PUSSY
25¢ in a dispenser
*Gulf* station, pinole

J Douglas says prisoners
use cardboard rolls, filled
with a greasy baggie,
surrounded by a hot wet
                              washcloth
"sure feels like pussy"

Playboy bunnies twitch their tails
bouncing squashedup titties
and grinning.

if you come in me
a child is likely to
come back out.
my name is Alta.
I am a woman.

[1969]

euch, are you having your period?
why didn't you tell me?
i shoulda fucked him ina dark.
he coulda thot bloody sheets
look ma a virgin

[1970]

penus envy, they call it
think how handy to have a thing
that poked out; you could just shove
it in any body, whang whang & come,
wouldn't have to give a shit.
you *know* you'd come!
wouldn't have to love that person,
trust that person.
whang, whang & come.
if you couldn't get relief for free,
pay a little $, whang whang & come.
you wouldn't have to keep, or abort.
wouldn't have to care about the kid.
wouldn't fear sexual violation.
penus envy, they call it.
the man is sick in his heart.
that's what I call it.

[1970]


## First Pregnancy

lonely and big
a couple of times i cried
hearing you
beating off under covers

[1970]

CAROLYN M. RODGERS

## U Name This One

let uh revolution come. uh
state of peace is not known to me
anyway
since I grew uhround in chi town
where
howlin wolf howled in the tavern on 47th st.
and muddy waters made u cry the salty nigger blues,
    where pee wee cut Lonnell fuh fuckin wid
    his sistuh and blood baptized the street
    at least twice ev'ry week and judy got
    kicked out grammar school fuh bein pregnant
    and died tryin to ungrow the seed
        we was all up in there and
        just livin was guerilla warfare, yeah.

let uh revolution come.
couldn't be no action like what
        i dun already seen.

[1969]

SUSAN SUTHEIM

# For Witches

today
i lost my temper.

temper, when one talks of metal
means strong,
perfect.

temper, for humans,
means angry
irrational
bad.

today i found my temper.
i said,
you step on my head
for 27 years you step on my head
and though I have been trained
to excuse you for your inevitable
clumsiness
today i think
i prefer my head to your clumsiness.

today i began
to find
myself.

tomorrow
perhaps
i will begin
to find
you.

[1969]

297

ELIZABETH FENTON

## Masks

Somehow it should have been
not quite so still. . . .
I watched the panes pale
into the morning city
the way a poet should
and heard the horns blow
all the way up Broadway
while you beside me
leaned on one elbow. . . .

I'd learned the whole act
and all variations
so I'd be applauded soundly
roses all round, white.
Whitened sheets, same ones
on which I am seen alive
as if for the first time
every time it happens:

*see, she is mellow & moves*
*see, she achieves her purpose*
*oh, most paradisical!*
*oh, woman in all her glory!*
Flesh makes me visible.
Nothing I am can do that.
The silence I sink in
is all you can hear now.

My nakedness the mask itself
covers the spirit completely.
I grow large and plastic
I am the enormous doll
and you dive into me
and hold on to limbs,

wriggling like a fish
and expire on my dry beach,
and never know I'm there.

My nakedness the mask itself,
Person and persona.
Yet somehow it should have . . .
In another country should have . . .
But you invented the word, *lovers*
You invented this body I wear.
The white rose closes on its wealth
My nakedness the mask itself.

[1970]

## Under the Ladder to Heaven

But when it was my turn to wrestle with the angel,
Farcical!
First thing, I had to tell him
To keep his hands where they belonged
And fight fair.

Lord, I asked
What kind of angel are you anyhow?
I thought you were serious.
Then he made for my right breast
And my head hit the ladder.
It all felt familiar.

Look, I said.
Where's God. Would he approve of this?
He pinned me to the ground,
And snapped, "My round."
I forgot all about asking questions.

O, my buttons were undone
And I couldn't remember
What it was I'd wanted.
The angel's breath was awfully hot,
For an angel,
But his eyes were the cool blue
Of a baby's night-light.
I held on to my soul with both hands.

Then when I'd unwound
His fingers from my thigh,
And backed off,
His wings went slack
And sank down gradually,
The glow escaping from them
Like air from a tire.
I felt like a discarded dishrag.
I was so tired.

The ladder to heaven swayed in the breeze.
Its light stung my eyes.
The angel asked if I wanted
Another go at it.
I said I didn't know,
But had to allow
That his style made me uneasy.
I didn't want to fall in with the wrong crowd.

That made the angel smile.
"Hell," he said, "I just work here
And that's the setup.
So what did you expect?
But you know, you're the first gal's
Ever objected."
So I left feeling pleased.

Later, I found
He told everyone that.

[1973]

NIKKI GIOVANNI

# Seduction

one day
you gonna walk in this house
and i'm gonna have on a long African
gown
you'll sit down and say "The Black . . ."
and i'm gonna take one arm out
then you—not noticing me at all—will say "What about
this brother . . ."
and i'm going to be slipping it over my head
and you'll rap on about "The revolution . . ."
while i rest your hand against my stomach
you'll go on—as you always do—saying
"I just can't dig . . ."
while i'm moving your hand up and down
and i'll be taking your dashiki off
then you'll say "What we really need . . ."
and i'll be licking your arm
and "The way I see it we ought to . . ."
and unbuckling your pants
"And what about the situation . . ."
and taking your shorts off
then you'll notice
your state of undress
and knowing you you'll just say
"Nikki,
isn't this counterrevolutionary . . . ?"

[1968]

301

# Woman Poem

you see, my whole life
is tied up
to unhappiness
its father cooking breakfast
and me getting fat as a hog
or having no food
at all and father proving
his incompetence
again
i wish i knew how it would feel
to be free

its having a job
they won't let you work
or no work at all
castrating me
(yes it happens to women too)

its a sex object if you're pretty
and no love
or love and no sex if you're fat
get back fat black woman be a mother
grandmother strong thing but not woman
gameswoman romantic woman love needer
man seeker dick eater sweat getter
fuck needing love seeking woman

its a hole in your shoe
and buying lil sis a dress
and her saying you shouldn't
when you know
all too well—that you shouldn't

but smiles are only something we give
to properly dressed social workers
not each other
only smiles of i know

your game sister
which isn't really
a smile

joy is finding a pregnant roach
and squashing it
not finding someone to hold
let go get off get back don't turn
me on you black dog
how dare you care
about me
you ain't got no good sense
cause i ain't shit you must be lower
than that to care

its a filthy house
with yesterday's watermelon
and monday's tears
cause true ladies don't
know how to clean

its intellectual devastation
of everybody
to avoid emotional commitment
"yeah honey i would've married
him but he didn't have no degree"

its knock-kneed mini skirted
wig wearing dyed blond mamma's scar
born dead my scorn your whore
rough heeled broken nailed powdered
face me
whose whole life is tied
up to unhappiness
cause its the only
for real thing
i
know

[1968]

303

# Beautiful Black Men

(with compliments and apologies to all not mentioned by name)

i wanta say just gotta say something
bout those beautiful beautiful beautiful outasight
black men
with they afros
walking down the street
is the same ol danger
but a brand new pleasure

sitting on stoops, in bars, going to offices
running numbers, watching for their whores
preaching in churches, driving their hogs
walking their dogs, winking at me
in their fire red, lime green, burnt orange
royal blue tight tight pants that hug
what i like to hug

jerry butler, wilson pickett, the impressions
temptations, mighty mighty sly
don't have to do anything but walk
on stage
and i scream and stamp and shout
see new breed men in breed alls
dashiki suits with shirts that match
the lining that compliments the ties
that smile at the sandals
where dirty toes peek at me
and i scream and stamp and shout
for more beautiful beautiful beautiful
black men with outasight afros

[1968]

# Adulthood

(for claudia)

i usta wonder who i'd be

when i was a little girl in indianapolis
sitting on doctors porches with post-dawn pre-debs
(wondering would my aunt drag me to church sunday)
i was meaningless
and i wondered if life
would give me a chance to mean

i found a new life in the withdrawal from all things
not like my image

when i was a teen-ager i usta sit
on front steps conversing
the gym teachers son with embryonic eyes
about the essential essence of the universe
(and other bullshit stuff)
recognizing the basic powerlessness of me

but then i went to college where i learned
that just because everything i was was unreal
i could be real and not just real through withdrawal
into emotional crosshairs or colored bourgeoisie intellectual pretensions
but from involvement with things approaching reality
i could possibly have a life

so catatonic emotions and time wasting sex games
were replaced with functioning commitments to logic and
necessity and the gray area was slowly darkened into
a black thing
for a while progress was being made along with a certain degree
of happiness cause i wrote a book and found a love
and organized a theatre and even gave some lectures on

Black history
and began to believe all good people could get
together and win without bloodshed
then
hammarskjold was killed
and lumumba was killed
and diem was killed
and kennedy was killed
and malcolm was killed
and evers was killed
and schwerner, chaney and goodman were killed
and liuzzo was killed
and stokely fled the country
and le roi was arrested
and rap was arrested
and pollard, thompson and cooper were killed
and king was killed
and kennedy was killed
and i sometimes wonder why i didn't become a debutante
sitting on porches, going to church all the time, wondering
is my eye make-up on straight
or a withdrawn discoursing on the stars and moon
instead of a for real Black person who must now feel
and inflict
pain

[1968]

SUSAN GRIFFIN

# I Like to Think of Harriet Tubman

I like to think of Harriet Tubman.
Harriet Tubman who carried a revolver,
who had a scar on her head from a rock thrown
by a slave-master (because she
talked back), and who
had a ransom on her head
of thousands of dollars and who
was never caught, and who
had no use for the law
when the law was wrong,
who defied the law. I like
to think of her.
I like to think of her especially
when I think of the problem of
feeding children.

The legal answer
to the problem of feeding children
is ten free lunches every month,
being equal, in the child's real life,
to eating lunch every other day.
Monday but not Tuesday.
I like to think of the President
eating lunch Monday, but not
Tuesday.
And when I think of the President
and the law, and the problem of
feeding children, I like to
think of Harriet Tubman
and her revolver.

And then sometimes
I think of the President
and other men,

men who practice the law,
who revere the law,
who make the law,
who enforce the law
who live behind
and operate through
and feed themselves
at the expense of
starving children
because of the law,
men who sit in paneled offices
and think about vacations
and tell women
whose care it is
to feed children
not to be hysterical
not to be hysterical as in the word
hysterikos, the greek for
womb suffering,
not to suffer in their
wombs,
not to care,
not to bother the men
because they want to think
of other things
and do not want
to take the women seriously.
I want them
to take women seriously.
I want them to think about Harriet Tubman,
and remember,
remember she was beat by a white man
and she lived
and she lived to redress her grievances,
and she lived in swamps
and wore the clothes of a man
bringing hundreds of fugitives from
slavery, and was never caught,
and led an army,

and won a battle,
and defied the laws
because the laws were wrong, I want men
to take us seriously.
I am tired wanting them to think
about right and wrong.
I want them to fear.
I want them to feel fear now
as I have felt suffering in the womb, and
I want them
to know
that there is always a time
there is always a time to make right
what is wrong,
there is always a time
for retribution
and that time
is beginning.

[1970]


## Song My

(Oh God, she said.)

It began a beautiful day by the sun up
And we sat in our grove of trees of smiles
Of morning eggs and toast and jam
and long talks, and baby babble
Becky sitting in her chair
spreading goo in her hair.

(Oh God, she said, look at the baby)

saying "hi" "ho" "ha" hi hi, goggydoggymamadada HI
and the light was coming through the window
through the handprints on the glass

making shadow patterns, and the cold day
was orange outside and they were muddling
in their underwear, getting dressed,
putting diapers on the baby,
slipping sandals on her feet.

(Oh God, she said, look at the baby
He has blood all over, she cried,)

Then the postman came,
And she went out on the steps
and got her magazine. They stood
by the stairs and looked, the baby
tugging at her skirt saying
mamamamama upupup mememe
and they looked at the pictures of Song My.

(Oh God, she said, look at the baby
He has blood all over, she cried,
Look at that woman's face, my God,
She knows she's going to get it.)

Going to get it, they knew
they were going to get it,
and it was a beautiful day,
the day that began in the fields
with the golden grain against the blue sky
the babies singing as if there were not
soldiers in the air.

[1971]

310

SANDRA MCPHERSON

## Pisces Child

Those calm swamp-green eyes,
Gliding like alligators,
Float to this shore
And bump awake.

Sea-legs jerk.
Hands swim still, submarine pink, the palms
Stretched out like starfish.
I'm the old wharf you live on.

Your tongue draws oceans in, not spitting
A word out. Quick, fluttery, slight
As a guppy,
Coercive as undertow.

Oh paramecium
I am your gross-pored mama. Hydra,
An elephant
Suckles you.

In the wilderness you are a spring.
You perpetually melt,
Lake and river maker, dedicated as the porpoise
To return to the sea.

Do you want both worlds?
I see you rooting,
Arms random, then possessive, like potatoes
Sprouting.

Or, needing, needing to need,
You cry yourself purple as eggplant.
You are wordless, but never mind:
You have your sort of song.

It can be heard above the breakers.
I watch you, you're far out on the horizon.
I am landlocked as a cat.
You will never run dry.

[1970]


## Pregnancy

It is the best thing.
I should always like to be pregnant,

Tummy thickening like a yoghurt,
Unbelievable flower.

A queen is always pregnant with her country.
Sheba of questions

Or briny siren
At her difficult passage,

One is the mountain that moves
Toward the earliest gods.

Who started this?
An axis, a quake, a perimeter,

I have no decisions to master
That could change my frame

Or honor.
Immaculate. Or if it was not, perfect.

Pregnant, I'm highly explosive—
You can feel it, long before

Your seed will run back to hug you—
Squaring and cubing

Into reckless bones, bouncing odd ways
Like a football.

The heart sloshes through the microphone
Like falls in a box canyon.

The queen's only a figurehead.
Nine months pulled by nine

Planets, the moon slooping
Through its amnion sea,

Trapped, stone-mad . . . and three
Beings' lives gel in my womb.

[1970]

SUSAN AXELROD

# The Home

### I

They walk dangerously
close tonight . . .
Those mad little girls
I can hear their voices going
The cat, sunk in his basket
                    never reeked
with quite such sour fury

And the program—
          that wall-eyed twig
of a momma
Miss Klister
dead on arrival
from Munich
What possible life
did she think she could glean
from
          a Peter-Pan Bra
Clairol
          and the dry-heaves
          at midnight
We were her specialty
delusions of poesy
              and the like
a delicacy among the street inclined
              and the asylum babies.

And how fine it was
to be not quite
                    really crazy
among all those
stately and profound insanities,
To be taken so seriously.

Can you remember
Claudia, edging into oblivion
                    sideways
        with bulging eyes
Watching it
            just below her right shoulder
slip up like the tide—
            talking all the way down.


Was it she
to whom
you gave Vaseline
with instructions
for Yusef
"that Arab"
She sat shiva
later
set fire to her room
mourning Claudia
who had somehow
got unstuck
                And Karen
big bosomed and foul
puffed-up like an adder
threatening imminent explosion.
With two bright
                discs of ire
she would hold you
secreting fluids all
the while
suffusing the room
                with a heavy
                aromatic damp
Red curls boiling
over a brow
            flawless
lucent
those perfect features
            untouched

I remember the bite
          of her nails
her thumb particularly
along the cheek
               up to the eyes.


                    II


In that room we shared
you slept
          badly
your bed
          in tight formation
          right angled to the wall
you took things as you found them
Mine—
          askew but slightly


That room;
oceanic,
we dove and surfaced,
as was officially encouraged—
the great mirror
a vague and
occasional shore.


All about
into the night
the ceaseless cry and cackle
of the sea-fowl
hunting
               there was never quiet
in our wallowing
               world


Who gave them first—
the land flowers
               ferns and dogwood
establishing a precedent

316

                    we looked at each other
                    with startled eyes
        and could not name it.

Say it now then
now that the danger is over
Speak of the resin and the burning pine
the rich and heady smoke
rising
            to shivering lips

We bore our love
like some strange
            transplanted organ
shameful,
            necessary—
Gills
to survive
immersion
in that deep
            wet world.

                    [1969]

RITA MAE BROWN

# Dancing the Shout to the True Gospel
*or*
# The Song Movement Sisters Don't Want Me to Sing

I follow the scent of a woman
Melon heavy
Ripe with joy
Inspiring me
To rip great holes in the night
So the sun blasts through
And this is all I shall ever know
Her breath
Filling the hollows of my neck
A luxury diminishing death.

[1970]

CATHLEEN QUIRK

# Another Night on the Porch Swing

in Pennsylvania; it's sort of like losing
baby teeth: the little ones waddle off
to make room for the bigger ones.
The thing to do is put them in a glass
of water, bury them under the back porch
and make a wish: a new dress, a
trip to the city.      No.
What actually happens is they become
a lover, hunched under the back steps
like a question mark; waiting for you
to come on out and hang the washing
on the high clothesline . . .
overalls, an undershirt, a sock.
Things he can put on to go around
and ring the front doorbell.
Someone you can finally bring home
to mother; along with a couple
of broken ribs, and probably a baby
or two; someone strange, respectable.

[1973]

SUZANNE BERGER RIOFF

## Cycles, Cycles

greasy oysters on friday nights
and a fight or two
before a steel-wool sleep
        darling
outside men are breaking themselves
everyone endures
the uncertain charity
of affecting
        each other
and this pain is a fix
there is only this thrill this tough miracle
of going apart
like scissor's edge
and back to simply
cut
    our guts in love

[1970]

# The Seduction

Open me like a meadow lily
examine me like an eel
for my mystery
my electric blue swim

Put me together
I am many chinks of broken light
Gently prod me to my country
where the mileage is green and wide
Gather my hills
to their plumpness
Name my rivers
Count the seconds
it takes to pry me open
to make me pour

Love, love me
Turn my thistle-cloth to satin
let us lie on the satin
like rosy Egyptian scarabs
Love me
for I am often singular
Alone, I steal and lie
and break, delinquent
Make me your moon-mate
your daughter
your prism
Mend my surfaces
be my mirror
my great silver hush

Be the light
by which my angles, my crevices
are explored

Miner, mine me
I am dark and rich
The caves are hung
with my secrets, my hair
Make me peaceful
make me chirp
Hide me
in the warm giant boot
of your human grace
Blush me
pull me out of pallor

Imagine me
in the white furry breath
of your dreaming
Make me still
Make me naked
Make me an animal
who loves its own tongue

[1973]

ALICE WALKER

# From "Love"

*ii*

An old man in white
Calls me "mama"
It does not take much
To know
He wants me for
His wife—
He has no teeth
But is kind.

[1968]

# From "Once"

*v*

It is true—
I've always loved
the daring
      ones
Like the black young
man
Who tried
to crash
All barriers
at once,
    wanted to
swim
At a white
beach (in Alabama)
Nude.

[1968]

# Chic Freedom's Reflection

*(for Marilyn Pryce)*

One day
Marilyn marched
beside me (demon-
stration)
and we ended up
at county farm
no phone
no bail
something about
"traffic vio-
lation"
which irrelevance
Marilyn dismissed
with a shrug
    *She*
had just got
    back
from
    Paris France
        In
      the
      Alabama
        hell
      she
      smell-
          ed
      so
      wonderful
like spring
& love
    &
freedom

            She
          wore a
        SNCC pin
      right between
        her breasts
          near her
            heart
      & with a chic
          (on "jail?")
      accent
          & nod of
      condescent
          to frumpy
          work-house
            hags
      powdered her nose
            tip-
                  toe
      in a badge.

              [1968]

# Medicine

Grandma sleeps with
my sick
grand-
pa so she
can get him
during the night
medicine
to stop
the pain

In
the morning
clumsily
I
wake
them

Her eyes
look at me
from under-
neath
his withered
arm

The
medicine
is all
in
her long
un-
braided
hair.

[1968]

INGRID WENDT

## The Newest Banana Plant Leaf

unfurls in rain
outside the window as
between the lips
of my cunt you
have just spoken
centuries
of promises
names like stars
on a flag someone
still believes in
raised at reveille
the year
the century this day
makes complete.

[1973]

# Personal Poem

It embarrasses,
                    I suppose,

to read another's sheets
                        dyed

with love
to learn
        my love

and I swam
                naked

behind bushes in a
                        public picnic

ground of a National Park.

That once again
                    at least in this a-

dult life we were

unreal

as a poem indelibly kept and
                                cut

off from news in a trailer
                            bound

by three feet of country snow, where

I first made you snow
                        angels, hollows

scooped from the crests
                        of drifts my arms

scraped like sky, like spell-

bound waves our dog

                    (our sunflower, sand

colored swimmer
                    turning

his fur a cluster
                    of berries white

in a bush of fire) plowed trails through,

spelling what scent he knew,

nosing foam to find a snow-
                              ball

white on white as one
                    as your skin

and mine the night we dared

frost and the moon,
                    two

shivering question marks,
                              periods

buried,
          luminous (your

thighs your chest your face and) the face

of the snow

we tossed at each other like
                              clouds,

like waves exploding,
                    bearing us

into our own motion again,
                              to sleeping

bag blankets,
          warm sheets,

to our mouths.

                    [1973]

## Ghetto Lovesong—Migration

She stood hanging wash before sun
and occasionally watched the kids
gather acorns from the trees,
and when her husband came,
complaining about the tobacco spit on him,
they decided to run North
for a free evening.
She stood hanging wash in the basement
and saw the kids sneak puffs from cigarettes,
fix steel traps with cheese
and when her husband came,
complaining of the mill's drudgery,
        she burst—
said he had no hunter's heart
beat him with a broom,
became blinded by the orange sun
racing into steel mill flames
and afterwards,
sat singing     spirituals to sons.

[1969]

NICOLE FORMAN

# Labour of the Brain, Ballad of the Body

I've thought of names
I say them
secretly in the bath, holding the little
sounds on my tongue and cooing
as one does over baby things—
pink, blue
spittle like lace
brown poo poo
booties, sand-dollar fists.
Even the dog is pregnant.
She rolls in the dust as if
it were nothing, her teats a
queer red corky colour and beginning
to dribble for the phantoms inside her.
(Mine are frail and vacant I
test them when no one looks running
loose piano fingers over my chest plucking
and pulling for pain a dim white nudge; if
they were flowers my milkmaid's hand
would kill them) In animal love
the dog shot her tail up and rocked
we watched from the window, mute sex dance
perhaps we were envious though outrage
was the word we used seeing our puppy ravaged
the obscene hang and grin of her suitor's jaw, his
balls swaying gaily as bells by her haunches.
He slunk off. Her neck bore toothmarks. I
thought of our nights, my clean skin, my
spread hair, the idol whose eyes I looked into
blinding me, wiping me
out in ecstasy. His lap was a seesaw, a carousel,
a herd of gaudy horses stampeding mechanical:
I grabbed at rings of tin, he
edged me on, solemn

civil till I screamed from the lung
(he from the crotch which
pleased him) then he fell
away. Every night. Every time.

The dog had it better I thought
lower, truer, and though the fur
grew back over her wounds I knew
they were there, hidden like lilies
in weeds and water. My neck was bare

and my belly
fed on tin rings, anguish,
empty as the names I chanted, silly
pottie rhythms pipe-flushed
each month.
Other women were a mystery, how
had my mother borne me, brought
me down the dark canal from one wet
moment? My brain had never wanted
a child, it didn't believe
in god or love scars but I
stopped listening, bitch hot
barren, I hung myself vulnerable
I began to pray
I lay
my dragon's womb on linen and stoked
the cold sleek scales with pearls.
Thumb-sucked, my body wouldn't work
the moon maneuvered me, shrank
me to a wintry scab. Curses
curses even my tears were red:
I broke and bled and went
on praying—make, take, slake.

God might suffocate
between these fingers.

[1973]

JEAN TEPPERMAN

## Witch

They told me
I smile prettier with my mouth closed.
They said—
better cut your hair—
long, it's all frizzy,
looks Jewish.
They hushed me in restaurants
looking around them
while the mirrors above the table
jeered infinite reflections
of a raw, square face.
They questioned me
when I sang in the street.
They stood taller at tea
smoothly explaining
my eyes on the saucers,
trying to hide the hand grenade
in my pants pocket,
or crouched behind the piano.
They mocked me with magazines
full of breasts and lace,
published their triumph
when the doctor's oldest son
married a nice sweet girl.
They told me tweed-suit stories
of various careers of ladies.
I woke up at night
afraid of dying.
They built screens and room dividers
to hide unsightly desire
sixteen years old
raw and hopeless
they buttoned me into dresses
covered with pink flowers.

They waited for me to finish
then continued the conversation.
I have been invisible,
weird and supernatural.
I want my black dress.
I want my hair
curling wild around me.
I want my broomstick
from the closet where I hid it.
Tonight I meet my sisters
in the graveyard.
Around midnight
if you stop at a red light
in the wet city traffic,
watch for us against the moon.
We are screaming,
we are flying,
laughing, and won't stop.

[1969]

# Going Through Changes

## 1

My head aches.
I love you.
How can you talk this way?
Afternoon light
falls gently in the parlor
you are groping—
the language is wrong.
Why don't you speak
Welsh/Swahili/Gaelic/Navajo?
You serve the man
drinks and dinner
then sit on his lap
and ask for a revolution—
just a little one
for being such a nice girl.
A plastic flower
grows out of my navel.
You are afraid
of what he will think of you.
I am afraid of you
when you talk like this.
You are ashamed of me.
You don't have nice friends.
I'm not a nice friend.
The honor system
sets its teeth in me.
I can't talk to you
I am failing us
again.

## 2

I used to get very big.
I used to be in rooms full of strangers
and questions made me into

China and Russia and Cuba
ten thousand teenage draft resisters
the history of the Communist Party
a lone terrorist in Oakland
the entire black population
and Marx and Engels.
I got so big
there were miles
from my mouth to your ear.
Today,
in my small natural body,
I sit and learn—
my woman's body
like yours
target on any street,
taken from me
at the age of twelve
like Venezuelan oil
with the same explanation
        You are ignorant
        let me show you
then sold back drop by drop
in pink-frosted bottles
by tiny merchants with big shadows
sitting behind the screens of Oz
and buying armies
with the profits.
I watch a woman dare
I dare to watch a woman
we dare to raise our voices
smash the bottles
learn.
Watch me learn to dare
my arms and legs feel awkward—
we came to ask your help.


3

I am not a lady

I live in an elevator
in a big department store America.
>"Your floor, lady?"
>"I don't have a floor,
>I live in the elevator."
>"You can't just live in an elevator."

They all say that
except for the man from *Time* Magazine
who acted very cool.
We stop and let people into
dresses, better dresses, beauty,
and on the top floor,
home furnishings and then
the credit office, suddenly stark
and no nonsense this is it.
At each floor I look out
at the ladies quietly becoming
ladies and I say "huh"
reflectively.
My hair is long and wild
full of little twigs and cockleburrs.
I visit the floors only for water.
I make my own food
from the berries and frightened rabbits—
I pray forgive me brother as I eat—
that grow wild in the elevator.
Once every three months,
solstice and equinox,
a cop comes and clubs me a little.
The man from *Time* says
I articulate my generation something
wobble squeegy squiggle pop pop
Yesterday pausing at childrens
I saw another lady
take off all her clothes
and go to live in #7.
We are waiting to fill
all thirteen.

[1969]

ANN GOTTLIEB

## Lady Luck

Falconers
have a way of lifting up
a hand, so that one bird
of the sky's indifferent handful
shifts its wing, turns
and drops like a stone:
why to him, who will only blind it
with a hood, whose gesture was
not even a command?

The city has drawn
a ring of tulips
around us, like a ring of lipstick.
We have been marked for
some event: something will fall
out of the sky, the lucky lightning
or a shower of little stones?

There's a good woman behind every man:
above our heads
Victory, Lady Luck with loco eyes,
drags General Sherman to his destiny.
Her brothers
are around somewhere, provocative
in bronze and denim, stirring up desire:
how good to be a god
on shore leave, sauntering, casual,
making an occasional pickup,
dropping a few divine
bastards as blessings in retrospect
on their gullible mothers, luck's ruins.

A pigeon lights on Victory's arm; her eyes
don't swerve. The old plush horses
shift in harness: where's our revelation?
You reach out a hand; I stoop for no
good reason, and we walk off arm in arm,
each other's windfalls, dodging the pigeons.

[1970]

MIRIAM PALMER

## Raccoon Poem

I

raccoons are selectively polygamous
they are fond of eggs, nestlings, corn and melons
their preferred den site
is a large, hollow branch of a tree
in very cold weather they sleep for extended periods
but do not hibernate in the sense of becoming torpid


II

underneath, in spring,
I have raccoon hands—
when I crouch over the sink
they scurry quickly across my scalp
my body smell sharpens
the head lies thick and furred
in the water
I have been sleeping through a long cold
in the hollow branch of my mother
it is time now to splash through
the thawed ice

[1971]

## "Vierge ouvrante"

Under her deep plush roof
she is water,
she runs in room after room,
so clear we see through her
like eyes or laughter.
Hers are the simplest desires
made visible
in coiled gold leaves
on picture frames and rococo
angel centerpieces.
She is never ashamed
of the obvious,
of calling her husband "Daddy"
or saying "those people" in conversation.

    "Can you imagine how horrible
      to wake up and find a black man in bed with you!"

She can't find her son or daughter anywhere,
she calls and calls in her sleep.
In the attic there is nothing but an old flute
and a football.
When her son married
there were no pretenses—
she sobbed through each night
to an exhausted morning, and prayed,
really believed
she could save him.
Now her fat,
mother-hollow body
shudders
as she catches his hand
on the girl's light breast,
and she is afraid.

"Oh I can't do anything. It's old age.
I can't even control my hands anymore."

And all her life it's been this endless tide
of pain, of not liking
her husband, children, garden
or even the piano,
of never knowing, only
that it was supposed to be that way.
She rearranges the heavy furniture
Mother gave her,
over and over, like a rosary,
and brings each stranger in to see,
to ask them, "is this the place?"
"Have I found it?"
"May I stop here?"

"This house is everything to us now,
we've worked so hard on it!"

But finally they all smile
and have to leave her.
She sits in Mother's rocker
and sinks herself back
to that just-beginning,
that blessed virgin
-ity, when the nuns
made a dresden magic over everything.
Flowers never died
and never bloomed, there were no necessities,
no demands
from husband-children-strangers,
her hands in their purity
never trembled on the keys
and the light
always followed her to mass.

[1971]

342

# What if jealousy . . .

What if jealousy is just a bad dream
that ran one night through the nursery?
Or if our marriage is not
water-soluble?
I feel only curious (proud even?),
strangely motherly
the nights you stay
with your soft hippie mistress.
Morning, I stop at her house
to be neighborly, watch
wonderfully her dress
the heavyslender blending of breasts
and body, like covering
a clutch of grapes with cloth
to stop them ripening in the sun.
I sense your swelling together
as though it were daffodils
or the warm honeylumps of wood
you carve.
I share with her
the light from our faces,
plans for the day. Our laughs are
belts of Indian bells as we walk.

[1972]

# Reflections

Clean thin hollow of breast
that I grew on, Mother,
what did you look like
when you were me?

Was your hair
long, were your eyes wild,
did you ride on Saturdays
through Prospect Park
on a silver mare? Did
all the black-eyed boys
in Brooklyn stare?

The summer
I doubled and tripled in you,
did you swim in the foam
at Brighton Beach
faster than dolphins? Slimmer
than sharks? Did the relatives
throw their hands up to God
when you rose like a fury
from weed and wave?

What
did you feed on? What
did you sip? October, November—
did you pray to the moon
when I whirled in you
like Autumn blood?

Whose were the fingers
that bubbled in you? Winding and whipping
your seasoned pulse?
Small, docile mother

with narrow hands. . . . I—
the gay poison
your bones expelled;
I drained the madness
from your womb.

[1970]

# Letter to a friend in an unknown place

For days I have been walking around
with a great bird tied to my neck.
His claws have taken on the thinness of my veins,
so that both of us are warmed
by the same blood, like trees
whose roots are knotted together beside a river.

He will not tell me who he is, or
what species of bird he belongs to, or
what is the country he comes from. I
cannot tell, by feeding him,
whether he is life-eater or death-eater,
flower- or fish-eater: Everything

I offer, he refuses. Still, he is growing.
The first day I called him my brother.
He was as small as my fist, and nested
like a weapon behind my shoulder. Later, he grew
to the size of my open hand; and his pulse
copied like tape the moon in my wrist.

Also, he has opened his eyes. I have tried writing down,
with their strange light behind me, all the things
I know about him. He has no song.
His wings must be bound, like the skin of an orange,
over his breast: there is no sound in his feathers
when the wind moves. He shows no interest in flying.

[1973]

## emigration

The words have all fled the country, they are not expected back

Some have gone to the desert others joined
the bands of hungry dogs two
have buried hammers
in their flesh two
have professed their belief in stone one
walks with a candle in his
groin a few three or four
have entered a monastery

none has married, none has had children

I saw them leave they were blessed
by the officials they were showered with
cherries a soprano
made love to a grain
of rice the laws were read again a
synthetic orchestra was arranged

it being a Sunday

they murmured among themselves I heard them they said
their eyes had grown thin they were unused
to the cold the fish
would grieve their passing they
had failed to convince the highway too many
of their number had been abandoned
to walls

I heard them their speech was foreign already
and blazed like the extinguishing of a mountain

[1973]

346

## September 7

Oh Beverly, do you remember
how we sat together in that brook, touching
our own bodies, wishing
we weren't wearing navy shorts, wishing
we could wear
only our own skin
like the silver birches
like the pebbles in the brook.

I was a pebble in that brook
a pebble with a pink band, and you
in your own skin
under those regulation campers' shorts
were a freckled pear.

The brook soaked through our shorts
and it should have been cold
it should have been too cold for two young girls
to put their bottoms in.

It should have been too cold
we should have gone back
back to change our wet shorts
and dry our private, barely hairy,
parts in towels that mother sewed our names in.

But we didn't.
We sat there where we were
not cold at all
singing softly madrigals

                    ride a cock horse
                    to banbury cross
                    to see a fine lady
                    ride on a white horse

                    ride on a white cock
                    ride on a fine lady
                    ride on, ride on

Singing madrigals and touching
bark and leaves and grass that grew beside the brook
wishing we were green and silver like the birch
green and brown like the dirt.

I put my head into a wide crack in the bank
and felt the coolness, dampness
of the earth against my cheeks
against my nose
smelled its dampness.

Like my opening
cool and damp
like the hole in the bank
grass growing around it
brown earthy hole and green grass.

We touched the earth
crumbled it in our hands
dug our fingers in the grass of the bank
caressed the silver bark of the birch
the dry pebbles in the sun
and the cold wet pebbles in the stream
held the pebbles in our hands
and ate the freckled pears.

                                        [1970]

# Partly to my cat

Walking, I heard the water dripping, running in the gutter
and I didn't walk on.
I stopped, standing in that snow,
> listening to that water,
> watching it through the grating of the gutter,
> watching the grating,
> and listening.
Later, I made dinner, cutting the ends from the string beans slowly,
> feeling the knife crunch neatly through the bean,
> slide across the wooden board.
And I was not so slow as it might seem.
Only, I did not hurry.
I took the garbage out, stepping through the snow,
> snow like string beans,
> crunching under my feet.


The next day I made a tuna fish sandwich,
not listening to the celery,
and the Prudential Center doorman wouldn't let me use his bathroom.
Oh when will I pee, quietly, smiling, on his red carpet?
I don't need a bathroom.
It can happen anywhere at all, like a sneeze.
But we are tied up with ribbons.
We live inside gift-wrapped packages,
> gummed with Christmas seals
> and tagged with the name of our donor,
> rustling about in the colored tissue paper,
> shredding it with our teeth,
> making our nest of scraps.
We live inside briefcases,
> chew the glue from the back of scotch tape,
> lick the ink from the navy blue signatures:
We are buckled in top-grade cowhide,
> smelling the warmth of the cow,

                    the grass,
                    the slightly soured milk.


Even with sandalwood incense burning at noon
                and oranges preserved in nutmeg and cloves,
even with apples smuggled in sweaters
with the fire from the old kitchen chairs
and the penny-eyed cat showing us how to sit on refrigerators,
we do not always hear.
We must stop:
                    stop eating dinner in the Star Market
                        and making love in subways
                    stop doing isometric exercises on the telephone
                    stop brushing our teeth at red lights.
This can't go on.


Cat: you are the animal that we forget to be.
Your stomach is your suitcase,
while I have 3 bathrobes and
                8 prs. of shoes,
                a checking account
                5 credit cards,
                and a AAA membership.
This breakfront staggers me.
I cannot carry the bookcases and drapes,
                the rugs, the linens, the dining room table.
This is no gear for a hike, for a life.
How can I leap to the heights of refrigerators weighted like this?


I will unload my relatives and toaster,
                my plumbing, my elevator, my degrees.
I will wash myself, slowly and completely, with my tongue.
I will run,
            like you cat,
                    making deep snow prints,
                            hearing the crunch.


                                        [1971]

# In Celebration*

Last night I licked
your love, you love,
like a cat. And
I watched you rise like
bread baking, like
a helium balloon, rise
with the skill of a soufflé,
your love, waving like
passengers on a boat coming in.
My cheek resting on your belly,
moist like a bathroom mirror, resting
in your hair like
dew grass, I drew
your love out like
the head of a turtle, like
an accordion, like
an expandable drinking glass.
I licked
you love, your love,
hard as a lollipop, plump
and tender as a plum.
I held you
like a mitten, like a cup,
and, like the crowds in the spray of a Yellowstone geyser,
like kids splashing in a July fire hydrant,
like a dinner guest biting in a whole tomato,
I gasped,
I laughed,
I feasted on your vintage.

[1973]

* Copyright © 1973 by Ellen Bass.

# Celia*

Celia, Celia, your name is like cilia,
fine hairs of a paramecium, flapping gently in unison
like a sunny day crew, cilia,
flapping gently like the arms of twenty ballerinas,
cilia, like a flock of gulls,
cilia, fine hair, like the down of your shoulder,
cilia, thick black hair of your lashes,
long fringe of your eyes, dark eyes of Arab women,
all that shows, all that shines, from the chaderi,
cilia, mane, black and wild, mad hair, crazy hair,
electric hair that shimmies like castanets.

Celia, as we smoke I feel the network of my veins,
spider web of capillaries carrying
hot rain mist, thick blood mist,
and the bones of my cheeks pulse
and the bones of my shoulders pulse.
I observe. I observe the fine curly thread snagged in my thumbnail,
delicate, fanned cirrus,
feathery arm of a white barnacle;
the smoke, rising, spiraling, transparent smoke twirling like these
    letters,
scribbles, lines that double back and swirl into words,
black wet lines, deep trails, like snakes through mud, winding,
flamenco lines that pulse like Celia's hair,
like my hair
that moistens, thick kinky hair,
hair that blows like sand across the desert,
blows like lean seaweed,
dense pelt of hair that
shields my quick life, stiff as a thumb,
straining to lie with you,
my lovelock to yours,
the throb of cilia with cilia.

[1973]

I am the sorrow in the wheat fields.

I am the chestnut hair, blowing at the trolley stop.

I am the shower curtain through the lighted bathroom window.

I am the "white sport coat and a pink carnation" that plays from the plumber's truck on Garfield St.

I am the garden we planted that never grew, a few tiny carrots the size of a thumb.

I am the telephone pole lights shining in the gutter puddles like the moon over Alabama.

I am the A&P truck and the mail truck.

I am the wine and I am the matzoh.

I am the wet black whale of asphalt.

I am the fox furpiece whose teeth grasp its tail.

I am a pair of pink satin toe shoes, the smell of them, the cotton, the rabbit's skin stuffed in the toes.

I am the Allegheny stewardess who calls me "honey would you like a magazine" and I am the child who calls her "waitress".

I am the potholes in the roads and I am the tar that fills the holes.

I am the pile of manure and I am the Rumanian who is disgusted.

I am the canned fruit and the lettuce and the salami in the delicatessen.

I am the first wondering kiss of a new lover and I am the hundred thousandth kiss of an old lover, familiar as my toothbrush.

I am the threadbare fields and I am the empty hen houses.

I am the dock where the boats line up evenly like teeth.

I am the lighthouse at the end of route 40.

I am the Central Vermont train that rusts on the tracks.

I am the highways crossing the land like palm creases, telling the future.

I am the tree, flapping its leaf-waved branches like a great bird.

I am my oldest from the 8th grade friend getting married in Columbia, Missouri where she's a maid in a Catholic girls' school.

I am Adrian who I followed across the African continent to wash his shirts in the bathtub.

I am the tobacco conventioneers and the Kiwanis Club and the Elks on the boardwalk in Atlantic City.

I am the mink-coated lady in the striped pants who pays the car hop by check.

I am the taxi driver who keeps waiting for one more passenger to fill an empty car.

I am the peasants and I am the soldiers and I am the mothers who mourn on tv.


I am the Tiger Rose and the Ripple under the rotting blackberry tree.

I am a night on the Provincetown dunes when the sound of the water is all that is real.

I am the disposable needle that is used and used again.

I am the contact and I am the rush.

I am the darkness that gathers in corners, that fills the trunk and the glove compartment.

I am the toll booth, the man with his hand out, the man who takes quarters to let you go by.


I am the wood and I am the leather. I am the clay that is fired in the kiln.

I am the plastic and I am the teflon. I am the naugahide, the cardboard, the foil.

I am the breasts and I am the bellies, the cock and the cunt and the smell of the semen.

I am the hot sweat of plowing and planting, the sweet smell that mixes with dirt smell and sun.

And I am the cold sweat of nightmare toward morning, the dampness of sheets and the panic of self, alone and peculiar, entire and full.

[1973]

MARGO MAGID

# Night Watch

for Jean

inside    the child
is motionless, or moves
by day, paces
almost human
at night drums
its tattoo softer
than moths'
wings beating
against a thin wall
or turns its eyes
inward, two smudges
cannot see, except
by your own sight
or waits
in perfect patience
webbed limbs coiled
in mollusk folds
as if asleep, or listening
or in prayer

seen, it can be loved
unseen, a lodestone,
a sentinel moving
in dark circles
a glimpsed shadow
tracing ancient maps
that lap like tidepools
the walls of its cave

[1973]

BEATRICE WALTER

## The Photograph the Cat Licks

"But, you're so
different," they said of
the photograph the cat licks,
because my face floated there,
like a pumpkin in the dark,
not my good-china face,
but the sister I never had.
She, who smiled with jagged teeth,
made love to spiders and laughed
to see them squirm, drank the sun's blood
on the back side of the moon—we thought
she was asleep—and cried
when she heard the field-birds scream
in last October's fire. She was caught,
she told me, when prowling the corners
one night with the cat, her brother.
The camera plucked her face
from the dark and pinned it
to the light. Only the cat,
who misses her,
licks it now and then.

[1970]

356

PEGGY HENDERSON

## The Serpent Muses

Carry your garden
the stalks pruned
better to bear cold
roots wrapped in earth
sunk in clay pots
to knock with your step

The seeds must sleep separate
with their dreams
each saved from a full
blossom
the sun will come into them again
ask the clouds
they also save their tears

The cosmos will open
lavender and red
blue vines trail the meadow
of your back
the serpent gives her blessing
as tomatoes give their juice
to her quick teeth
she lies long in the sun
slides among the roots
and muses

[1973]

## MARGO TAFT

i have been my arm
resting on the side of a truck
carrying a cigarette
to my mouth
my hand like an animal
that can not see or feel.

[1973]

## One, The Other, And

One

That sound like the scratch
scratch of an old recording
the static and scratch of an
old recording that tight
scratch was the sound of her
hands in her head and that
contracted scratch was the
scar of her mouth and her
eyes

That was she standing like
a phone booth at the corner;
folding door that groaned
and doubled at a man straddling
the rusty seat, facing a limp
phone, dialing a number's
name. A number and name
scratched on the wall of her
booth. A girl's name
scratched in an obscene erect
heart

And she began to think she
was that name, that girl. She
took her phone off the hook
and let the air wheeze out
the nozzle of her heart. Hid
her nickels and dimes. She took
time and more time to smile
the stitches of her mouth
and without bothering to file
her nails she folded
her hands in her
head

The Other

She made no sound
but held her body as
a driveling wind
held her own body in
and rocked it like a
painted rocking horse
she rocked like a huge
autistic child she rocked
a peeling circus pony
rocked with a bit
in her mouth painted
shut

She sat in the circus
and stood by the gorge.
Stood like a side show
hung in a wail
of the carnival wheel;
the jester laughing
blue bells on his toes
rapier in one blue glove.
Woman wearing a golden
mask and the lie
of one red plume.
Woman without nose.
Jester with curling toes.
Masquerade cursed
and carnival time.
The fault and a
face noosed by
darkness

And she thought she'd
noose the circus wheel and

waited to slash the glove
and all she had to do
was find the woman's
unborn nose, stamp the
jester's ringing toes.
But she waited by the chasm
holding body like a chill
fastening still ribs of pain,
biting noose in a mouth painted
shut. Playing with bright
blue carnival pills to rock
to rock to rock her slowly
stop


And


they hadn't known
of the gardens
the opalescent gardens
that swayed
behind their eyes
as tenuously as dew

that grew delicate leaves
shyly as the doe's eyes

They hadn't known
for so much frost
for bone cold fingers
of the stunting hand
and stings of the
ice bee

they hadn't known
but gathered themselves
unto one another
gathered their selves

into such a wholeness
they took
the blue knife
and slit the belly of night
spinning the sun into life

hands
stirring to opening
unwove the noose
and the sound of the scratch
and the scars
dissolved in the warming
of breaths
loosened like music

They hadn't known
that lovers touch
for love
not for province
that water intermingles
boundlessly with
water

And
the gardens unfolded
slendering
in sundance

the lovers
lay at one
another's breasts
and their hair
joined
like swiftly running
rivers
the dark murmur
and splashed gems
of deepest waters

while from their
very eyes
        the garden

        the greenest
            singing leaves

                grew
                    tendresses
                        of trust

                    [1970]

## thoughts for you
## (when she came back from the mountains)

1.

you are
getting free

i'm glad.
   it makes me
     free
  sometimes
       (i'm sure it will)

you've been climbing mountains

i've been making substitutes.

2.

you've been climbing mountains
    singing all the way down in the fog
smiling when you told me

       i said i'd made love to one
       you said that you'd had four

somehow i had expected it
as if i had been with you the whole time

      i always knew we were one
you made everything else unimportant
there was so much comfortable silence

3.

you have been climbing mountains
    while i've been trying to climb out of my holes
and then when i am sitting looking down at my holes
you will be hitchhiking to the west
        with a friend of yours from montana

and the flies will still be sitting on me

4.

you asked me to go to the mountains
      the ones you had been climbing

             i never answered
     forgive me

5.

    you are a mountain

                    [1973]

## poem about a seashell

it is rough
      like my edges

      [1973]

*Biographies*

## HELEN ADAM 1909

Helen Adam was born in Glasgow, Scotland. She attended Edinburgh University and worked as a journalist in Edinburgh and London. She came to the United States in 1939, worked summers in the land army during the war, and moved west in 1949. She is now living in New York. She has written two books, *Ballads* and *Onaisis,* and the play, *San Francisco's Burning,* which was produced at the Judson Memorial Church in New York. She has received the Ingram Merrill Award. See page 86.

## ALTA 1942

Alta lives in California with her two daughters. She is founder and director of the Shameless Hussy Press, which publishes women's writing, and has edited *Remember Our Fire,* an anthology of poetry by women. Among her books are *Freedom's In Sight, Letters to Women, Song of the Wife/Song of the Mistress, No Visible Means of Support, Poems and Prose, Burn This and Memorize Yourself.* See page 294.

## MARGARET ATWOOD 1939

Margaret Atwood lives in Canada. She has had poems in *The New Yorker, The Atlantic Monthly, Poetry,* and *Mademoiselle.* Her volumes of poetry include *The Animals in That Country, The Circle Game, The Journals of Susanna Moodie, Procedures for Underground,* and *Power Politics.* She has also published a novel, *The Edible Woman,* which is going to be made into a film; a second novel, *Surfacing,* will appear this year. She has also recently published a non-fiction work, *Survival: A Thematic Guide to Canadian Literature.* See page 269.

## SUSAN AXELROD 1944

Susan Axelrod was born in Brooklyn and lives on the Lower East Side. She has studied with John Logan, Diane Wakoski, Harriet Sohmers Zwerling and admires Williams and Ginsberg. She began writing "The Home" during her early teens. See page 314.

## ANITA BARROWS 1947

Anita Barrows received her B.A. from San Francisco State College and her M.A. from Boston University. She has published poetry in *Aphra, Grécourt Review, Dryad, Invisible City, Transfer, New Magazine,* and *University of Kansas City Review.* Her translation of a novel by Marguerite Duras and one by Didier Coste are scheduled to be published in England. She has worked as poetry editor for Radio KPFA in Berkeley; as teacher/administrator for the Poetry In The Schools Project in California; and has taught a course on Anaïs Nin and the Surrealists for the University of California Extension. She is now living and writing in London. See page 344.

## ELLEN BASS 1947

Ellen Bass received her B.A. from Goucher College and an M.A. in creative writing from Boston University. She has had poems in *Preface, Softball, Women: A Journal of Liberation, Earth's Daughters,* and *Prickly Pear* and edited the feminist issue of *New Magazine,* titled "If you want something done, do it yourself." She lives in Cambridge and works at Project Place leading groups, one of which uses writing and acting out poetry as a medium for exploring feelings. She also leads poetry workshops at the Cambridge and Boston Centers for Adult Education. See page 347.

## PHYLLIS BEAUVAIS 1940

Phyllis Beauvais was born in Nebraska. She received her B.A. from Loretto Heights College, her M.A. from San Francisco State College, and is now working toward a Ph.D. at the Hartford Seminary Foundation. She is married, has two children, and works as a psychotherapist at The Country Place in Litchfield, Connecticut. Her private practice includes consciousness-raising groups for women. See page 287.

## LOUISE BOGAN 1897-1970

Louise Bogan was born in Maine and educated at Girls' Latin School in Boston and at The Western College for Women in Oxford, Ohio. She lived most of her life in New York City, working as an editor and writer for the *New Yorker*. While she received several honors in her lifetime—the Chair of Poetry at the Library of Congress (1946-47), the Bollingen Prize, and an award from the Academy of American Poets, for example—her work as a poet has still to receive proper recognition. She is better known as a critic, especially for the useful volume, *Achievement in American Poetry*. Her titles include *Body of This Death, Dark Summer, The Sleeping Fury,* and *The Blue Estuaries: Poems/1923-1968*. See page 69.

## KAY BOYLE 1903

Kay Boyle was born in St. Paul, Minnesota, and has lived half her life in France, Austria, England, and Germany. She teaches at the University of California at San Francisco. Among her awards are Guggenheim Fellowships in 1934 and 1961, and the O. Henry Memorial Prize for Best Short Story of the year in 1934 and 1941. She is a member of the National Institute of Arts and Letters. In 1971 she received an honorary degree of Doctor of Letters from Columbia College, Chicago. Kay Boyle has written thirty books: novels, stories, poetry, children's books, and a volume of essays. Among the titles are: *Year Before Last, The Smoking Mountain, Nothing Ever Breaks Except the Heart, Testament for My Students,* and *The Long Walk at San Francisco State*. See page 74.

## GWENDOLYN BROOKS 1917

Gwendolyn Brooks is the most distinguished living black poet. She was born in Kansas, graduated from Wilson Junior College in 1936, and has always lived in Chicago. Among her awards are the American Academy of Arts and Letters Award, the Pulitzer Prize, and two Guggenheim Fellowships. She is Poet Laureate of Illinois, succeeding Carl Sandburg. Her books include *In the Mecca, A Street in Bronzeville, Annie Allen, The Bean Eaters, Maud Martha,* a novel, *Riot, Family Pictures, Aloneness,* and *Bronzeville Boys and Girls.* Her autobiography, *Report from Part One,* was published in 1972. See page 116.

## RITA MAE BROWN 1944

Rita Mae Brown was born in Hanover, Pennsylvania. She went to the University of Florida, was expelled for civil rights activities, and later received her B.A. from New York University. She dropped out of graduate school to build a counter-culture to oppose the war-oriented male culture. She has been active in the women's liberation movement for five years and is currently working with the movement in Washington, D.C. Her essays have appeared in *Rat, Liberation, Off Our Backs,* and *Women: A Journal of Liberation.* She recently finished a first novel, tentatively titled *Molly Bolt* . . . and she wishes you all Kisses and Revolution! See page 318.

## HELEN CHASIN 1938

Helen Chasin's book of poems, *Coming Close,* was published in the Yale Series of Younger Poets. She has been a Fellow in Poetry at the Bread Loaf Writers' Conference, a Radcliffe Institute Fellow, and the recipient of a Howard Foundation fellowship. She has taught literature and writing at Emerson College, led a poetry workshop for teachers sponsored by the New York City Board of Education and the Academy of American Poets, and been a Visiting Lecturer at the Iowa Writers' Workshop. She lives with her two children in New York City. See page 261.

# CAROLE GREGORY CLEMMONS 1945

Carole Gregory Clemmons was born and raised in Youngstown, Ohio. In 1968 she graduated from Youngstown State University. At the age of sixteen she started writing poetry simply because she hated school so much. At the present time she is teaching at the Martin Luther King Opportunities Program at New York University and studying in the Masters of Fine Arts Program at Columbia University. Her thesis will be a volume of her own poetry. Her poems have appeared in *Nine Black Poets, Galaxy of Black Writing, The New Black Poetry,* and *Black Review.* See page 330.

# LUCILLE CLIFTON 1936

Lucille Clifton was born in Depew, New York, and attended Howard University and Fredonia State Teachers College. She has published poems in *The Negro Digest* and *The Massachusetts Review* and has read her poems at various colleges and universities. In 1969 she participated in the YM-YWHA Poetry Center's Discovery Series. Her first book of poetry is titled *Good Times.* Presently she lives in Baltimore with her husband and six children. See page 229.

# JANE COOPER 1924

Jane Cooper writes, "In my twenties I wrote a book of poems—perfectly serious work—but was sufficiently torn between my concepts of 'poet' and 'woman' that I never tried to publish. Teaching brought me back to poetry through a different door." In 1968 her first published book, *The Weather of Six Mornings,* was the Lamont selection of the Academy of American Poets. She has held grants from the Ingram Merrill and Guggenheim Foundations. She teaches at Sarah Lawrence College and is currently working on a collection that will probably include "both new poems and some of those old, early, angry pieces." See page 161.

## RANICE HENDERSON CROSBY 1952

Ranice Crosby lives in Baltimore. She received the Pee/Reese prize for poetry upon graduation from Western High School. See page 364.

## H.D. 1886–1961

Hilda Doolittle, known as H.D., was born in Pennsylvania and attended Bryn Mawr College. In 1911, she went abroad for a visit and never returned to live in the U.S. She married one of the original members of the imagist group, a British poet named Richard Aldington, and later divorced him. Her first volume of poems appeared in 1916, and more than seven others at generous intervals through the twenties, thirties, and forties won for her a reputation as "the only true Imagist." Her titles include *Sea Garden, Hymen, Heliodora and Other Poems, Red Roses for Bronze, The Walls Do Not Fall, Tribute to the Angels,* and *The Flowering of the Rod.* In addition, she published translations from the Greek, several volumes of prose, and a play. See page 52.

## MADELINE DEFREES 1919

Madeline DeFrees was born in Ontario, Oregon. She is a Professor of English in the Creative Writing Program at the University of Montana. A member of the Washington Province of the Sisters of the Holy Names, she published a collection of poems, *From the Darkroom,* under her former name of Sister Mary Gilbert. A second collection of poems is ready for publication. See page 120.

## DIANE DI PRIMA 1934

Diane Di Prima was born in New York. Her books include *This Kind of Bird Flies Backward, Various Fables from Various Places, Dinners and Nightmares, Earthsong, The New Handbook of Heaven, The Calculus of Variation, Spring and Autumn Annals, Some Haiku,* and *Poems for Freddie.* In 1965 she received a grant from the National Institute of Arts and Letters. She was editor of *The Fleating Bear* for five years, *Kulchur* for one year, and has been associate editor of *Signal Magazine* since 1963. See page 224.

## MARI EVANS  birth date unavailable

A native of Toledo, Ohio, Mari Evans was a John Hay Whitney Fellow, 1965–66, and a Consultant for the National Endowment of the Arts. Her poetry has been used extensively in textbooks and anthologies. Producer/director of a weekly half-hour television series, "The Black Experience," she is Writer-in-Residence and Assistant Professor of Black Literature at Indiana University, Bloomington. Her first volume of poetry, *I Am a Black Woman,* appeared in 1970. See page 275.

## RUTH FAINLIGHT 1931

Ruth Fainlight was born in New York City and attended Birmingham and Brighton Colleges of Arts and Crafts in England. She has traveled in France, Spain, and Morocco. Her volumes include *A Forecast, A Fable, Cages,* and *18 Poems from 1966.* See page 204.

## ELIZABETH FENTON 1943

Elizabeth Fenton attended Catholic schools and the University of Chicago. She is active in women's liberation and now teaches in the Feminist Studies program at the Cambridge-Goddard School for Social Change. She has had poems published in the Free Press anthology of women's poetry, *New Magazine, The Harvard Advocate, Hanging Loose, Women: A Journal of Liberation,* and *Women/Poems.* She also works as a typist and astrologer. See page 298.

## NICOLE FORMAN 1945

Nicole Forman was born in New York City and educated at the University of Wisconsin and Barnard College, where she studied art history. In 1967 she moved to London, which has been her home ever since. She is married to the Czech photographer Werner Forman, and is currently working with him on a book entitled *Cities of the Thousand and One Nights* (part of which deals with the position of women in the *Arabian Nights*). She expects to complete a series of poems early in 1973. See page 331.

## KATHLEEN FRASER 1937

Kathleen Fraser graduated from Occidental College. With her five-year-old son, David, she lives in San Francisco where she teaches and directs The Poetry Center at San Francisco State College. Her first collection of poems, *Change of Address*, was published by *Kayak* in 1966. *Stilts, Somersaults & Headstands*, a children's book of game chants and play poems, appeared in 1968, *In Defiance (of the Rains)* in 1970, and *Little Notes to You from Lucas Street* in 1972. In 1973, she will publish *New and Selected Poems*. See page 252.

## CAROLE FREEMAN 1941

Carole Freeman is a resident of northern California. Her works are included in numerous anthologies. She is the winner of the 1972 Mary Merritt Henry prize for excellence in verse awarded by Mills College of Oakland. She has one play in production at Grove Street College. See page 291.

## NIKKI GIOVANNI 1943

Nikki Giovanni was born in Knoxville, Tennessee. Her books are *Black Feeling Black Talk/Black Judgement, Re:Creation, Spin a Soft Black Song,* and *Gemini*. Her album, *Truth Is on Its Way*, was a best seller. She now lives in New York with her son, writing and lecturing. See page 301.

## ANN GOTTLIEB 1946

Ann Gottlieb was born in Chicago. She received her B.A. from Radcliffe in 1967 and attended Columbia School of the Arts in writing. She worked for two years as an assistant editor and now free-lances as a critic and editor in New York. She has published poems in *The American Scholar, Diné Baa-Hani,* and *The Massachusetts Review,* and reviews in *The Village Voice* and the New York *Times.* See page 338.

## JUDY GRAHN 1940

Judy Grahn was born under the sign of Leo and raised in New Mexico. She has worked as a waitress, fry cook, meat wrapper, WAF, maid, typist, medical secretary, file clerk, lab technician, social service worker, sandwich maker, barmaid, poet, and barbarian. She is a lesbian and is committed to women's liberation. Her poems have appeared in *It Aint Me Babe, Aint I a Woman, The Sadder, Rat, Woman to Woman, Women: A Journal of Liberation,* and she has published one book, *Edward the Dyke and other poems.* She does readings for money or love. See page 285.

## SUSAN GRIFFIN 1943

Susan Griffin has a B.A. in English and has worked as a waitress, switchboard operator, artist's model, teacher, and, most recently, wife, from which position she resigned. Presently she is looking for work, trying to stay off welfare, and living through child support, occasional earnings as a writer, foodstamps, and the love and care of another woman with whom she shares her home. She has been published in *Aphra, Ramparts, The Tribe, The Guardian, Space City, Metamorphoses, It Aint Me Babe, Aint I a Woman, The Woman's Rights Law Reporter, Freedom News, The Wildcat, Woman to Woman, Everywoman, Remember Our Fire, Off Our Backs,* and *Aldebaran Review.* Her first collection of poems, *Dear Sky,* was published by the Shameless Hussy Press. She is now working on a trilogy of novellas about the marriage, divorce, and motherhood of a young woman. See page 307.

## ANNE HALLEY 1928

Anne Halley was born in Germany. She was educated in the United States, lives in Amherst, and teaches English at Holyoke Community College. Remembering certain editorial comments from the fifties—"all that kitchen sink imagery!"—"too much female self-pity!"—she is committed to, and at least sporadically active in, the women's movement. Her most recent publication is a chapter from a novel, *Confessions of Mother Goose*, in *The Massachusetts Review*, Spring 1972. She spent last year in Berlin, and her translation of Kurt Tucholsky's *Deutschland, Deutschland über alles* has been published by U. Mass. Press in August 1972. *Between Wars and Other Poems* (1965) was published in the United States and in England, where it was the Poetry Society's Summer Recommendation. See page 181.

## PEGGY HENDERSON 1949

Peggy Henderson was born in Monterey, California, and raised in southern California and northern Virginia. She received her B.A. from Goucher College and her M.A. from Johns Hopkins University. She was a Johns Hopkins Teaching Fellow in 1971 and a Watson Fellow in 1972. Her poem, "Night Angel," was anthologized in *Pendulum*. See page 357.

## SANDRA HOCHMAN 1936

Sandra Hochman was born in Manhattan. She received her B.A. from Bennington College and did graduate work at Columbia University and the Sorbonne. She has traveled in Europe and has been an actress and a teacher. Her first volume, *Manhattan Pastures*, was the Yale Younger Poet selection. She has also written *Love Letters from Asia*, *The Vaudeville Marriage*, and *Voyage Home*. See page 231.

COLETTE INEZ 1931

Colette Inez was born in Belgium and brought up in a Catholic home for children; she now lives in Orangeburg, New York, with her husband. Her poems have appeared in several anthologies, including *Quickly Aging Here, Anthology of Christian Poets,* and *Live Poetry Anthology,* and some sixty national and international poetry publications, including *Antioch Review, Prairie Schooner, Poetry Northwest, Southern Poetry Review, New York Poetry,* and *The Nation.* See page 205.

JUNE JORDAN 1936

June Jordan was born in Harlem, studied at Barnard College and the University of Chicago, and has taught at Sarah Lawrence, City College of New York, and Connecticut College. She has received a Rockefeller Foundation grant and the Prix de Rome in Environmental Design. She co-founded the Voice of the Children writing workshop for black and Puerto Rican kids. Her essays have been published in *Esquire, Mademoiselle, The Nation, The Village Voice, Evergreen Review,* and the New York *Times.* She edited the anthology *Soulscript* and co-edited *The Voice of the Children.* Her own publications include *Who Look At Me* and *Some Changes* (poetry), *His Own Where* (a novel), a biography of Fannie Lou Hamer, and a hip history comparing Reconstruction to the civil rights era. Presently she lives in New York where she is working on her second novel. See page 233.

LENORE KANDEL  birth date unavailable

Lenore Kandel was born in New York City and is a Capricorn. She says, "I am no longer a professional belly dancer, school-bus driver, or choir singer. I stand witness for the divine animal and the possibility of the ecstatic access of enlightenment. My favorite word is YES!" Her books include *Love Poems* and *Word Alchemy.* She is now living in San Francisco. See page 277.

## SHIRLEY KAUFMAN 1923

Shirley Kaufman won the Academy of American Poets prize at San Francisco State while getting her M.A. there, and has read at the Discovery Series of the YM-YWHA Poetry Center as well as in schools around the country. She has published poems in *The Atlantic Monthly, Harper's, Kayak, The Nation, The New Yorker,* and *Poetry.* Her book, *The Floor Keeps Turning,* won the U.S. Award of the International Poetry Forum and was a National Council on the Arts selection. She translated Israeli poet Abba Kovner's volumes, *My Little Sister* and *A Canopy in the Desert.* Born in Seattle, she now lives in San Francisco with her husband and three daughters. She says, "I think poetry is sort of organized irrationality, like trying to become human. Or being a woman." See page 138.

## FAYE KICKNOSWAY 1936

Faye Kicknosway has published poems in *Prairie Schooner, Tri-Quarterly, New York Quarterly,* and *Alternative Press.* Her first book, *O. You Can Walk on the Sky? Good.,* was published in December by the Yes! Press in Portland, Oregon. Her second book, *Poems From,* will be published next year. She teaches creative writing at Wayne State University in Detroit and spends time driving back and forth between Detroit and San Francisco. See page 238.

## CAROLYN KIZER 1925

Carolyn Kizer was born in Spokane and educated at Sarah Lawrence and Columbia University; she has traveled widely. She founded *Poetry Northwest* in Seattle and edited it for seven years. She was the Director of Literary Programs for the National Endowment for the Arts from the beginning until the Nixon administration. Presently, she is lecturing in poetry at the University of North Carolina at Chapel Hill. Recently she was Visiting Hurst Professor of Literature at Washington University in St. Louis and she participated in the Spring Lecture Series at Barnard. Her volumes include *The Ungrateful Garden, Knock upon Silence, Midnight Was My Cry,* and a work in progress, *Funnylove.* See page 169.

## MAXINE KUMIN 1925

Maxine Kumin received her B.A. and M.A. from Radcliffe College and has taught at Tufts University, Newton College of the Sacred Heart, and the University of Massachusetts. Among her awards are the Lowell Mason Palmer Award and the William Marion Reedy Award from the Poetry Society of America and a grant from the National Council on the Arts and Humanities. She was also a Scholar at the Radcliffe Institute for Independent Study. She has published numerous books, among them *The Privilege, The Nightmare Factory,* and *Up Country* (poetry), *Through Dooms of Love, The Passions of Uxport,* and *The Abduction* (novels), and many children's books. See page 177.


## DENISE LEVERTOV 1923

Denise Levertov was born in England and educated privately. She came to the United States in 1948 with her husband Mitchell Goodman. She has one son, Nikolai. She has been a Guggenheim Fellow, an Associate Scholar at the Radcliffe Institute, and Poetry Editor of *The Nation.* She has been published in many periodicals and her volumes include *The Double Image, With Eyes at the Back of Our Heads, The Jacob's Ladder, O Taste and See, The Sorrow Dance, To Stay Alive, Relearning the Alphabet, Footprints,* and the translation *Selected Poems of Guillevic.* See page 147.


## AUDRE LORDE 1934

Audre Lorde was born in Manhattan. She went to Hunter College and then to Columbia University, where she received her master's degree. After a year at the University of Mexico, she became Poet-in-Residence at Tougaloo College in Jackson, Mississippi. She now teaches at the City University of New York. She says of herself, "I am Black, Woman, and Poet;—fact, and outside the realm of choice. I can choose only to be or not be, and in various combinations of myself." See page 221.

## AMY LOWELL  1874–1925

A member of the illustrious Lowell family, Amy Lowell was born in Brookline, Massachusetts and educated privately at home and abroad. When at the age of twenty-eight she decided to become a poet, she spent the following eight years reading in preparation for the task. Her first poem appeared in 1910, her first volume two years later, and a succession of six others between then and 1921. Three more volumes of poems were published posthumously, the first of which, *What's O'Clock*, received the Pulitzer Prize for 1925. She was a popularizer of imagism and an early proponent of *vers libre*. In addition to poetry, she wrote three volumes of literary criticism and a biography of John Keats, published early in the year of her death. Her titles include *A Dome of Many-colored Glass, Sword Blades and Poppy Seed, Men, Women and Ghosts, Can Grande's Castle, Pictures of the Floating World, Legends, East Wind,* and *Ballads for Sale*. See page 37.

## CYNTHIA MACDONALD  1932

Cynthia Macdonald was born in New York City. She received her B.A. from Bennington College. In the middle of a career as an opera singer, she began to write poetry. When poetry began to dominate music, she gave up singing to allow more time for writing. She received her M.A. degree from Sarah Lawrence College in 1970 and now is a member of the writing faculty there. Her first book, *Amputations,* was published in 1972. She is married and has two children. See page 207.

## MARGO MAGID  1947

Margo Magid was born under a Taurus sun, Gemini moon, and Leo rising. She attended Goucher College and Johns Hopkins and was a Fulbright Fellow in 1970–71. Her poems have appeared in *pyx, Survival Manual, Women: A Journal of Liberation,* and the anthology *New Women.* She has recently returned from a kibbutz in Boit Shoan Valley, Israel, where she counted caterpillars, studied Hebrew with a saint, lived in a water tower, and completed her first and last novel, *window water baby moving.* She currently lives in a blue house in South Hampton, New York, with Neil and both plan to return to caterpillars any day. See page 355.

## PHYLLIS MCGINLEY 1905

Phyllis McGinley was born in Ontario, Oregon. She was graduated from the University of Utah and attended the University of Southern California. Before her marriage, she taught school in Utah and New Rochelle (New York) and was a staff writer for *Town & Country*. Her numerous collections of short verse include *On the Country, A Pocketful of Wry, A Short Walk from the Station,* and *Love Letters of Phyllis McGinley*. She has also written many books for children, magazine articles, and a collection of essays called *The Province of the Heart*. Her many awards include the Pulitzer Prize in 1961 for a collection of verse, *Times Three*. She once said, "I've always read poetry. I read it for enjoyment, for delight, to get drunk on. . . ." See page 83.

## SANDRA MCPHERSON 1943

Sandra McPherson was born in California. She received her B.A. in English from San Jose State College and later studied writing at the University of Washington. She was guest editor of *Poetry Northwest* in 1971 and received the Helen Bullis Prize from the magazine in 1968. Her book, *Elegies for the Hot Season*, was chosen as a Selection of the National Council on the Arts Program. Her poems have appeared in *The New Yorker, The New Republic, The Nation, Poetry, New American Review, The Iowa Review,* and *Field*. In 1972 she received a grant from the Ingram Merrill Foundation. See page 311.

## EVE MERRIAM 1916

Eve Merriam was born in Philadelphia. She is a prolific writer who can claim more than seventeen volumes, including poetry and fiction for young people. She wrote feminist books before they were fashionable (*After Nora Slammed the Door*) and has recently produced an anthology of nineteenth century autobiography and memoirs (*Growing Up Female in America*). Her first volume of poetry won the Yale Younger Poets Prize in 1946. Since then, her titles have included *Basics, The Inner City Mother Goose,* and *The Nixon Poems*. See page 115.

# EDNA ST. VINCENT MILLAY 1892–1950

Edna St. Vincent Millay was born and raised in Maine and received a degree from Vassar College in 1917. Her first long poem, "Renascence," published in 1912 when she was nineteen, has endured its early acclaim. For a time, she lived in New York City, wrote short stories under pseudonyms and worked with the Provincetown Players as actress and playwright. After her marriage in the twenties, she moved to the Berkshires where she continued to write poems. Between 1917 and 1942, she published ten volumes of poetry and several plays. Her poem, "The Harp Weaver," won the Pulitzer Prize in 1924. Among her titles are *Renascence, A Few Figs from Thistles, Second April, The Buck in the Snow and Other Poems, Fatal Interview, Wine from These Grapes, Huntsman, What Quarry? Make Bright the Arrow,* and *The Murder of Lidice*. See page 64.

# VASSAR MILLER 1924

Vassar Miller was born in Houston, Texas. She received her B.S. and M.A. from the University of Houston and taught creative writing from 1964 to 1966 at St. Johns School in Houston. Among her awards are three from the Texas Institute of Letters. Her books include *Wage War on Silence, My Bones Being Wiser, Adam's Footprint,* and *Onions and Roses*. She is now working on a novel. See page 166.

# MARIANNE MOORE 1887–1972

Marianne Moore was born in St. Louis, Missouri and educated at Bryn Mawr College. She worked for nearly two decades first as a teacher of stenography to American Indians, then as a librarian in New York City, and from 1925–1929 as an editor of *The Dial*. She won recognition early in the twenties from poet friends who successfully published her work, and in her lifetime received many honors, including three in a single year (1951): the Pulitzer Prize, the Bollingen Prize, and the National Book Award. In 1944, Louise Bogan called her "our most distinguished contemporary American poet." She has had many admirers, but few imitators. Her volumes include *Poems, Observations, The Pangolin and Other Verse, What Are Years?, Like a Bulwark, O To Be A Dragon,* and *A Marianne Moore Reader*. See page 56.

## ROBIN MORGAN 1941

Robin Morgan was born in Florida and grew up in Mt. Vernon, New York. She has been active in the women's movement for five years. A feminist militant, she co-founded N.Y. Radical Women, WITCH, and was a member of the *Rat* collective. She edited the anthology, *Sisterhood Is Powerful,* and has poems in *The Yale Review, The Atlantic Monthly, The Ladder,* and *Feminist Art Journal.* She is now living in New York and has just published a book of poems called *Monster.* See page 293.

## PAULI MURRAY 1910

Pauli Murray is a poet and a lawyer. She has been active in the civil rights movement and the women's movement. Born in Baltimore, she received her B.A. from Hunter College, her LL.B. from Harvard University, her LL.M. from the University of California, and her J.S.D. from Yale University. She is now Stulberg Professor of Law and Politics at Brandeis University. Among her honors are the Eugene Saxton Award and a Ford Fellowship. Her books include *Proud Shoes, States' Laws on Race and Color, The Constitution and Government of Ghana* (co-author), *Human Rights USA: 1948–1966,* and *Dark Testament,* a new volume of poems. See page 91.

## ROCHELLE OWENS 1936

Born in Brooklyn, Rochelle Owens now lives in New York City with her husband, poet George Economou. Her innovative and controversial plays are produced throughout the world. A collection of five plays, *Futz and What Came After,* was published in 1968. She has published four books of poetry, her latest being *I Am the Babe of Joseph Stalin's Daughter.* Her new plays include *He Wants Shih!, Kontraption,* and *The Karl Marx Play.* She edited *Spontaneous Combustion Plays.* She is a founding member of the New York Theatre Strategy and The Women's Theatre Council. Presently, she is in the process of writing *The Joe 136 Creation Poems,* and a play, *Baal Shem.* See page 239.

## GRACE PALEY 1922

Grace Paley was born and still lives in New York City. She teaches experimental writing at Sarah Lawrence College. Her volume of short stories, *The Little Disturbances of Man,* was published in 1960, and she has published other stories in the *New American Review,* the *Atlantic, Esquire,* and many little magazines. On a recent trip to North Vietnam, she began to write poems. About the last ten years, she says: "The Vietnam War has taken my energy, time, interest, and emotion." See page 136.


## MIRIAM PALMER 1946

Miriam Palmer has lived in Missouri, Greece, Ohio, and is now living in Maine. She holds a degree in German from Oberlin, but does odd jobs for money in order to have time for writing poems and working for women's liberation. She has published several poems in magazines and a book, *Mothers and Daughters,* which she printed herself. She has recently organized a writing workshop for women in Brunswick, Maine. She is writing a biography of Victoria Woodhull for The Feminist Press. See page 340.


## MARGE PIERCY 1936

Marge Piercy was born in a working-class neighborhood in Detroit during the depression and believes more in ecology than in post-scarcity. She was the first person in her family to go to a university and took five years to recover. She was a member of SDS and is very active in the women's movement. Her poems have appeared in *The Carleton Miscellany, The Transatlantic Review, Tri-Quarterly,* and many other magazines and underground papers. Her volumes include *Breaking Camp* and *Hard Loving* (poetry), *Going Down Fast* and *Dance the Eagles to Sleep* (novels). She lives in Wellfleet, Massachusetts, and is writing a novel about ten years in the lives of two women. See page 243.

## SYLVIA PLATH 1932–1963

Sylvia Plath was born in Boston and lived in England with her husband Ted Hughes and their two children. She received her B.A. from Smith College and her M.A. from Newnham College, Cambridge, where she was a Fulbright Scholar. Among her awards are the Irene Glascock Poetry Prize, the Bess Hokin Award from *Poetry* magazine, and the Eugene F. Saxon Fellowship. She wrote a great many poems, most of which have appeared posthumously in the volumes *The Colossus and Other Poems, Ariel, Crossing the Water,* and *Winter Trees.* A novel, *The Bell Jar,* appeared in 1963, the year she committed suicide. See page 210.

## CATHLEEN QUIRK 1944

Cathleen Quirk was born in Erie, Pennsylvania. She received her B.A. from Duquesne University and her M.A. in English from the University of Wisconsin. She has taught English and creative writing at Emerson College in Boston and presently teaches at Northeastern University. She has poems in *New American and Canadian Poets, East Coast Poets,* and *Ploughshares,* and has published a broadside of her poem "The Only Child." She says, "I will not rest until I get to Africa!" See page 319.

## JULIA RANDALL 1923

Julia Randall was born in Baltimore. She received her B.A. from Bennington and her M.A. from Johns Hopkins and presently teaches at Hollins College. She has received grants from the National Foundation on Arts and Humanities and from the National Institute of Arts and Letters; she has been a Sewanee Review Fellow. Her poems have appeared in *Poetry, Sewanee Review,* and *The American Scholar* and her books include *The Puritan Carpenter, The Solstice Tree,* and *Adam's Dream.* See page 158.

## JUDITH RECHTER 1937

Judith Rechter has two daughters, a master's degree in English, and a cat named Bathsheba. This year she has been studying poetry with Donald Finkel. She is enrolled as a graduate student in comparative literature at Washington University and teaches part time at a junior college in St. Louis. Her poems have been published in *Focus Midwest, Perspective, Poetry and Audience,* and *New Magazine.* See page 257.

## NAOMI REPLANSKY 1918

Naomi Replansky was born and grew up in the Bronx. She has lived in France and California and now lives in Manhattan. She began to write poetry when she was ten, was published in *Poetry* (Chicago) when she was fifteen. Since then, her poems and translations (mostly from the German) have appeared from time to time in magazines and anthologies. A collection of her poems, *Ring Song,* was published in 1952; it was nominated for the National Book Award that year. She is now completing a second book of poems. See page 118.

## ADRIENNE RICH 1929

Adrienne Rich was born in Baltimore and attended Radcliffe College. Her awards include the Yale Series of Younger Poets, two Guggenheim Fellowships, the National Institute of Arts and Letters grant for poetry, and the Amy Lowell Traveling Scholarship. She teaches Basic Writing in the SEEK program at City College and has worked with a tenant squatters' movement in New York, with an alternate high school and on a committee for women prisoners. She has three sons. Her work has appeared in numerous periodicals and her books of poetry are *A Change of World, The Diamond Cutters, Snapshots of a Daughter-in-Law, Necessities of Life, Leaflets,* and *The Will to Change.* In 1972–73 she will be teaching at Brandeis University as the Fannie Hurst Visiting Professor of Creative Literature. See page 193.

WENDY G. RICKERT   birth date unavailable

Wendy Rickert was an English major at the University of Chicago and has studied poetry at New York University. See page 280.

SUZANNE BERGER RIOFF 1944

Suzanne Berger Rioff was born in Texas and raised in Chicago, London, and Cleveland. She attended Smith College, Northwestern University, and Johns Hopkins University. She has been a VISTA volunteer, a barmaid, and a Head Start teacher, and presently teaches English at a community college in Boston. She participates in the Poetry In The Schools program. Her interests are modern art, piano, and teaching kids how to write poetry, and she loves the ocean. See page 320.

CAROLYN M. RODGERS 1942

Carolyn M. Rodgers was born and raised in Chicago where she now lives. An active member of OBAC (Organization of Black American Culture), she has traveled around the country reading her poetry. In 1968 she won the first Conrad Kent Rivers Writing Award. She has taught Afro-American literature at Columbia University and at City College of New York. Her volumes include *Paper Soul, 2 Love Raps,* and *Songs of a Blackbird.* See page 296.

MURIEL RUKEYSER 1913

Muriel Rukeyser is a poet, lecturer, and teacher. She was born and raised in New York and attended Vassar College and Columbia University. She is a member of the National Institute of Arts and Letters and is on the board of directors of the Teachers-Writers' Collaborative. Her awards include a Guggenheim Fellowship, the National Institute Award, and a fellowship from the American Council of Learned Societies. In addition to five volumes of prose and a number of children's books, she has published more than a dozen volumes of poetry, including *Theory of Flight, Soul and Body of John Brown, Beast in View, The Green Wave, Body of Waking,* and *The Speed of Darkness.* Her work has been translated into ten languages. See page 92.

## SONIA SANCHEZ 1937

Sonia Sanchez was born in Birmingham and studied at New York University and Hunter College, where she received a B.A. She has taught creative writing at San Francisco State College and to elementary school children in New York City. She has been published in *Negro Digest* and the *Journal of Black Poetry* and in the anthologies *Black Fire* and *The New Black Poetry*. See page 259.

## E. N. SARGENT 1934

E. N. Sargent says, "I was born to starving parents in West Virginia and adopted by more comfortable people at the age of two. For some years I did not speak, but I speak now, and although my work is hated by many, especially by the male pervert literary establishment (please note I don't hate them; they hate me), it is also loved by quite a few." She is a dancer and a prose writer as well as a poet and has published three books, *The African Boy, Love Poems of Elizabeth Sargent,* and *The Magic Book of Love Exercises.* She lives with her husband and children in New York. See page 228.

## ANNE SEXTON 1928

Anne Sexton was born in Newton, Massachusetts, and attended Garland Junior College. In 1961–63 she was a Scholar at the Radcliffe Institute and presently she teaches creative writing at Boston University. Among her awards are a Robert Frost Fellowship at the Bread Loaf Writers' Conference, an American Academy of Arts and Letters Traveling Fellowship, the Pulitzer Prize, and a Ford Foundation grant for a year's residence with the theater. Her books include *All My Pretty Ones, To Bedlam and Part Way Back, Love Poems, Live or Die,* and *Transformations.* She lives in Weston, Massachusetts, with her husband and children. See page 188.

# KATHLEEN SPIVACK 1938

Kathleen Spivack's first volume of poetry, *The Jane Poems*, reveals contemporary life as viewed through the eyes of a female persona. Her poems have appeared in *The New Yorker, The Atlantic Monthly, Harper's, Poetry, Encounter*, as well as in *The Young American Poets, The New Yorker Anthology*, and *Best Poems of 1971*. She was one of the winners of the Discovery prize of the YM-YWHA in 1972 and for the past two years has been a Fellow at the Radcliffe Institute in the writing of poetry. She is married and has two young children. See page 264.

# GERTRUDE STEIN 1874–1946

Gertrude Stein was born in Pennsylvania, studied psychology at Radcliffe College and medicine at Johns Hopkins University. With her brother Leo, in 1903 she went to Paris where they came to know Matisse, Picasso, Braque, and a wide circle of Europeans and American expatriates. She never returned to live in the U.S., and, like the painters she came to know, she pushed "abstraction to its farthest limits" in language. She is rarely, if ever, included in anthologies of poetry, though her experimental volume of prose poems, *Tender Buttons*, was published in 1914. Her other innovative volumes include *Three Lives, The Autobiography of Alice B. Toklas, Everybody's Autobiography, The World is Round*, and *Stanzas in Meditation*. See page 45.

# JANE STEMBRIDGE 1936

Jane Stembridge was born Aries in Georgia and says, "By the grace of God, I'm still alive to receive the joy of earth and the community of man. Any statement about me that is at all relative must include the names of the human saints who've shared the Light and the Agony and the Joy . . . they are Barbara Deming, Paul Salstrom, Alex Durham, Clint McCormick, Rita Heffren, the Kings, the Herrins, Tom Heffren, Jane Verlaine, my family and Casey, Sam Shirah, Dove Greene and Bob Moses. . . . If I have an autobiography, it is just a facet of the one shining body we all are." See page 250.

## ANNE STEVENSON 1933

Anne Stevenson was born in England and grew up in the United States. She was educated at the University of Michigan, where she three times won the Avery Hopwood Award for Poetry. She has published two volumes of poetry, *Living in America* and *Reversals,* and a critical study, *Elizabeth Bishop.* Her two new collections of poems are *Traveling Behind Glass* and *Correspondences,* a sequence of dramatic monologues about an American family. She has taught at Westminster School and at the Cambridge School of Weston. She was a Fellow at the Radcliffe Institute in 1970 and is presently living in Scotland, where she teaches at the University of Glasgow. She has three children. See page 220.

## RUTH STONE 1915

Ruth Stone was born in Roanoke, Virginia. A graduate of the University of Illinois, she has taught at several colleges, was Poet-in-Residence at the University of Wisconsin, and has been a member of the Radcliffe Institute. Her work has appeared in *Kenyon Review, Poetry, The New Yorker, Accent,* and *Partisan Review.* In 1958 her first volume of poems, *In an Iridescent Time,* appeared; her second, *Topography,* in 1970. In 1971 she received a Guggenheim Fellowship in creative writing. She lives in Brandon, Vermont, with her three daughters. See page 106.

## LYNN STRONGIN 1939

Lynn Strongin was born and raised in New York City. She went to Hunter College, lived on the West Coast for seven years, and is presently teaching at the University of New Mexico. She won a Creative Writing Grant from the National Endowment for the Arts. *The Dwarf Cycle,* her first book of poems, was recently published by Thorp Springs Press. Her poems have been included in *31 New American Poets, American Literary Anthology, 3, Green Flag, Mark in Time, Sisterhood Is Powerful, Rising Tides: Contemporary American Women Poets,* and *The Touch of the Poet.* She has also published poems in *Poetry, New York Quarterly, The Ladder, Aphra, Hyperion,* and *Manroot.* Five of her poems have been choreographed and danced in New York this year. See page 274.

## LYNN SUKENICK 1937

Lynn Sukenick was born and raised in New York. She graduated from Brandeis University and received her "penultimate and ultimate degrees" from City University of New York. After a long silence, she began writing poems again—in the woods of Connecticut. She taught at Cornell University and now teaches writing and literature at the University of California, Irvine. She lives in Laguna Beach, California, and is completing her first book, *Houdini and Other Poems*. See page 260.

## SUSAN SUTHEIM 1942

Susan Sutheim was the news editor for *The Guardian*. She is a former regional staff member for New York SDS and is active in women's liberation. See page 297.

## MAY SWENSON 1919

May Swenson was born and raised in Utah and graduated from Utah State University. Among her awards are a Robert Frost Fellowship, a Rockefeller Foundation Fellowship, a Guggenheim Fellowship, an Amy Lowell Traveling Scholarship, and a Ford Foundation Poet-Playwright Grant. In 1966 she was Poet-in-Residence at Purdue University. In 1970 she was elected to membership in the National Institute of Arts and Letters. She has written several volumes of poetry including *To Mix with Time, Half Sun Half Sleep*, and *Iconographs*, as well as several children's books and an experimental play, *The Floor*. See page 122.

## MARGO TAFT 1950

Margo Taft graduated in 1972 from Radcliffe College, where she majored in visual and environmental studies. She has studied with Denise Levertov and Sidney Goldfarb. See page 358.

## JEAN TEPPERMAN 1945

Jean Tepperman is currently in graduate school studying to become a high school teacher. Active in the student movement at college, she later worked in an SDS community-organizing project in Chicago. She was a staff member of *The Old Mole,* an underground newspaper in Cambridge, and was a part of Bread and Roses, a socialist women's liberation group in Boston, now dead. Her poems have appeared in *Lion Rampant, Motive, The Old Mole, The Red Pencil,* and the anthology, *Sisterhood Is Powerful.* See page 333.

## MONA VAN DUYN 1921

Mona Van Duyn was born and educated in Iowa. She has taught at the University of Iowa, the University of Louisville, and Washington University, St. Louis. She helped to found and is co-editor of *Perspective: A Quarterly of Literature.* She has been published in dozens of magazines, including *Poetry, The New Yorker, New American Review, Kayak, Sewanee Review,* and *Poetry Northwest.* Her first two books are *Valentines to The Wide World* and *A Time of Bees.* In 1971 her third book, *To See, To Take,* won both the Bollingen Prize and the National Book Award. See page 129.

## ALICE WALKER 1944

Alice Walker was born in Georgia and graduated from Sarah Lawrence College. She has been a Scholar at the Bread Loaf Writers' Conference, a fellow at the McDowell Colony and at the Radcliffe Institute, and has received a grant from the National Endowment for the Arts. Her publications include *Once* and *Revolutionary Petunias,* books of poems; *The Third Life of Grange Copeland,* a novel; *Langston Hughes,* a biography for young children; and *In Love & Trouble, Stories of Black Women,* to be published in 1974. She has also published stories, poems, and essays in numerous magazines and anthologies. She has worked in voter registration in the South for many years and has taught courses in writing, black literature, and women writers. She is married, has a daughter, and lives in Cambridge. See page 323.

## MARGARET WALKER 1915

Margaret Walker was born in Birmingham, Alabama. She attended Northwestern University and received her M.A. from the School of Letters of the University of Iowa. She has taught at Livingstone College and Jackson State College and has worked also as a typist, reporter, and editor. Among her awards are the Yale Younger Poets Prize for *For My People* in 1942 and the Houghton Mifflin Literary Fellowship for her novel, *Jubilee*. *Prophets for a new day*, her newest volume of poetry, appeared in 1970. See page 110.

## BEATRICE WALTER 1948

Beatrice Walter received her B.A. in English from Boston University. She spent one year working at the Harvard Business School, helping students learn how to write, and is presently working as a free-lance writer. She has had poems published in *New Magazine* and *An Anthology of College Poetry*. See page 356.

## INGRID WENDT 1944

Ingrid Wendt was educated at Cornell College, Iowa (B.A.), and the University of Oregon (M.F.A.), and writes, "I've learned most from my experiences as a church organist, rinky dink piano player, waitress, assistant file clerk, magazine editor, and assistant professor at Fresno State College, where I taught poetry writing and women's studies courses. I have been writing and publishing poems and stories in literary journals. Right now I'm learning to be a mother to Erin Marie (born 1971), and getting into photography, fishing, landscaping, and housebuilding with my husband, writer Ralph Salisbury, in Eugene, Oregon—where we're in the process of reclaiming and moving an old house across town from a future McDonald's Hamburgers parking lot." See page 327.

## WENDY WIEBER 1951

Wendy Wieber lives in Boston. See page 359.

# ELINOR WYLIE 1885–1928

Elinor (Hoyt) Wylie was born in New Jersey of an old, socially prominent Pennsylvania family and raised in Washington, D.C. Her exceptional private life, which included three marriages, one of them an elopement with a married man, and the abandonment of her first husband and child, has received more attention than her writing. Her first book, *Incidental Numbers,* was published privately and anonymously in England in 1912, but she did not begin to take herself seriously as a writer until 1921. For the next seven years until her death at age forty-three, she worked passionately at both poetry and prose and produced some eight volumes. Among her titles are *Nets to Catch the Wind,* her first and most acclaimed book of poems, *Black Armour, The Venetian Glass Nephew, The Orphan Angel,* and *Mr. Hodge and Mr. Hazard.* More of her work was published posthumously in *Angels and Earthly Creatures, Collected Poems,* and *Collected Prose.* See page 47.